MORTALITY PATTERNS IN NATIONAL POPULATIONS

With special reference to recorded causes of death

STUDIES IN POPULATION

Under the Editorship of: H. H. WINSBOROUGH

Department of Sociology
University of Wisconsin
Madison, Wisconsin

Samuel H. Preston, Nathan Keyfitz, and Robert Schoen. Causes of Death: *Life Tables for National Populations.*

Otis Dudley Duncan, David L. Featherman, and Beverly Duncan. Socioeconomic Background and Achievement.

James A. Sweet. Women in the Labor Force.

Tertius Chandler and Gerald Fox. 3000 Years of Urban Growth.

William H. Sewell and Robert M. Hauser. Education, Occupation, and Earnings: *Achievement in the Early Career.*

Otis Dudley Duncan. Introduction to Structural Equation Models.

William H. Sewell, Robert M. Hauser, and David L. Featherman (Eds.). Schooling and Achievement in American Society.

Henry Shryock, Jacob S. Siegel, and Associates. The Methods and Materials of Demography. *Condensed Edition by Edward Stockwell.*

Samuel H. Preston. Mortality Patterns in National Populations: *With Special Reference to Recorded Causes of Death.*

In preparation

Robert M. Hauser and David L. Featherman (Eds.). The Process of Stratification: *Trends and Analyses.*

MORTALITY PATTERNS
IN
NATIONAL POPULATIONS
With special reference to recorded causes of death

SAMUEL H. PRESTON

Center for Studies in Demography and Ecology
Department of Sociology
University of Washington
Seattle, Washington

ACADEMIC PRESS   New York   San Francisco   London

A Subsidiary of Harcourt Brace Jovanovich, Publishers

ACADEMIC PRESS, INC.
111 Fifth Avenue, New York, New York 10003

United Kingdom Edition published by
ACADEMIC PRESS, INC. (LONDON) LTD.
24/28 Oval Road, London NW1

Library of Congress Cataloging in Publication Data

Preston, Samuel H
    Mortality patterns in national populations.

    (Studies in population series)
    Includes bibliographical references.
    1.   Mortality.   2.   Vital statistics.   I.   Title.
II.   Series: Studies in population.
HB1321.P74   1976   301.32'2   75-40612
ISBN 0–12–564450–7

PRINTED IN THE UNITED STATES OF AMERICA

Contents

Preface

Demographers have developed an inclination to view the worth of research in terms of the policy relevance of its results. This inclination has been accompanied by, and is largely responsible for, the decline of mortality studies. Mortality is presumed to be outside the policy sphere, since nations will (or at least should) never spend less than the maximum they can afford to promote human health and longevity.

An alternative criterion for evaluating research is its contribution to an understanding of social reality and social change: how we came to be where we are. If this criterion were in effect, current trends in demographic research would be exactly reversed. Mortality has been the volatile feature of population change during the twentieth century. Life expectancy for the world as a whole has increased from about 30 years in 1900 to an estimated 53 years in the late 1960's (United Nations, 1971, p. 32), producing population growth rates that are historically unparalleled. Since life expectancy for the human population has probably never been much below 20 on a sustained basis, it is clear that over two-thirds of the improvement in longevity from prehistoric times to the present has occurred in the very brief span of time since 1900. Birth rates in the meantime for the world population have declined from perhaps 38 per 1000 to perhaps 34 per 1000, forming a relatively insignificant chapter in social history.

Even if policy relevance is accepted as the appropriate criterion, mortality research appears to be relatively neglected. The notion that mortality is outside the policy domain cannot be seriously entertained. Nations and individuals do not devote maximum amounts to health-related expenses but divert portions of discretionary funds to schools, roads, houses, and recreation—items that make life more pleasant or productive while not necessarily prolonging it. Mortality levels are inevitably a product of social and individual choice made under budget constraints and in the presence of competing alternatives. They have probably been a focus of group decision-making as long as fertility levels have. Not only are mortality levels determined in part as a matter of policy but the available policies appear to be much more effective than fertility policy in terms of demographic responsiveness.

The two American institutions that have maintained a tradition of international research in mortality are the Office of Population Research of Princeton University and the University of California at Berkeley. Both played an important role in the genesis of this volume. Professor Ansley Coale of Princeton proposed a comparative study of mortality, conducted by the author, that served to demonstrate the feasibility of cross-national mortality research. At Berkeley, Nathan Keyfitz, Robert Schoen, and Verne Nelson collaborated with the author in a large-scale effort to process and publish data on mortality patterns for many different populations. This work resulted in the volume, *Causes of Death: Life Tables for National Populations* (1972), that provides the bulk of the data analyzed herein. That endeavor was supported by grants from the Ford Foundation and the National Institute of Child Health and Human Development (HD00375), administered by Judith Blake. The author is grateful to each of these individuals and institutions for making the present work possible.

Principal support for the present volume was provided by National Science Foundation Grant GS 33864 to the University of Washington. Additional support was provided by NSF Grant GZ-995, NICHD grant HD 00375, and National Institute of Mental Health grant MH-11673.

Major sections of this work were previously published elsewhere: Chapter 2 is primarily extracted from "Structure and Change in Causes of Death: An International Summary," *Population Studies* Vol. 28(1), November, 1974, pp. 19–51 (with Verne E. Nelson); portions of Chapter 3 appeared in "Cause of Death Life Tables: Application of a New Technique to Worldwide Data," *Transactions of the Society of Actuaries* Vol. XXV, Meeting No. 72, December, 1973, pp. 83–109 (with Nathan Keyfitz and Robert Schoen); most of Chapter 4 was originally published as "The Changing Relation between Mortality and Level of Economic Development," *Population Studies* Vol. 29(2), July, 1975, pp. 231–248; some sections of Chapter 5 appeared in "Influence of Cause-of-Death Structure on Age-Patterns of Mortality," in T. N. E. Greville, editor, *Population Dynamics*, Academic Press, New York, 1972, pp. 201–250; and most of Chapter 7 was originally published as "Demographic and Social Consequences of Various Causes of Death in the United States," *Social Biology* Vol. 21(2), Summer, 1974, pp. 144–162. Permission to reproduce parts of these papers is gratefully acknowledged. Although the sections appearing here were written by the present author, they are based upon work that would surely not have been completed without the collaboration of those listed above.

Many persons made suggestions that enriched portions of this analysis. Most notably, James McCann and Avery Guest read every chapter, several of them twice, and invariably offered cogent comments. Hubert M. Blalock, Irvin Emanuel, John McDonald, Alberto Palloni, Lincoln Polissar, and James Weed offered valuable detailed comments on sections of the work, which also profited from exposure in colloquia presented at the University of Wisconsin, Harvard University, the University of North Carolina, and the University of Washington. James Weed's contributions to Chapter 6 were major enough to deserve special mention. The computational assistance of Shun-er Huang and William Grady, the typing of Sunny Raynes, and the programming of Verne Nelson, Robert Lundy, John McDonald, and James Weed was of uniformly high quality. Most of these individuals are associated with the University of Washington, to which a large debt is owed for providing not only requisite personnel but a congenial and productive working environment.

CHAPTER 1

Introduction

Of the many social, economic, and political "revolutions" of the past two centuries, probably none has had a more salutary effect on the conditions of everyday life than the radical improvement in health and mortality. Because of traditionally strong public concern with matters of health and because death certification has been required for administrative purposes in many populations, we are left with a richer and more detailed record of this revolution than of many others. This costly legacy is especially valuable in the detail it provides on the age, sex, and cause of death of the decedent.

The present volume is an attempt to interpret the account left by millions of death certificates that have been recorded in forty-three nations over the past century. The account is translated into the language of demographers. Its concerns are the typically demographic ones of explaining variation in vital rates and in the structure of those rates, and its principal method is the workhorse in the demographer's analytic stable: decomposition. This is not to say that work in related fields such as epidemiology is ignored or that nondemographers will necessarily find the work void of interest. But the explicandum here is variation in national mortality patterns, from which the account occasionally works down, rather than a disease process from which the account occasionally works up.

The work is focused upon the contribution of various underlying causes of death to variation in the level and structure of mortality. Ignoring causes of death in the study of mortality is somewhat akin to ignoring fecundity, exposure, contraceptive effectiveness, and fetal wastage in the study of fertility. Both sets represent biological variables through which all social and

1

environmental influences must necessarily operate. Since underlying cause is conventionally defined in such a way that the several causes are mutually exclusive and exhaustive, any variation in mortality from all causes combined is necessarily attributable to variation in mortality for one or more causes of death. These causes manifest among themselves important differences in etiology and in implications for population structure, so that a recognition of the role of the causes moves us one step closer to a thorough understanding of determinants and consequences of mortality structure in human population. Causes are undoubtedly recorded with considerable inaccuracy and interpopulation incomparability, and these problems have discouraged the exploitation of cause-of-death statistics. But demographic data are never perfectly accurate, and the choice is between neglecting them altogether and producing qualified statements about the tendencies they suggest. Obviously, the latter course is pursued here.

Nature of the Data Base

In 1970 the author undertook a project jointly with N. Keyfitz and R. Schoen to prepare life tables by cause of death for certain human populations. An attempt, largely but not completely successful, was made to process information for every national population that could provide the appropriate data on mortality rates jointly by age, sex, and cause of death. When cause of death data were available only in broad categories, they were graduated to five-year intervals, primarily by indirect standardizations specific to each cause. But the major problem was to achieve maximum comparability in the cause-of-death categories utilized. The raw data were organized according to six different classifications of *International Lists of Diseases, Injuries, and Causes of Death* (World Health Organization, 1948), to lists unique to Scandinavian countries, and to lists unique to individual populations. The final categories used had to be broad enough to be constructed from data provided in each of these classifications. The determination of these categories was sensitive to diagnostic and coding differences likely to be encountered within the set of populations and to the desirability of providing an etiologic rather than an anatomical axis of classification. With the aid of D. Krueger and I. Moriyama of the United States National Center for Health Statistics, a final list of 12 categories was adopted.

This classification was applied to all assembled national data and the resulting mortality rates examined for gross error (e.g., a decline in death rates with age after 50, or an implausible life expectancy). Data for the 180 populations that passed these permissive tests were published in *Causes of*

Death: Life Tables for National Populations.[1] This volume includes a discussion of the accuracy and comparability of cause-of-death assignments and a presentation of the classification used in terms of the various *International Lists.* It demonstrates the implications of each cause of death for survivorship and for life expectancy in each of these populations considered separately.

For purposes of the more highly aggregated analysis pursued here, an additional 15 of these populations were excluded: West Berlin because of its subnational status; United States (total) 1920 and 1950 because of redundancy with the United States white and nonwhite populations that were separately represented in those years; Ceylon (1960), El Salvador (1950), France (1926, 1931, 1936), Greece (1928), Japan (1899), Mauritius (1960, 1964), the Philippines (1964) and Portugal (1920) because of exceptionally high proportions of deaths ascribed to "other and unknown causes" for a population at their respective mortality levels. The remaining 165 populations, representing 43 nations, that form the basis of this analysis are the following:

Australia: 11, 21, 33, 40, 51, 60, 64
Austria: 61, 64
Belgium: 60, 64
Bulgaria: 64
Canada: 21, 31, 41, 51, 60, 64
Chile: 09, 20, 30, 40, 50, 59, 64
Colombia: 60, 64
Costa Rica: 60, 64
Czechoslovakia: 34, 60, 64
Denmark: 21, 30, 40, 60, 64
England and Wales: 1861, 71, 81, 91, 1901, 11, 21, 31, 40, 51, 60, 64
Finland: 51, 60, 64
France: 58, 60, 64
Germany (F.R.):   60, 64
Greece: 60, 64
Guatemala: 61, 64
Hong Kong: 60, 64
Hungary: 60, 64
Iceland: 64
Ireland: 51, 61
Israel (Jewish population):   51, 60, 64

[1] Preston, Keyfitz, and Schoen (1972), in collaboration with V. E. Nelson. A population is defined as the aggregate of individuals alive within national boundaries during a particular year.

Italy: 1881, 91, 1901, 10, 21, 31, 60, 64
Japan: 08, 40, 51, 60, 64
Malta and Gozo: 64
Mexico: 60, 64
Netherlands: 31, 40, 50, 60, 64
New Zealand: 1881, 91, 1901, 11, 28, 26, 36, 45, 51, 64
Northern Ireland: 60, 64
Norway: 10, 20, 30, 46, 51, 60, 64
Panama: 60, 64
Poland: 60, 64
Portugal: 30, 40, 60, 64
Puerto Rico: 60, 64
Scotland: 51, 60, 64
Republic of South Africa (coloured and white):   41, 51, 60
Spain: 30, 40, 60
Sweden: 11, 20, 30, 40, 51, 60, 64
Switzerland: 30, 40, 51, 60, 64
Taiwan: 20, 30, 36, 60, 64
Trinidad and Tobago: 63
U.S.A.:   00, 10, 30, 40, 60, 64
U.S.A. (white and nonwhite):   20, 50
Venezuela: 60, 64
Yugoslavia: 61, 64.

The regional and temporal distribution of these populations is shown in
Table 1.1. Obviously, the sample of populations studied is not randomly
drawn from the universe of all populations. Rather, it is representative—
indeed, very nearly a complete sample—of populations for which the appropriate data are available. As such, it is biased toward states with relatively
stable and well-developed governmental machinery, towards populations in
which the exceptional peaks in mortality associated with epidemics are
largely absent, and towards European experience.

Twelve cause-of-death groupings are identified for study. The principal
criterion for combining specific causes into a broader group was their
etiological similarity, but important elements of an anatomical classification are necessarily present because of their persistence in the *International
Classification of Diseases, Injuries, and Causes of Death*. The causes employed in this study, and their corresponding numbers in the A- or B-list
of the Sixth and Seventh Revisions of the *International Lists of Diseases,
Injuries, and Causes of Death* (World Health Organization, 1948) are:
respiratory tuberculosis (B1); other infectious and parasitic diseases (B2-17);

Table 1.1

Distributions of populations on which analysis is based

	Pre-1900	1900–1935	1936–1951	1952–1960	1961–1964	Total
Northern and Western Europe	4	14	15	12	14	59
Southern and Eastern Europe	2	7	2	7	11	29
Overseas Europe[a]	2	14	12	4	4	36
Africa, Asia, Latin America[b]		6	8	11	16	41
Total	8	41	37	34	45	165

[a] Includes Republic of South Africa (White) and United States (nonwhite).

[b] Includes Israel (Jewish population) and Republic of South Africa (Coloured).

malignant and benign neoplasms (B18-19); cardiovascular disease (B22, 24–29; A85, 86); influenza, pneumonia, bronchitis (B30–32); diarrhea, gastritis, enteritis (B36); certain chronic diseases (B20, 33, 37, 38) (these numbers represent, respectively: diabetes mellitus, ulcer of the stomach and duodenum, cirrhosis of the liver, and nephritis and nephrosis); maternal mortality (B40); certain diseases of infancy (B42–44); motor vehicle accidents (BE47); other accidents and violence (BE48–50); and all other and unknown causes.

As a sobering introduction to these categories, it is useful to review the major problems of accuracy and comparability that they are likely to present. The following summary is abstracted from Chapter III of *Causes of Death: Life Tables for National Populations* where a more detailed discussion and appropriate references may be found.

(1) *Respiratory Tuberculosis:* Relatively easy to diagnose, recognized in all populations; one of the most robust of categories.

(2) *Other Infectious and Parasitic Diseases:* Probably somewhat under-recorded in statistically poor populations because of a tendency to assign deaths to terminal conditions (e.g., pneumonia) or to symptoms (e.g., fever) rather than to specific underlying cause.

(3) *Neoplasms:* Unquestionably underrecorded in statistically poor populations because of poor diagnosis; many deaths from neoplasms appear in the categories of "senility" or "unknown cause" (category 12).

(4) *Cardiovascular Diseases:* Also underrecorded in statistically poor populations and assigned instead to senility or cause unknown. About 2%

of deaths from the cause disappeared when the Fifth Revision of the *International Lists of Diseases, Injuries, and Causes of Death* was instituted. Frequent association with other chronic conditions—nephritis, bronchitis, diabetes—renders death rates from the cause susceptible to national coding idiosyncracies.

(5) *Influenza/Pneumonia/Bronchitis (Respiratory Diseases):* Probably inflated in statistically poor populations because of tendency to assign deaths to symptomatic and terminal conditions. There appears to be a tendency in England and Wales, Australia, and New Zealand to assign to chronic bronchitis deaths that would elsewhere be assigned to cardiovascular diseases. About 5% of the deaths in the category disappeared at the time of the Sixth Revision when deaths from pneumonia under age 5 weeks were transferred to certain diseases of early infancy.

(6) *Diarrheal Diseases:* Are some times confused with specific infectious diseases. About 16% of deaths in the category were lost when the Sixth Revision transferred deaths under 5 weeks of age to certain diseases of early infancy. Diarrheal deaths are often understated in Latin America below age 1, having been improperly transferred to certain diseases of early infancy.

(7) *Certain Chronic Diseases (Diabetes, Nephritis, Stomach Ulcers, Cirrhosis of Liver):* Variations in diagnostic and coding fashions render this a very imprecise category. Transfer of terms to nephritis at the time of the Fifth Revision caused a growth of about 10% in this category as a whole. With the Sixth Revision and its changed method of assigning multiple causes of death, diabetes deaths were reduced substantially and nephritis deaths were raised. Diabetes trends are nevertheless biased upwards by increasing levels of diagnostic accuracy. A high frequency of association with other causes of death renders death rates in the category susceptible to variation in methods of multiple-cause assignment.

(8) *Maternal Mortality (Complications of Pregnancy):* Lost 8–9% of its deaths when the method of coding multiple causes changed at the Sixth Revision. Probably some deaths in statistically poor populations are improperly assigned to infectious diseases.

(9) *Certain Diseases of Early Infancy:* The number of deaths increased by about 10% as a result of the transfer of deaths from pneumonia and diarrhea under 5 weeks of age at the Sixth Revision. The category often is inflated in Latin America at the expense of diarrhea.

(10) *Motor Vehicle Accidents:* The number of deaths is considerably understated in Latin America.

(11) *Other Accidents and Violence:* Seems to be a fairly robust category.

(12) *Other and Unknown Causes:* Ill defined and unknown conditions, especially those assigned to senility, inflate this category markedly in statistically poor populations.

Scheme of the Analysis

Chapter 2 provides the basic groundwork for the remainder of the volume. It is addressed to identifying the role played by various causes of death in interpopulation variation in the level of mortality from all causes combined. It is designed particularly to provide statistical generalizations regarding the contribution of various causes to changes in mortality levels. It suggests that the experience most commonly cited, that of England and Wales in the latter half of the 19th century, was highly atypical with regard to the cause-structure of mortality decline. Its somewhat unusual suggestion, based on a variety of indirect evidence, is that cardiovascular diseases have in general been important contributors to mortality change, more important than the specific infectious diseases of childhood exclusive of tuberculosis. The chapter also demonstrates that the structure of causes at a particular mortality level varies among geocultural regions, and furthermore that specific infectious and parasitic diseases are less important contributors to a particular level of mortality the later is that level intersected by a population.

Chapter 3 provides a brief set of empirical generalizations regarding the role of various causes of death in producing a particular mortality level. It is similar to Chapter 2 but its emphasis is on the chance of dying from a particular cause (in the probabilistic sense) and on the life-shortening effects of that cause at various levels of mortality. It thus serves as a short summary of the life tables presented in Preston *et al.* (1972). Diseases of an infectious nature are shown to have a more important impact on life expectancy than on age-standardized death rates.

Chapter 4 returns to the theme of factors responsible for changing levels of mortality. It addresses the question that currently seems most central to sociological and economic analyses of mortality regardless of the era investigated: how much of the improvment in mortality levels is in general attributable to improvements in living standards and how much to changes in health levels at a particular standard? The analysis concludes that the large majority of mortality improvement for the world as a whole during the 20th century is attributable to noneconomic factors, particularly but not exclusively as they impinge on infectious diseases.

The demographic structure of mortality, rather than its level, is the subject of Chapters 5 and 6. The aim is to describe the contribution of various causes of death to variation in age patterns of and sex differentials in mortality. In both cases a statistical, rather than a biological, model of "normal" demographic patterns is adopted and deviations from these normal patterns become the center of attention. Chapter 5 demonstrates that interpopulation differences in recorded age-patterns of mortality, holding mortality level constant, can for the most part be attributed to variation in the cause-of-death structures to which those populations are subject. It illustrates this point by showing that age-pattern differences among representatives of different mortality "families" previously identified by Coale and Demeny can be reliably predicted from knowledge of their cause-of-death patterns. These results should assist demographers in making choices among the various available models when faced with the frequently encountered task of estimating demographic parameters from incomplete data. The chapter concludes with some suggestions regarding the construction and use of model life table systems that recognize causes of death.

Chapter 6 shows that instances of higher female than male mortality are common at ages 1–40, especially in high mortality populations and from infectious diseases. It develops a new technique for measuring sex mortality differentials and identifies thereby powerful and persistent regional differences in the value of the differential and also a strong tendency toward substantial increase in the value of the differential over time. Cardiovascular disease, cancer, and influenza/pneumonia/bronchitis are shown to be the causes principally responsible for variation in sex mortality differentials among populations; mortality relations between the sexes for most of the infectious diseases are so regular as to cause little disruption in relations for all causes combined. Indicators of national levels of economic modernization—especially the participation rate in primary industries—are shown to be closely associated with the masculinity of mortality.

Finally, Chapter 7 is concerned with the contribution of causes of death, not to mortality level or structure, but to demographic, social, and economic processes. The strategy is to estimate what difference it would make in future U.S. populations if mortality from a particular cause were immediately eliminated altogether rather than continued at its current level. Implications are drawn out for population size, growth, age–sex structure, kinship relations, and per capita income. The assumption underlying the calculations is that, age by age, causes of death are independent both of one another and of fertility rates. The sensitivity of results to changes in fertility rates is demonstrated. The results are not directly applicable to any other population, but it is clear from Chapter 3 that populations at higher mortality levels would generally experience consequences that were greater from "eliminating" infectious diseases and smaller from eliminating degenerative diseases.

CHAPTER 2

Structure and Change
in Causes of Death:
An International Summary

The sources of declining death rates during the vital revolution appear reasonably intelligible, especially in contrast to the factors underlying fertility reductions. Reasons for the plague's disappearance and the importance of medical factors in mortality declines during the eighteenth century are still matters of debate. But for the twentieth century, when well over half of the worldwide progress from traditional to modern levels has occurred, the sources of decline appear readily discernible, although precise estimates of impact are lacking. A large degree of the success achieved can be attributed to the existence of national records of mortality by cause of death. Despite their considerable inaccuracy, such records provide indispensable clues regarding environmental factors in mortality change since these factors themselves often leave markedly different impressions on different causes. Probably the most successful example of using cause-of-death records to infer the role of environmental factors in mortality change has been by McKeown and Record (1962).

The purpose of the present chapter is to establish a "model" of the cause structure of mortality at various levels of mortality from all causes combined, to use the model to make statements about typical patterns of mortality change, and to identify and interpret regional and temporal differences in the cause structure of mortality. The initial model will be based upon data for the 165 populations identified above, undifferentiated by period or region. When a change or decline in mortality is referred to, it denotes a change in the value of a variable in the model, rather than an event in an actual population. Thus, the constructions provide a model of the cause structure of mortality change in exactly the same sense that model life tables offer an indication of the age pattern of mortality change. In both cases an observation is dissociated, at least initially, from the nation and period to which it refers; in neither case does the model provide information on the pace of change. Later sections examine the extent to which individual populations or groups of populations deviate from the norms established. The intent is not to offer a substitute for detailed epidemiological investigations focusing upon a particular country, but rather to permit the placement of such studies in a broad comparative framework.

Linear Model of Variation in the Cause Structure of Mortality

The mean and standard deviation of death rates in the 165 populations for each cause and for all causes combined are presented in Table 2.1. Here and throughout much of the volume, death rates have been age-standardized on the basis of an age distribution that is expressed in five-year age intervals.[1] A particular death rate, M_j, is thus properly interpreted as the rate that would have been recorded for all ages combined in population j if its age structure had been identical to that of the standard. Age standardization is desirable in order to reduce the 68,970 observations on age, sex, and cause-specific death rates by a factor of 19, the number of age groups originally identified. Chapter 5 demonstrates the regularity of age patterns of mortality from the various causes and thereby implies that significant losses are not incurred by collapsing age groups in this fashion. The average age-standardized death rate for all causes combined is 12.25 for females and 15.20 for males. The *range* for females extends from 5.90 (Iceland, 1964) to 36.87 (Taiwan, 1920). The mean is thus about double the minimum and one-third of the maximum, indicating correctly that these populations are concentrated at lower levels of death rates. A convenient starting point for studying the cause structure of mortality at various levels is a scatter diagram of the relationship between the death rate from a specific cause and the death rate from all causes com-

---

[1] The standard age distribution is that of a "West" model female stable population with $e_0{}^0 = 65.0$ and $r = 0.01$. From Coale and Demeny (1966). This same age distribution is applied to age-specific death rates from all causes combined and from each specific cause. Age intervals 0–1 and 1–5 are treated separately; the terminal age category is 85+, which comprises .0039 of the standard population. The rates for individual countries may be found in Preston *et al.* (1972) as Standardized Rate (2).

Table 2.1

Means and standard deviations of age-standardized death rates from particular causes. 165 populations (annual deaths per 1000 population).

	Females			Males		
		Standard deviation	$\dfrac{\sigma_i}{\sigma_{all}}$		Standard deviation	$\dfrac{\sigma_i}{\sigma_{all}}$
	Mean	σ_i		Mean	σ_i	
Respiratory tuberculosis	0·58	0·72	0·12	0·76	0·81	0·14
Other infectious and parasitic	0·65	0·91	0·16	0·74	0·98	0·16
Neoplasms	1·30	0·30	0·05	1·51	0·51	0·09
Cardiovascular	3·56	0·93	0·16	4·33	1·23	0·21
Influenza, pneumonia, bronchitis	1·41	1·54	0·26	1·74	1·79	0·30
Diarrheal	0·53	0·76	0·13	0·57	0·80	0·13
Certain chronic	0·48	0·33	0·06	0·63	0·40	0·07
Maternal	0·12	0·13	0·02	—	—	—
Certain diseases of infancy	0·48	0·32	0·05	0·60	0·36	0·06
Violence	0·35	0·11	0·02	0·99	0·34	0·06
Residual	2·78	2·18	0·37	3·34	2·37	0·40
All causes	12·25	5·87	1·00	15·20	5·94	1·00

bined. Figure 2.1 presents these diagrams for the 12 causes identified above for female populations only. All death rates appearing on the graphs are age-standardized in five-year age intervals. Some of the 165 observations for a particular cause fail to appear because they fall outside the defined plotting range. Since a wide range of cause-specific rates had to be accommodated, and since the scales on the axes are identical for each cause of death, the y-axis is logarithmic. Consequently, what appears on the graphs to be a curvilinear relationship may be linear on a strictly linear scale, as noted below. The lines drawn on the figures are second-degree polynomials fitted to the data by least-squares regression. They are discussed in a later section, along with the general question of curvature.

Visually striking differences among causes appear with respect to both the slope and tightness of fit of their relationship with all causes. Nor do these two features always bear a close correspondence to one another. The slopes of the curves for the diarrheal and respiratory tuberculosis relationships are quite similar, but much more scatter is apparent in the diarrheal graph. These features are efficiently summarized by a correlation coefficient, measuring degree of association, and the slope of a regression line, measuring the average change in a cause-specific rate per unit change in the rate from

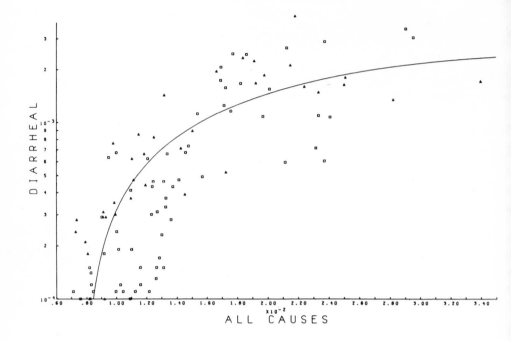

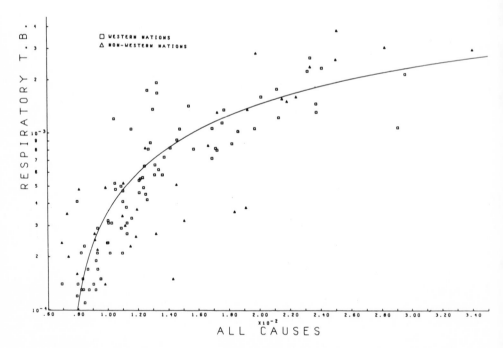

Figure 2.1 Scatter diagrams and regression lines for relationships between deaths from all causes combined and deaths from a particular cause.

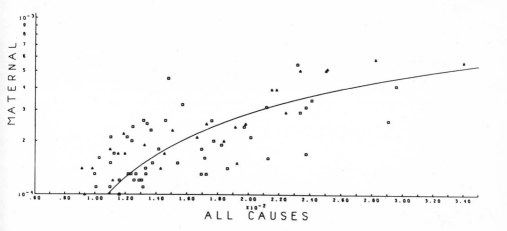

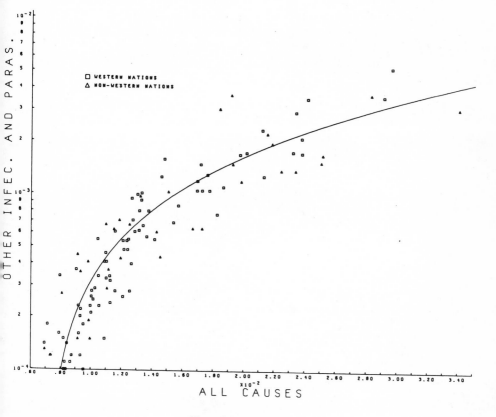

Figure 2.1 (continued)

13

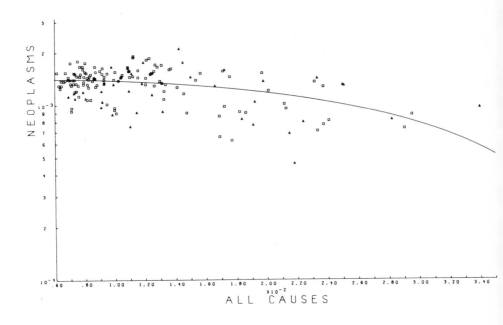

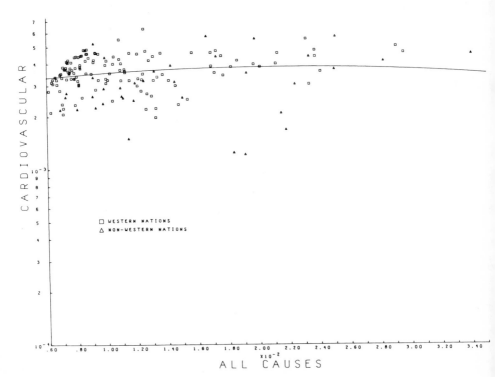

Figure 2.1 (continued)

14

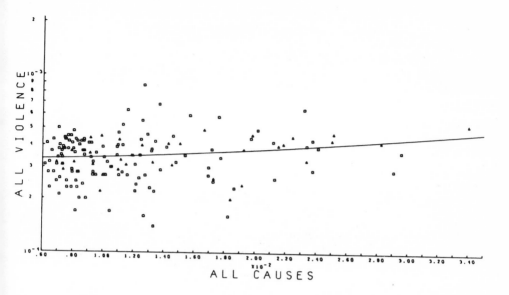

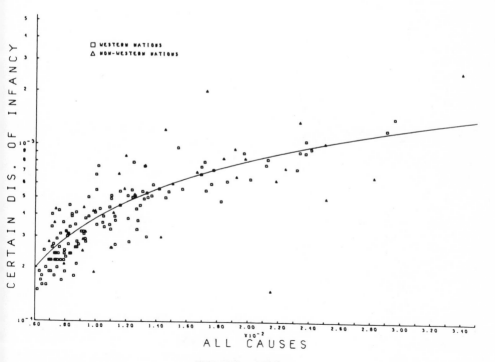

Figure 2.1 (continued)

15

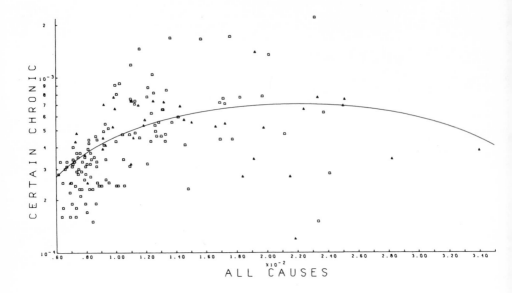

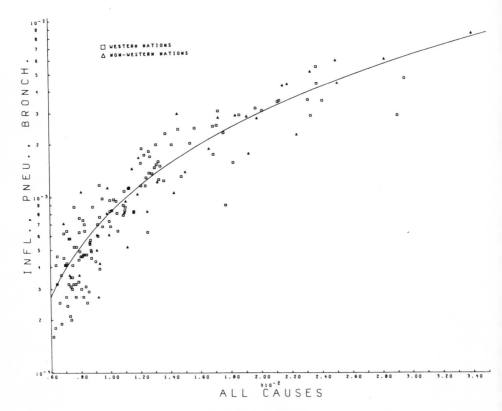

Figure 2.1 (continued)

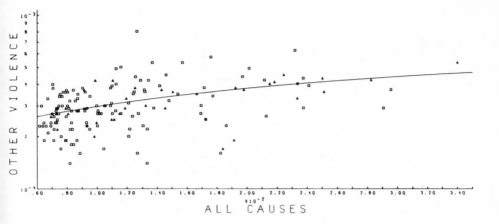

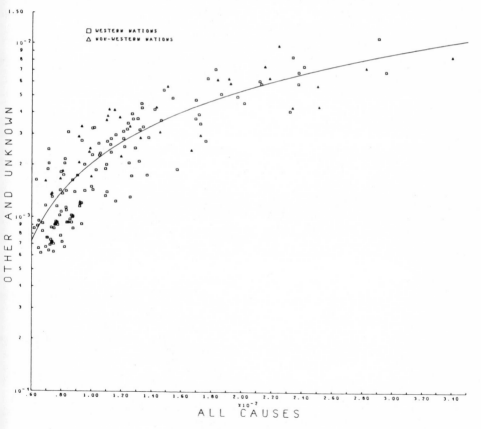

Figure 2.1 (continued)

17

all causes. Table 2.2 presents these parameters for eleven causes of death for both females and males. For most of the remainder of this chapter, motor vehicle accidents and "other violence" have been combined into one category: "violence." It must be borne in mind that the figures in the table depend upon the standard age distribution employed. Had we used a younger standard age distribution, for example, the results would be more reflective of cause-of-death patterns at younger ages.

The correlation coefficients for both sexes arrange themselves into two groups. One set is always above $+.73$ and the other always below $+.48$.

Table 2.2

Coefficients of correlation and parameters of linear regressions relating death rates from each cause to those from all causes combined*

Cause of death, i	Coefficient of correlation with death rate, all causes combined		Parameters of the simple linear regression of the form,[a] $M_i = a_i + b_i \cdot M$. (Standard error of b_i in parentheses)			
			Females		Males	
	Females	Males	a_i (intercept)	b_i (slope)	a_i (intercept)	b_i (slope)
Respiratory tuberculosis	0·860	0·866	−0·0007	0·1059 (0·0049)	−0·0011	0·1188 (0·0054)
Other infectious and parasitic	0·905	0·880	−0·0011	0·1398 (0·0052)	−0·0015	0·1458 (0·0062)
Neoplasms	−0·477	−0·664	0·0016	−0·0245 (0·0035)	0·0024	−0·0569 (0·0050)
Cardiovascular	0·113	−0·153	0·0033	0·0179 (0·0123)	0·0048	−0·0316 (0·0160)
Influenza/pneumonia/ bronchitis	0·926	0·938	−0·0016	0·2434 (0·0078)	−0·0026	0·2831 (0·0082)
Diarrheal	0·804	0·782	−0·0007	0·1041 (0·0060)	−0·0010	0·1050 (0·0066)
Certain chronic	0·291	0·308	0·0003	0·0165 (0·0043)	0·0003	0·0206 (0·0050)
Maternal	0·890	—	−0·0001	0·0197 (0·0008)	—	—
Certain diseases of infancy	0·765	0·733	0·0000	0·0422 (0·0028)	−0·0001	0·0447 (0·0033)
Violence	0·224	0·404	0·0003	0·0041 (0·0014)	0·0006	0·0232 (0·0041)
Other and unknown (residual)	0·892	0·872	−0·0013	0·3307 (0·0131)	−0·0020	0·3475 (0·0153)
Sum			0·0000	0·9998	0·0002	1·0002

[a] All parameters refer to calculations performed on data in their decimal form, representing the annual number of deaths per member of the population.

The group displaying a close positive association with death rates from all causes combined consists of respiratory tuberculosis, other infectious and parasitic diseases, influenza/pneumonia/bronchitis, diarrheal diseases, maternal mortality, certain diseases of infancy, and "all other and unknown." Since we will have later occasion to refer to this set of causes, we will name them the "motile" group. The second group, having a much weaker association with overall mortality, consists of neoplasms, cardiovascular diseases, certain chronic diseases, and violence. For both sexes, death rates from neoplasms are *negatively* associated with death rates from all causes; for males the negative association also appears in cardiovascular diseases.

More interesting than the degree of association is the extent to which a particular cause contributes to change in death rates from all causes combined. Linear regression proves to be a very convenient device for providing this information. We have estimated for each of the 11 causes, i, equations of the form

$$M_i = a_i + b_i M,$$

where a_i, b_i are fitted constants for cause of death i, M the death rate from all causes combined, and M_i the predicted death rate from cause i. Using the least-squares regression technique, Nicholson (1949) and Espenshade (1973) have shown that, except for rounding errors,

$$\sum b_i = 1.0000, \qquad \sum a_i = 0.0000.$$

As a result of this convenient property, we can choose any value of M, insert it into each of the 11 cause-specific equations, and produce predicted values of M_i which sum to the original value of M. Moreover, since the predicted change in M_i per unit change in M is b_i, the predicted changes summed over all i must equal 1.0000 per unit change in M. In this manner a change in the death rate from all causes can be precisely ascribed to its individual components. The set of b_i's is probably the best single indicator of the cause structure of mortality variation. Of course, it measures only the contribution made by a cause in its "underlying" role. The actual contribution made by a disease to mortality change includes whatever impact it may have on mortality from other underlying causes.

Table 2.2 presents b_i coefficients for the 11 causes of death for each sex. Sex differences in the b_i's are relatively small in absolute value, never amounting to as much as 0.04. Ignoring temporarily "other and unknown," we note that the cause of death which declines the most when death rates from all causes decline is "influenza, pneumonia, and bronchitis." About 25% of the change in death rates from all causes can, on average, be ascribed to changing death rates from this cause. Another 10% is due to the category, "diarrheal diseases." Both of these categories work principally through the death rates of children under 5 years. Both are produced by microorganisms that are exceedingly diverse and often difficult to identify and both causes have consequently proved resistant to attack through any one specific medical instrument (McDermott, 1966). Together, they account for considerably more of the decline in mortality than all of the well-defined infectious diseases combined, a category which includes tuberculosis, typhus, typhoid, diphtheria, dysentery, measles, and whooping cough.

McDermott (1966) argues that the importance of the "name" diseases has been overemphasized in high-mortality populations, and contends that it is incorrect to think of such populations as being dominated by diseases that Western populations have "learned" to control. The respiratory and diarrheal diseases of early life have indeed come under control, but it is not clear that, apart from listing a large number of factors that "must have" been involved, we can say how we did it. These results tend to confirm McDermott's contention and caution to some extent against optimism regarding the decipherability of factors in mortality change.

The well-defined infectious diseases—respiratory tuberculosis and "other infectious and parasitic diseases"—account for about one-quarter of the mortality decline, of which fraction approximately 40% is specifically attributable to respiratory tuberculosis. Altogether, the diseases of infectious origin account for approximately 60% of the change in death rates from "all causes." Almost all of the remainder is due to changing death rates from the category, "all other and unknown causes." Leaving one-third of the total movement to be explained by an essentially residual component is scarcely satisfactory. However, evidence to be presented implies that a majority of change in death rates from the residual category should be ascribed to change in cardiovascular disease.

We can note at this point that the mortality changes in England and Wales between 1851–1860 and 1891–1900, carefully examined by McKeown and Record (1962), are quite exceptional. During this period 43.9% of the decline in age and sex standardized death rates could be ascribed to changing rates from respiratory tuberculosis, compared to the normal 11–12%. The proportion of decline in England attributable to other infectious and parasitic diseases was also exceptionally high at 47.6%, compared to the standard 14%. Influenza, pneumonia, and bronchitis—typically the largest contributor to mortality change—was virtually constant during the period in England and Wales. Unfortunately, the country with the most satisfactory early data appears to offer an atypical account of mortality decline, a record that may be largely responsible for prevailing representations of mortality reduction that stress the role of specific and readily identified infectious diseases of childhood and early adulthood.

Association among Causes; with Emphasis on Cardiovascular Disease and "Other and Unknown Causes"

A tendency towards positive correlation between death rates from a particular cause and death rates from all causes combined is produced by the additive inclusion of the cause-specific rate in the "all cause" rate. For example, if only one cause of death were responsible for movements in death rates from "all causes," then these two series would be perfectly correlated (and every other cause would have zero correlation with "all causes").

Estimating the expected amount of this internally generated correlation, due to the additive nature of the all-cause category, can proceed as follows.

Let X_j, Y_j, Z_j be the death rate from causes X, Y, and Z for the jth population. Assume that we are distinguishing only two causes of death (e.g., cancer and "all other causes"), labeled X and Y, and that for all populations j,

$$X_j + Y_j = Z_j.$$

Assume further that no correlation exists from population to population between X_j and Y_j. Then it is readily shown that the coefficient of correlation between X_j and Z_j, r_{XZ}, is equal to σ_X/σ_Z (Preston and Nelson, 1974, pp. 24–25). That is, the amount of internally generated correlation between X and Z is equal to the ratio of the standard deviations of X and Z. These ratios may be found in Table 2.1. It is clear from a comparison of Tables 2.1 and 2.2 that the amount of internally generated correlation for diseases in the "motile" group is in all cases less than half the total correlation, and is more commonly around 20% of that figure. Subtracting one figure from the other reduces the correlation below .66 for only one of these cause-of-death categories—the residual, discussion of which is again deferred.

Thus the close association between death rates from a cause in the motile group and death rates from "all causes" is not primarily a spurious result of the nature of the variables. Rather, it reflects close associations among individual causes of death within this group. This assertion is supported in Table 2.3, where linear correlations between each pair of cause-specific death rates are presented. For both males and females, correlations between any two diseases in the "motile" group—tuberculosis, other infectious and parasitic, influenza/pneumonia/bronchitis, diarrheal, maternal, certain diseases of infancy, and other unknown—are usually above .70 (21 cases out of 36) and always above .59. At the same time, causes outside this special group are typically poorly correlated both with those in the group and among

Table 2.3

Interpopulation coefficients of correlation between cause-specific death rates

(Upper triangle: FEMALES; lower triangle: MALES)

	Respiratory tuberculosis	Other infectious and parasitic	Neoplasms	Cardiovascular	Respiratory	Diarrheal	Certain chronic	Maternal	Certain diseases of infancy	Violence	Residual
Respiratory tuberculosis		0·748	−0·391	0·094	0·793	0·618	0·244	0·837	0·635	0·174	0·720
Other infectious and parasitic	0·739		−0·547	−0·077	0·826	0·757	0·136	0·800	0·661	0·128	0·859
Neoplasms	−0·590	−0·750		0·265	−0·430	−0·618	0·098	−0·376	−0·298	0·191	−0·617
Cardiovascular	−0·217	−0·353	0·448		0·019	−0·005	0·170	0·027	0·111	0·309	−0·229
Respiratory	0·806	0·821	−0·585	−0·211		0·674	0·252	0·848	0·715	0·214	0·790
Diarrheal	0·663	0·774	−0·708	−0·300	0·679		0·058	0·652	0·604	0·036	0·769
Certain chronic	0·287	0·167	−0·264	0·010	0·249	0·085		0·417	0·167	0·444	0·138
Maternal	—	—	—	—	—	—	—		0·683	0·279	0·763
Certain diseases of infancy	0·608	0·667	−0·540	−0·180	0·673	0·591	0·234	—		0·091	0·633
Violence	0·338	0·302	−0·225	0·028	0·320	0·197	0·441	—	0·432		0·025
Residual	0·738	0·837	−0·757	−0·494	0·794	0·748	0·174	—	0·600	0·214	

themselves. As a result, they bear little relation to the category, "all causes combined."

The figures in Table 2.3 do not indicate the presence of direct causal relations among different diseases. Instead, they reflect variations in antecedent health conditions that tend to affect several causes of death simultaneously. Nutritional standards directly affect death rates from both tuberculosis and diarrheal diseases. Progress in chemotherapy reduced mortality from many infectious diseases as well as from pneumonia. To control in a crude way for these antecedent conditions, we can compute partial correlations between two causes, holding constant the death rate from all causes combined, which we assume is an accurate proxy for these antecedent conditions. Table 2.4 demonstrates that such a control severly reduces the correlations among diseases in the motile group. All zero-order correlations between two diseases in the group were above $+.59$, but none of the partial correlations are above $+.32$.

One outstanding feature emerges from Table 2.4: a very high negative partial correlation between death rates from cardiovascular diseases or neoplasms and "all other and unknown." In other words, when a population's death rate from cardiovascular diseases in unusually low relative to its predicted value, "other and unknown" rates tend to be unusually high. The further a population lies below the cardiovascular regression line, the higher it tends to lie above the "other and unknown" regression line. The four partial correlations between cardiovascular diseases or neoplasms and "other and unknown," in fact, are the highest in absolute value of any of the 100 entries in the table.

These relationships suggest that a large proportion of deaths which should have been assigned to cardiovascular diseases and neoplasms were in many instances assigned instead to "other and unknown causes." Such errors would cause an artificial inflation of the latter death rate and a deflation of the former, creating a negative partial correlation. Misassignment of deaths to "senility" seems the mechanism most likely to be operating.

In order to support this interpretation, we must once again deal with the argument that the result is merely a statistical artifact. A negative partial correlation between two diseases, holding constant death rates from all causes combined, is to be expected since death rates from one disease cannot be increased, while holding constant death rates from all causes combined, without reducing death rates from some other cause. In order to estimate the size of the expected negative partial correlation, we expand upon the earlier result. Suppose there are three causes of death in a population and we denote death rates from these causes as X, Y, and P. Their death rates sum to the death rate from Z, all causes. The partial correlation coefficient

Table 2.4

Interpolation coefficients of partial correlation between cause-specific death rates, holding constant the level of mortality from all causes combined

	Respiratory tuberculosis	Other infectious and parasitic	Neoplasms	Cardio-vascular	Respiratory	Diarrheal	Certain chronic	Maternal	Certain diseases of infancy	Violence	Residual
Respiratory tuberculosis		−0·138	0·042	−0·006	−0·014	−0·242	−0·012	0·306	−0·069	−0·038	−0·202
Other infectious and parasitic	−0·098		−0·307	−0·424	−0·072	0·117	−0·311	−0·026	−0·112	−0·180	0·272
Neoplasms	−0·039	−0·466		0·365	0·036	−0·449	0·282	0·122	0·118	0·348	−0·481
Cardiovascular	−0·170	−0·466	0·469		−0·228	−0·161	0·143	−0·163	0·039	0·293	−0·734
Respiratory	−0·036	−0·028	0·145	−0·198		−0·316	−0·049	0·136	−0·026	0·017	−0·210
Diarrheal	−0·047	0·190	−0·405	−0·293	−0·252		−0·310	−0·238	−0·030	−0·249	0·192
Certain chronic	0·042	−0·232	−0·083	0·061	−0·124	−0·263		0·364	−0·091	0·406	−0·281
Maternal	—	—	—	—	—	—	—		0·005	0·177	−0·153
Certain diseases of infancy	−0·80	0·067	−0·106	−0·101	−0·062	0·042	0·012	—		−0·127	−0·170
Violence	−0·026	−0·124	0·063	0·099	−0·187	−0·209	0·363	—	0·218		−0·398
Residual	−0·071	0·300	−0·488	−0·746	−0·141	0·218	−0·204	—	−0·118	−0·309	

(Upper triangle: FEMALES; lower triangle: MALES)

between X and Y, holding constant Z, if there were *no* zeroth-order correlation between X and Y, X and P, and Y and P (no relationship among individual causes of death), would then become (Preston and Nelson, 1974, p. 28)

$$r_{xy \cdot z} = \frac{\sigma_x \sigma_y}{\{(\sigma_y^2 + \sigma_p^2)(\sigma_x^2 + \sigma_p^2)\}^{1/2}}.$$

That is, the expected partial correlation depends upon the size of the standard deviation of P (the excluded cause) relative to that of X and Y. As σ_p gets smaller and smaller in relation to σ_x and σ_y, the partial correlation gets closer and closer to -1.00. As σ_p rises, the partial correlation approaches zero.

Applying this formula to the problem and data at hand, let X be the death rate from cardiovascular diseases, Y the death rate from the residual, P the death rate from all other causes than cardiovascular disease and the residual, and Z the death rate from all causes $= X + Y + P$. Then

$$r_{xy \cdot z} = -.141 \text{ for males}$$

$$= -.114 \text{ for females.}$$

It is clear that the actual $r_{xy \cdot z}$'s of $-.746$ and $-.734$ are far greater than would be expected on the basis of these purely statistical considerations.

Because of the size and variability of death rates in the residual, their strong negative relationship with cardiovascular rates becomes of major interpretive concern and bears further elaboration. Table 2.5 is a cross-

Table 2.5

Average death rates from cardiovascular diseases in female populations classified according to death rates from "all causes" and "all other and unknown causes"

Death rates (per 1,000) from "all other and unknown causes"	Death rate (per 1,000) from "all causes" [a]				All
	< 8	8 – 10·999	11 – 13·999	14+	
< 1	3·56	4·52	—	—	3·79
	(26)	(8)			(34)
1 – 1·999	2·90	4·09	4·84	4·60	3·82
	(13)	(23)	(5)	(1)	(42)
2 – 3·499	2·15	3·08	3·48	4·65	3·42
	(2)	(17)	(19)	(6)	(44)
3·5+	—	2·92	2·31	3·53	3·27
		(1)	(9)	(35)	(45)
All	3·28	3·79	3·37	3·72	3·56
	(41)	(49)	(33)	(42)	(165)

[a] Number of populations in parentheses.

classification of the 165 populations by the level of "all causes" and of "other and unknown," with the mean value of cardiovascular death rates computed for populations falling into each cell. Clearly, cardiovascular disease varies positively with "all causes," holding constant the level of "other and unknown." It is equally clear that, at a certain level of death rates from all causes, high death rates from "other and unknown" are associated with low cardiovascular rates. These results represent a striking instance of the need to consider simultaneously the influence of two variables upon a third. The proportion of variance in female cardiovascular death rates "explained" by the female rate from either "all causes" or "other and unknown" acting alone is, respectively, .013 and .051. Acting simultaneously, however, they account for .545 of the total variance.

The slope of the cardiovascular versus all-causes regression is altered substantially when "other and unknown" enters as an independent variable.

The new regressions are

Females

$$M_1 = 0.00247 + 0.2456M - 0.6888M_2, \qquad R^2 = 0.545$$
$$ (0.0186) \quad\ \ (0.0501)$$

Males

$$M_1 = 0.00330 + 0.2390M - 0.7788M_2, \qquad R^2 = 0.566$$
$$ (0.0218) \quad\ \ (0.0547)$$

where M_1 is the death rate from cardiovascular disease, M_2 that from other and unknown causes, and M that from all causes combined. In both cases the coefficients of the "all-causes" rate become large and positive, implying that cardiovascular disease is typically an influential contributor to mortality decline. Holding constant the death rate from "other and unknown" causes, when death rates from all causes decline by one unit, cardiovascular diseases decline by a quarter unit. The category attains an importance in mortality variation equal to that of "influenza, pneumonia, bronchitis," or the combination of tuberculosis and all other infectious and parasitic diseases.

These statistical results must be treated cautiously, of course, particularly since they are so strikingly opposed to conventional wisdom. In support of the validity of the result, it can be argued that deaths coded to senility and ill-defined conditions at older ages must have been caused by some disease process that is currently specifiable, and cardiovascular diseases (along with cancer) is the most plausible candidate. Even taking no account of declining death rates from "other and unknown" causes, the female death rate from cardiovascular diseases already tends to fall with mortality level. Moreover, this fall is extremely pronounced at younger ages, as will be demonstrated in Table 5.1. In fact, cardiovascular disease is shown there to be the leading source of mortality decline at ages 45–64 when life expectancy increases from the range of 45–54.99 to one of greater than 70. It is only above age 70, where ascription of death to senility would be most common in high-mortality populations, that average death rates from cardiovascular disease are higher in female populations with life expectancy above 70 than in those with life expectancy below 45.

Why should cardiovascular death rates fall in step with death rates from other causes? Certainly one reason is that many forms of cardiovascular disease that were formerly prevalent, such as rheumatic heart disease and bacterial endocarditis, were infectious in origin. Death rates from these diseases were affected by many of the same factors influencing other infectious diseases, especially decreased crowding, improved nutrition, and antibiotics.[2] Even where heart disease is not of infectious origin, infectious diseases, particularly those with respiratory complications, can precipitate a cardiovascular incident. It is also possible that improved standards of living and decreased hours of work and fatigue have exercised some beneficial effect. According to Keys *et al.* (1950, pp. 202, 617), cardiac atrophy is a regular result of undernutrition and starvation, and premature senility may be a common occurrence. However, some types of cardiovascular disease seem to decrease under famine conditions, particular coronary disease and myocardial infarction (Keys *et al.,* 1950, pp. 617–618). There are suggestions that fatigue resulting from extremely hard physical labor can speed the aging process (Dublin, Lotka, and Spiegelman, 1949, p. 233; Dublin, 1919, p. 24), although this is probably not a major factor in most of the populations under study here. Whatever the combination of reasons, our results are reflected in continuing social class differentials in cardiovascular mortality in the United States. Death rates from cardiovascular disease tend to show an important inverse relationship with social class, a gradient which is particularly strong for females of all ages and for males between ages 25 and 64 (Kitagawa and Hauser, 1973, chap. 2). The search for an adequate explanation of these tendencies is perhaps one of the most important tasks facing mortality analysis.

Contribution of Various Causes to Mortality Decline as a Function of Mortality Level

Up to this point, we have summarized the cause structure of mortality variation by means of linear regression. In a straight-line relationship, of

---

[2] For a review of rheumatic heart disease trends and related factors, see Moriyama, Krueger, and Stamler (1971, chap. 7). See also Campbell (1963).

course, the amount of change in one variable per unit change in the other remains constant through the whole range of their relationship. If linear regression proved to be the best method of representing the relationships considered here, we could conclude that the cause structure of mortality change was essentially invariant with respect to the level of mortality: the same causes would be responsible for a decline in M from 30 to 20 as for a decline from 20 to 10, and the size of the contribution of a particular cause would be identical.

For the most part, the amount of curvature in the relationships proves to be insubstantial. That this should be true is hardly surprising in view of the high linear correlation coefficients between many of the individual causes and "all causes." Several different methods of nonlinear curve fitting were tried, including logarithmic and second-, third-, and fourth-degree polynomial regressions. The gain in explanatory power resulting from the addition of terms beyond the linear was very small. Almost all of the observed gain resulted from the addition of the second-degree term in a polynomial expression. Table 2.6 displays the coefficients of second-degree polynomials of the form

$$M_i = a_i + b_i \cdot M + c_i \cdot M^2.$$

Although the coefficients of the second-degree term are typically larger than those of the first, it should be noted that they are multiplying a variable whose average value is only .015 of the average value of the first-degree term.

The importance of nonlinearities depends in part on the measure used. It is clear from a comparison of the coefficients of correlation in Tables 2.6 and 2.2 that the gain from introducing the second-degree term is typically quite small, exceeding .05 in only one case—certain chronic diseases for females. However, when measured against the *unexplained* variance, and in view of the large number of observations, even small improvements can be statistically significant. In eleven cases out of 21, the reduction in unexplained variance caused by the introduction of the second-degree term is statistically significant at the 5% level.[3] Perhaps a more informative test is the relative importance of the first- and second-degree terms in the polynomial, as indicated by their respective β weights.[4] In 17 of the 21 sets of

---

[3] The reduction in unexplained variance from the introduction of the second-degree term is statistically significant at the 5% level in the following cases: other infectious and parasitic (females); neoplasms (males and females); influenza/pneumonia/bronchitis (males and females); diarrheal (males and females); certain chronic diseases (males and females); certain diseases of infancy (males); violence (males).

[4] This is the slope coefficient multiplied by the ratio of the standard deviation of the independent variable to that of the dependent variable. It can be interpreted as the amount of change in the dependent variable (in standard deviation units) per unit change in the independent variable, also in standard deviation units. See Blalock (1960, pp. 345–346).

Table 2.6

Parameters of the curvilinear regression relating death rates from each cause to those from all causes combined and coefficients of multiple correlation for both sexes

Cause of death, i	Parameters of the curvilinear regression of the form, $M_i = a_i + b_i \cdot M + c_i \cdot M^2$ (standard errors of b_i and c_i in parentheses)						Coefficient of multiple correlation with death rate, all causes combined R_i	
	Females			Males				
	a_i	b_i	c_i	a_i	b_i	c_i	Females	Males
Respiratory tuberculosis	−0·00096	0·1421 (0·0207)	−1·0672 (0·5926)	−0·00141	0·1601 (0·0217)	−0·9937 (0·5053)	0·8628	0·8697
Other infectious and parasitic	−0·00065	0·0786 (0·0213)	1·8046 (0·6108)	−0·00127	0·1221 (0·0251)	0·5702 (0·5849)	0·9097	0·8811
Neoplasms	0·00140	0·0056 (0·0148)	−0·8863 (0·4229)	0·00272	−0·0964 (0·0203)	0·9488 (0·4729)	0·4981	0·6738
Cardiovascular	0·00288	0·0855 (0·0519)	−1·9961 (1·4888)	0·00396	0·0763 (0·0648)	−2·5922 (1·5095)	0·1536	0·2023
Respiratory	−0·00019	0·0404 (0·0286)	5·9920 (0·8189)	−0·00050	0·0486 (0·0276)	5·6354 (0·6428)	0·9449	0·9585
Diarrheal	−0·00124	0·1768 (0·0249)	−2·1452 (0·7127)	−0·00196	0·2111 (0·0254)	−2·5496 (0·5925)	0·8156	0·8070
Certain chronic	−0·00011	0·0735 (0·0174)	−1·6822 (0·4987)	−0·00006	0·0638 (0·0201)	−1·0382 (0·4684)	0·3804	0·3490
Maternal	−0·00015	0·0246 (0·0033)	−0·1423 (0·0953)	—	—	—	0·8920	—
Certain diseases of infancy	−0·00009	0·0491 (0·0118)	−0·2025 (0·3380)	−0·00042	0·0831 (0·0129)	−0·9222 (0·3013)	0·7656	0·7499
Violence	0·00033	−0·0003 (0·0006)	0·1292 (0·1685)	0·00026	0·0658 (0·0164)	−1·0260 (0·3829)	0·2318	0·4459
Residual	−0·00127	0·3248 (0·0557)	0·1739 (1·5953)	−0·00123	0·2658 (0·0622)	1·9626 (1·4499)	0·8919	0·8734
Sum	−0·00005	1·0007	−0·0221	−0·00001	1·0003	−0·0049		

29

coefficients in Table 2.6, the β weight of the first-degree, or linear term, exceeds that of the second-degree term.[5] Perhaps the most sensible procedure is to present the graphs of the polynomial equations and let the reader judge the importance of nonlinearities. Figure 2.2 displays these lines, identical to those previously presented in Figure 2.1 but now on a linear rather than a log–linear scale. Obvious nonlinearities are clearest for cardiovascular diseases, a result which is plausibly attributed to their deficient coding in high-mortality populations. There is also a tendency for influenza/pneumonia/bronchitis to contribute more to declines at higher rather than at low levels, which may reflect overassignment of deaths to terminal causes in statistically poor populations. In general, the causes responsible for mortality decline do not appear to vary substantially over the range of mortality which we are observing. However, while linear relationships provide a reasonably accurate characterization of the past, they cannot obtain in the future. Countries currently at the lowest levels of mortality will be forced to utilize a different set of causes in order further to reduce mortality, since death rates from the causes previously responsible for change are now virtually zero.

Populations with Unusual Cause-of-Death Structure

No population has a cause-of-death structure identical to that predicted by the regression equations. Variation from the norm can reflect either real differences in the prevalence of the several causes or coding idiosyncracies. In the remainder of the chapter we are primarily concerned with identifying consistent regional or temporal discrepancies in the cause structure of mortality. As a preliminary step, we will examine the degree to which individual populations adhere to the predicted relationships. In all cases, the predictions are derived from the polynomial equations in Table 2.6. For convenience, we deal only with female populations.

We will utilize the following index of dissimilarity in order to identify those populations with the most deviant cause-of-death structures:

$$D_j = \frac{50 \sum_i |M_{ij} - \hat{M}_{ij}|}{\sum_i M_{ij}},$$

where D_j is the index of dissimilarity for population j, M_{ij} the death rate from cause i in population j, and M_{ij} is the predicted death rate from cause

---

[5] The interested reader may derive the β weights for himself by combining the figures of Tables 2.1 and 2.6. The standard deviation of (all causes)^2 is 0.00020 for females and 0.00025 for males.

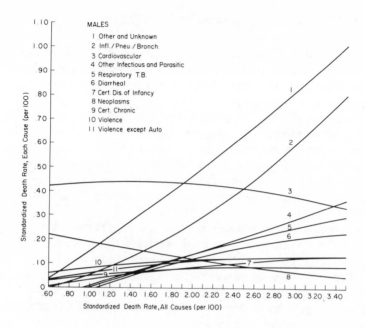

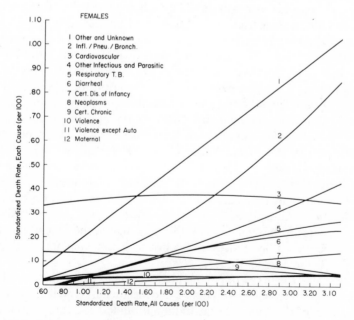

Figure 2.2   Polynomial regression of the relationships between death rates from a particular cause and from all causes combined, plotted on a linear scale.

i, based on polynomial regressions of Table 2.6 and death rate from all causes in *j*. Since $\sum \hat{M}_i = \sum M_i = M$, the measures can take values between 0 and 100. D_j is thus interpretable as the percentage of the maximum possible deviation in its cause structure of mortality achieved by population *j*.

Table 2.7 displays the value of D_j for each female population in which it exceeds 19.0, and identifies the four largest contributing causes of death to the overall discrepancy. The grand mean of D_j for all populations is 12.6. A wide range of mortality is represented among these deviant populations, extending from a death rate of 6.29 to one of 19.8 (only 1.8% of all 165 populations fall below this minimum and 10.9% above the maximum). The geographical and temporal range is also broadly representative of that in the entire sample, except for a moderate overrepresentation of "non-Western" countries.

The most striking result depicted in Table 2.7 is the importance of deviations from predicted values of cardiovascular diseases and "other and unknown" (O + U). For every one of the populations listed, these are two of the three most deviant causes of death, and in most cases they are the leading two. Deviations for the two causes are always opposite in sign. These findings give flesh to the previously noted negative partial correlation between cardiovascular diseases and "other and unknown." For the most part, they are reasonably attributed to improper diagnostic and coding practices, wherein deaths which should have been assigned to cardiovascular disease are allocated instead to the "other and unknown category." In 12 of the 18 cases, death rates from cardiovascular diseases are below predicted levels and those from the "other and unknown" category are above. A country that is particularly assiduous in reporting cardiovascular deaths would appear as a positive deviation from the norm for this disease. It is possible that the United States, from which three of the remaining six populations are drawn, is such a country. However, it is also possible that cardiovascular disease has been overreported here. According to the report of the *Vital Statistics of the United States, 1950:* "Heart disease was probably overreported as a cause of death during the first two decades of the century in that many deaths were improperly returned as some ill-defined heart disease when actually they were due to an undiagnosed condition other than heart disease" (United States Public Health Service, 1950, p. 171). But since death rates from senility were still quite high in the U.S. populations, what may be true of heart disease may not be true of the more aggregative category, "cardiovascular disease."

An international survey of coding practices sheds some light on whether these discrepancies are due to coding idiosyncrasies, as well as on certain other features of the table. For attribution of underlying cause, 1,032 death certificates listing multiple causes were sent to 18 predominantly Western

Table 2.7

Index of dissimilarity (D_j) of cause of death structure, and most deviant causes of death for all female populations where (D_j) exceeds 19.0

Country (i)	Year	Age-standardized crude death rate	D_j	Largest absolute deviation from predicted value[a] (deaths per 100,000)			
				1st	2nd	3rd	4th
Greece	60	712	27·0	136 (O+U)	−132 (Card)	−47 (Canc)	20 (Diar)
U.S. (non-white)	50	1255	26·3	266 (Card)	−157 (O+U)	−63 (Resp)	−55 (Diar)
Greece	64	714	25·4	−116 (Card)	93 (O+U)	−43 (Canc)	23 (Resp)
Mexico	64	1152	25·3	−211 (Card)	159 (O+U)	−44 (Canc)	38 (Resp)
Guatemala	64	1840	24·2	−254 (Card)	164 (I+P)	138 (O+U)	102 (Diar)
Guatemala	61	1915	23·6	−258 (Card)	215 (I+P)	121 (O+U)	−99 (TB)
France	64	629	23·6	−116 (Card)	93 (O+U)	−43 (Canc)	23 (Resp)
Malta and Gozo	64	921	22·7	173 (Card)	−55 (O+U)	−33 (Canc)	−42 (Resp)
Hong Kong	64	693	22·2	−119 (Card)	58 (O+U)	33 (Resp)	27 (Canc) / 27 (TB)
Norway	10	1330	21·9	−169 (Card)	137 (O+U)	118 (TB)	−41 (Diar)
Hong Kong	61	808	20·4	−123 (Card)	54 (Resp)	44 (O+U)	36 (TB)
Scotland	51	1091	20·2	191 (Card)	−101 (O+U)	−34 (Diar)	−27 (I+P) / 27 (Canc)
Poland	60	843	20·2	155 (O+U)	−89 (Card)	−31 (Canc)	−24 (Chron)
U.S.	40	1159	20·1	−133 (O+U)	100 (Card)	93 (Chron)	−40 (Diar)
S. Africa (coloured)	51	1981	19·4	−304 (O+U)	172 (Card)	139 (TB)	−43 (I+P)
N. Zealand	81	1480	19·3	176 (O+U)	−138 (Card)	67 (I+P)	−41 (Resp)
U.S.	30	1365	19·3	−149 (O+U)	108 (Chron)	91 (Card)	−50 (Diar)
Norway	20	1268	19·1	−144 (Card)	107 (TB)	99 (O+U)	−51 (Diar)

[a] $M_{ij} - \hat{M}_{ij}$, where $\hat{M}_{ij} = a_i + b_i \cdot M_j + c_i \cdot M_j^2$.

countries in 1935 (U.S. Bureau of the Census, 1938). The median number of deaths ascribed to cardiovascular disease for all countries was 185. Of nations appearing in Table 2.7, Scotland and the Republic of South Africa were quite close to the median at 179 and 191, respectively. The United States was above it at 203 and Norway below it at 159.[6] The tendencies in the United States and Norway correspond to their positions in Table 2.7, and support the statements in the previous paragraph. In addition, Norway showed the strongest tendency to assign deaths to tuberculosis. (The Republic of South Africa, another highly tubercular population in Table 2.7, showed no such tendency.)

However, it would probably be an error to conclude that a majority of the abnormality in Norwegian tuberculosis rates in 1910 and 1920 or in the United States and Norwegian death rates from cardiovascular disease was a result of coding peculiarities. The Norwegian age curve of mortality in 1910 and 1920 is one of the most unusual ever recorded, a phenomenon almost certainly resulting principally from extremely high tuberculosis mortality, as demonstrated in Chapter 5 (see also Springett, 1960). Cardiovascular deaths rates have remained much higher in the United States than in Norway up to the present, while international coding practices have surely attained greater uniformity. The twelve per cent higher age-standardized crude death rate from all causes among United States females in 1964 compared to Norwegian must be due to *some* cause of death, and none seems as plausible as cardiovascular diseases (Preston *et al.*, 1972). It seems likely that the actual prevalence of a disease in a country may condition the certifier's alertness to it, perhaps producing an exaggeration of national differences but not accounting for all of them. This contention receives some support from a later and much smaller study of national coding practices. In this study, certifiers from several nations were unwilling to ascribe aortic aneurysm to syphilis, as suggested by international coding procedures, on the grounds that syphilis was rare in their country (World Health Organization, 1967, pp. 12–13).

The high death rates from infectious and parasitic diseases in Guatemala are confirmed by an investigation by the Pan American Health Organization of the accuracy of death certification among adults in Guatemala City in the period 1962–1964. The reviewers, in fact, assigned a slightly higher number of deaths to this cause than did the original certifiers. However, they discovered that diarrheal diseases were overrecorded by a factor of 2 or 3, so that this abnormality in the table is plausibly attributed to coding

---

[6] United States Bureau of the Census (1938, pp. 391–392). These figures cannot be applied to national death rates for purposes of adjustment. They undoubtedly overstate proportionate national differences because the sample is composed only of certificates where confusion is likely to occur.

inaccuracies. It is important to note that Guatemala City was the exception in Latin America, with the other nine cites examined showing only "a small net increase or decrease" in adult deaths from this cause after the review of certification (Puffer and Griffith, 1967, pp. 238, 327).

The Pan American Health Organization study also discovered a slight tendency to underrecord cardiovascular mortality in Mexico City (by about nine per cent) and overassign deaths to ill-defined conditions. These results may be associated with Mexico's abnormally low death rate from cardiovascular conditions and high rate from "other and unknown" causes. With regard to France and Greece, each of which appears in the table of deviant cases twice, and would have appeared more frequently had not earlier data been excluded at the outset, it is obvious that cause of death assignment is unusually imprecise. The proportion of deaths assigned here to ill-defined conditions is much higher than normal for a population of reasonably low mortality.

We may conclude this brief discussion of unusual cause-of-death structures by saying that some features of Table 2.7 apparently represent "real" differences in the incidence of death from a particular cause, but that the composition of the table is largely dominated by variation in methods of assigning deaths to cardiovascular diseases and to "other and unknown" causes. Moreover, even when differences are "real," they may be exaggerated by the influence of actual disease prevalence on the certifier's alertness to it.

Populations with highly "normal" cause-of-death structures form a much more coherent bloc, one that contains important implications for age patterns of mortality. Populations with the least deviant cause-of-death structures for females are, in order: Netherlands (1950); Belgium (1964); United States Registration Area (1900); Sweden (1960); Germany (Federal Republic, 1960); Canada Registration Provinces (1921); Japan (1960); Israel (Jewish population, 1951); Canada (1964); Australia (1921 and 1933); Austria (1964); New Zealand (1926); and England and Wales (1881). This list is distinguished by the absence of Southern/Eastern European countries and of any but the most developed of the non-Western bloc. With only two exceptions—Austria and West Germany—the list is confined to members of the Coale–Demeny "West" model of age patterns of mortality. Since this region exhibited an age pattern closer than any other to the norm for all countries combined, the two sets of results are mutually supportive. A concentration of postwar Western European populations is evident, perhaps representing the greater uniformity of cause structures following the successful application of health measures to what may have been local anomalies. Former English colonies in the first third of this century are also overrepresented. In the case of New Zealand and Australia, this may reflect a method of assigning multiple causes that was quite close to the norm for that era (Preston *et al.*, 1972, p. 40). England and Wales during the last half of the nineteenth century also appear in the list, and their cause structure in 1871, 1891, and 1901 also displayed below average deviance. The cause structure of *change* was so peculiar because death rates from tuberculosis and other infectious diseases went from exceptionally high values in 1861 to average values (other infectious diseases) or below average values (tuberculosis) in 1901.

Regional Variation in Cause-of-Death Structure

For the purpose of studying regional variation in cause-of-death structure, we employ the four regions distinguished in Table 1.1. The most straight-forward means of determining whether a region differs significantly from others in its cause structure is to recompute the regression lines relating each cause to all causes, adding the region from which an observation derives as an independent, explanatory variable. We recomputed each regression line ($N = 165$) four times, on each occasion employing a dummy variable representing a different region. The dummy variable took the value 1 if an observation were in the region and 0 otherwise. The coefficient of the dummy variable thus indicates by how much, on the average, death rates from cause *i* in a particular region lie above or below death rates from that cause in all other regions, once mortality level from all causes combined is controlled.

Table 2.8 presents all coefficients of the regional dummy variables that are significant at a 0.05 level, for both males and females. Of the possible 84 coefficients, 35 are significant, or about 40%. That is, in 60% of the cases, information about the region from which an observation is derived is of no significant additional value for predicting a population's cause-specific death rate. The absence of regional significance is much more pronounced for the leading causes of death. Of the six causes of death with the largest mean value—cardiovascular, other and unknown, respiratory, neoplasms, other infectious and parasitic, and tuberculosis—only 13 of 48 regional co-efficients, or 27%, are significant.

The cause of death displaying the most persistent regional differences, for both sexes, is diarrheal disease. Each region differs significantly from all others combined in regard to death rates from this cause. Controlling for mortality level, diarrheal death rates are higher than average both in Southern/Eastern Europe and in non-Western areas, and below average in Northern/Western Europe and in countries of overseas European settlement. By itself, this evidence suggests that Southern and Eastern Europe in general provide a more appropriate "model" of mortality patterns for non-Western countries than do other European areas, and may explain

Table 2.8

Significant coefficients of regional dummy variables (d_i) in regressions relating death rates from a particular cause to death rates from all causes combined. $M_i = a_i + b_i \cdot M + c_i \cdot (M)^2 + d_i \cdot D$, where $D = 1$, if observation is in the region, and 0, otherwise (standard errors of coefficients in parentheses). All numbers refer to death rates per person)

Cause of death	FEMALES				MALES			
	Non-West	Overseas Europe	Northern and Western Europe	Southern and Eastern Europe	Non-West	Overseas Europe	Northern and Western Europe	Southern and Eastern Europe
Respiratory tuberculosis								
Other infectious and parasitic								
Neoplasms			0·00015 (0·00006)			−0·00014 (0·00007)	0·00021 (0·00006)	
Cardiovascular	−0·00061 (0·00017)	0·00049 (0·00017)	0·00016 (0·00004)	−0·00017 (0·00005)	−0·00068 (0·00022)	0·00075 (0·00022)		
Respiratory				−0·00020 (0·00010)			0·00018 (0·00009)	
Diarrheal	0·00020 (0·00008)	−0·00020 (0·00008)	−0·00027 (0·00007)	0·00035 (0·00008)	0·00022 (0·00009)	−0·00022 (0·00009)	−0·00026 (0·00008)	0·00033 (0·00009)
Certain chronic		0·00035 (0·00005)	−0·00013 (0·00005)	−0·00020 (0·00006)		0·00037 (0·00007)	−0·00019 (0·00006)	−0·00019 (0·00007)
Maternal	0·00003 (0·00001)	0·00005 (0·00001)	−0·00003 (0·00001)	−0·00005 (0·00001)	—	—	—	—
Certain diseases of infancy								
Violence		0·00008 (0·00002)		−0·00005 (0·00002)		0·00022 (0·00006)	−0·00014 (0·00005)	
Residual		−0·00065 (0·00018)				−0·00069 (0·00021)		

why the "South" model of Coale and Demeny often provides a superior representation of age patterns of mortality to that of the "West," particularly at ages under 5 (Adlakha, 1972). This point is further elaborated in Chapter 5.

Extended studies by Gordon and his co-workers in Guatemala (1964), and by Moore and collaborators in Costa Rica (1965a,b; 1966a,b), are instructive regarding the causative agents in cases of and deaths ascribed to diarrheal diseases. In both sets of studies, the primary factors implicated were insufficient and/or contaminated food and water, striking with particular virulence at newly-weaned children. According to Moore *et al.,* "more than one-half of the deaths from diarrhea in childhood might more appropriately have been attributed to preexisting malnutrition or severe undernutrition" (1965a, p. 160). Gordon *et al.* (1964) stress the importance of personal hygiene and water availability, along with nutrition. Countries in both the non-Western and Southern/Eastern European blocs appear to score lower on average than the remainder both in calorie or protein intake and in educational attainment of the adult population, which may be associated with personal hygienic practices. Italy, Spain, Portugal, and Greece had the lowest calorie consumption per head of any countries in Europe, North America, or Oceania during 1960/61, and along with Yugoslavia, they were also lowest in quantity of animal protein consumed. Countries in Asia, Latin America, and Africa, even those with reasonably complete vital registration, were also subnormal in these respects. In addition, Italy and Portugal have the highest proportion of adults in Europe who have failed to complete primary school, about 50% (United Nations, 1963b, pp. 44–45; United Nations, 1966, pp. 68–73). Sloan (1971) reports on a cross-regional analysis of death rates in early childhood in Costa Rica, Mexico, East Pakistan, and Puerto Rico. Nutritional standards and female literacy are identified as the most successful predictors. Although causes of death are not distinguished, much of the impact of these variables probably makes itself felt through diarrheal diseases.

Warm climate may also predispose to diarrheal disease and forge an additional link between Southern/Eastern Europe and many non-Western nations. The incidence of all the well-defined intestinal diseases, such as Asiatic cholera, dysentery, and typhoid, is typically highest in the late summer (Tromp, 1963, pp. 522–25), a condition recognized by one term for diarrhea in earlier International Lists as "summer complaint." More to the point, Buck, Sasaki, and Anderson (1958, p. 96) report that in Peru, diarrhea in children is more frequent in tropical than in nontropical villages.

Differences in habits and conditions of life may also account for the excessively high death rates from cardiovascular disease in overseas European countries, and for the low rates in non-Western countries. The United States, Canada, Australia, and New Zealand have the highest cigarette consumption per adult in the world, and also rank high in consumption of other commodities believed deleterious to health, such as animal fats (Preston, 1970, Appendix F). Non-Western countries show relatively low consumption of cigarettes and animal fats.[7] The regional differential in Table 2.8 is greater for males, the sex whose cardiovascular mortality has proved generally more vulnerable to these environmental risks. Climatic and genetic factors cannot be ruled out, however. Moreover, their significant negative deviations for the residual category suggest that recorded mortality from cardiovascular diseases may be overstated in the overseas European region relative to death rates elsewhere. However, Stock's (1969) analysis of the PAHO data strongly indicates that divergent coding practices are not of central importance to these differentials in recorded cardiovascular mortality.

Overseas European countries also exhibit unusually high death rates from violence. It is tempting to attribute such rates to some component of national character produced by the migration or settlement process. However, it should first be noted that about one-third of the excess is attributable to unusually high death rates from automobile accidents in these countries, reflecting primarily high standards of living. Such a statement is possible because computations were performed separately for mortality from automobile accidents and from other forms of violence.[8] In recent years, automobile deaths account for all of the excess in these countries. Death rates from other forms of violence, in fact, tend to fall short of expected levels. The total excess in recent years is, in any case, minor, and does not support the contention that any one of these countries has remained unusually violence-prone. Almost all of the excess in violent mortality in these countries occurred late in the nineteenth or early in the twentieth centuries or is currently due to automobile accidents.

Northern and Western Europe exhibit high death rates among females from respiratory tuberculosis (led by Norway in 1910 and 1920) and among males from influenza/pneumonia/bronchitis (led by England and Wales in the postwar period). A climatic explanation seems plausible in the case of influenza/pneumonia/bronchitis, on the basis of the observed seasonal incidence of death from the diseases and the effect of severe winters (Tromp, 1963, pp. 250, 499–501; Daw, 1954). The suggestion has been made that

---

[7] For figures on cigarette consumption in several non-Western countries, see Todd (1963).

[8] The coefficients of the overseas European dummy variable for automobile accidents were .00007 for males and .00003 for females; for other violence, they were .00015 and .00006. These two sets of coefficients sum to the figures appearing in Table 2.8 for the category, "all violence."

Table 2.9

Comparison of death rates from respiratory tuberculosis, other infectious and parasitic diseases, and diarrheal diseases in non-Western populations in the 1960s with those in Western populations at equivalent mortality levels

FEMALES	All causes	Respiratory tuberculosis	Other infectious and parasitic	Diarrheal
	Age-standardized death rate from specified cause (per 100,000)			
Guatemala, 1964	1840	36	305*	231*
(England and Wales, 1901)	(1971)	(106)	(169)	(107)
(U.S. (Registration Area), 1910)	(1760)	(114)	(129)	(115)
South Africa (coloured), 1960	1666	85	64	194*
(England and Wales, 1911)	(1715)	(82)	(148)	(124)
(France, 1926)	(1625)	(115)	(53)	(47)
Mauritius, 1964†	1222	7	23	74*
(Denmark, 1930)	(1247)	(65)	(55)	(46)
(Netherlands, 1931)	(1217)	(55)	(48)	(11)
Chile, 1964	1196	37	43*	44*
Colombia, 1964	1188	26	71*	66*
Ceylon, 1960†	1155	15	48*	49*
Mexico, 1964	1152	23	63*	85*
(Ireland, 1951)	(1211)	(54)	(26)	(8)
(Sweden, 1930)	(1159)	(105)	(61)	(15)
(U.S., 1940)	(1159)	(33)	(28)	(12)
(Netherlands, 1940)	(1128)	(31)	(32)	(9)
Trinidad and Tobago, 1963	966	8	15	30*
Taiwan, 1964	988	49*	19	35*
Costa Rica, 1964	982	14	41*	76*
(New Zealand, 1936)	(1006)	(31)	(28)	(5)
(Australia, 1940)	(996)	(24)	(23)	(11)
(France, 1951)	(993)	(29)	(22)	(5)
Venezuela, 1964	932	22*	36*	29*
Malta and Gozo, 1964	921	0	5	10*
Panama, 1964	913	27*	45*	29*
(England and Wales, 1951)	(932)	(17)	(12)	(6)
(New Zealand, 1945)	(930)	(21)	(20)	(8)
(Switzerland, 1951)	(921)	(19)	(16)	(5)
Israel (Jewish Pop.), 1964	796	2	6	4
Japan, 1964	792	16*	9	21*
(Northern Ireland, 1964)	(793)	(3)	(4)	(4)
(Netherlands, 1950)	(790)	(12)	(16)	(4)
Puerto Rico, 1964	727	20*	12*	28*
(New Zealand, 1964)	(727)	(1)	(5)	(4)
(Canada, 1960)	(722)	(3)	(5)	(5)
Hong Kong, 1964	693	24*	13*	6*
(England and Wales, 1964)	(693)	(2)	(3)	(5)
(Norway, 1951)	(692)	(14)	(14)	(4)

* Death rate exceeds average for Western populations at that level.
† Population excluded from original sample of 165.
Death rates for Western countries are in parentheses

many deaths assigned to bronchitis in England and Wales may elsewhere have been ascribed to cardiovascular disease, but this interpretation has recently been called into question (Preston *et al.*, 1972, pp. 5–7). A climatic explanation for the observed regional variation in respiratory tuberculosis is not persuasive. Tuberculosis morbidity and mortality are typically highest in May, and sanatoria are often designed to protect the patient from direct sunlight (Tromp, 1963, pp. 502–05). The excess from this cause in the Northern/Western European group is completely attributable to exceptionally high rates in Norway and Sweden throughout the twentieth century, but especially in its earlier years. The search for a satisfactory explanation will have to focus on these populations.

The higher death rates from maternal causes in non-Western and overseas European populations probably reflect in part the unquestionably higher level of fertility in these populations at a given level of mortality. It need not reflect a higher risk of maternal death per confinement. Since the deviations for this cause form a very small proportion of total mortality, we make no attempt to test this assertion.

Certain coefficients are noteworthy for their lack of significance in Table 2.8. Death rates from "other infectious and parasitic diseases" do not differ significantly from one region to another in their contribution to mortality from all causes combined. It was anticipated that the non-Western populations, for which the bulk of data relates to the postwar period, would display exceptionally low death rates from infectious diseases because of their well-publicized access to "Western" health technologies and to international aid designed primarily to combat these diseases. But this expectation is not verified. Table 2.9 provides additional detail on this matter by comparing death rates from respiratory tuberculosis, other infectious and parasitic diseases, and diarrheal diseases in certain non-Western countries during the 1960's to the same rates in those Western populations that are closest to that country in overall mortality level (excluding candidates from Southern/ Eastern Europe).

In every non-Western population, diarrheal death rates either equal or exceed the average rates among the Western populations used as a standard, even when mortality has fallen to very low levels. In 10 of 17 non-Western populations, death rates from "other infectious and parasitic diseases" are also above the Western referent. The basic point to be made, elaborated upon in Chapter 4, is that improved medical and public health technologies have revolutionized the role of infectious diseases in mortality structures of all populations, no less in Western than in non-Western areas. Only in the case of respiratory tuberculosis in those non-Western populations still at relatively high mortality levels is their comparative advantage manifest. If we sum the rates from respiratory tuberculosis and other infectious and parasitic diseases, we find no systematic difference in the importance of the specific infectious diseases in mortality structures of non-Western as opposed to Western countries at comparable overall levels.

Changes in Cause-of-Death Structure

The final question to be considered is whether the cause structure of mortality has changed systematically over time, apart from those changes that "normally" accompany declines in mortality. Two measures of time are employed: the year of observation; and a dummy variable, equal to unity for observations after 1945 and zero otherwise. The latter variable permits inferences regarding the extent to which abrupt changes occurred after World War II, when sulfa drugs, antibiotics, and effective antimalarial measures were all deployed extensively for the first time and when the Sixth Revision of the *International Classification of Diseases, Injuries, and Causes of Death* was introduced with its major modification of procedures for assigning deaths to underlying cause where several terms were listed on a death certificate.

The measure of the importance of changes in cause structure will be the coefficient of partial correlation between these measures of time and the death rate from a particular cause. In one instance we will control mortality level from all causes combined (represented both by the death rate from all causes and by the death rate from all causes squared). In the other instance we will control both mortality level from all causes and the regional composition of populations, using the dummy variables described in the previous section. The results of this procedure are displayed in Table 2.10.

Specific Infectious Diseases.   The categories, respiratory tuberculosis and other infectious and parasitic diseases, display coefficients of the time variables that are consistently negative and usually significant. The negative coefficients for these relationships in Table 2.10 do *not* mean that these diseases have declined over time; such an observation is scarcely worth making. Instead, they mean that, as time progressed, the infectious and parasitic diseases have made a smaller and smaller contribution *to a particular level of overall mortality* (lie further and further below the polynomial regression line computed for the infectious and parasitic diseases).

This result would appear to reflect an accelerating rate of medical progress in combating infectious and parasitic diseases, in relation to the rate of progress against other diseases that have also been important contributors to mortality decline. An outline of the basic developments is available in any text on the history of medicine or public health. It would include the

Table 2.10

Coefficients of partial correlation between death rates from a particular cause and two measures of time

Cause of death	FEMALES				MALES			
	Controlling mortality level from all causes (a)		Controlling mortality level from all causes and regional composition (b)		Controlling mortality level from all causes (a)		Controlling mortality level from all causes and regional composition (b)	
	Years since 1900	Post-war dummy	Years since 1900	Post-war dummy	Years since 1900	Post-war dummy	Years since 1900	Post-war dummy
Respiratory tuberculosis	−0·204	−0·185	−0·235	−0·216	−0·036	−0·068	−0·148	−0·178
Other infectious and parasitic	−0·225	0·081	−0·274	0·116	−0·373	−0·101	−0·442	−0·104
Neoplasms	−0·069	−0·187	0·140	−0·066	0·318	0·178	0·496	0·253
Cardiovascular	0·050	0·045	0·337	0·271	0·231	0·230	0·531	0·470
Respiratory	0·122	−0·064	0·137	−0·121	0·000	−0·140	0·032	−0·158
Diarrheal	0·339	0·274	0·169	0·136	0·191	0·107	−0·015	−0·064
Certain chronic	0·007	−0·270	0·169	−0·229	0·009	−0·221	0·084	−0·197
Maternal	−0·060	−0·151	−0·127	−0·214	—	—	—	—
Certain diseases of early infancy	0·146	0·196	0·073	0·159	0·020	0·088	−0·068	0·039
Violence	0·008	−0·078	0·159	0·026	0·030	0·081	0·121	0·070
Other and unknown	−0·111	0·015	−0·369	−0·150	−0·288	−0·171	−0·520	−0·330

Note: Significant at 5 per cent: ±0·154.

evolution of vaccines, toxoids, antibiotics, and chemotherapy; implementation of community programs of water purification, disease surveillance, and insect control; and improvements in personal sanitary and nutritional practices. Almost all these developments are direct descendants of the germ theory of disease, and the changing cause-of-death structure testifies to the absence of similar intellectual breakthroughs with respect to noninfectious causes. The relative unimportance of economic changes for these developments is suggested by the analysis in Chapter 4.

The linear form of the time variable is the more significant for these diseases. In fact, the postwar dummy coefficients are positive for females. This evidence implies that the acceleration in progress against these diseases has been steady rather than abrupt, an implication again confirmed in Chapter 4. The period during which infectious disease death rates fell furthest below expected levels is 1935–1945, when 15 of the 17 observed deviations for females are negative. Once again, the results reflect the diffuseness and scope of changes in methods of combating infectious diseases and serve to refute the supposedly exceptional character of postwar changes in non-Western countries.

Diarrheal Diseases.   What diseases have begun "replacing" infectious diseases in cause-of-death structures? Table 2.10 suggests that a common successor has been diarrheal disease, although the change is much more pronounced for females. The later the date to which an observation refers, the greater the relative contribution of diarrheal diseases to a particular level of mortality. This observation has been made, in slightly different terms, at the local or national level as well. In reference to Costa Rica, Moore writes that: "this disquieting lag in the decline of mortality from diarrhea has persisted in the face of considerable increase in the medical and public health services available to the population" (1966a, p. 276). The fundamental problem is that the disease can be neither prevented nor cured by injections or other direct remedies readily dispensed through public health programs. Even purification of water supplies has had limited benefits. Diarrheal disease is prompted by poverty and ignorance and it remains closely connected to a nation's level of social and economic development.

However, it is important to note that a majority of the trend in the contribution of diarrheal diseases is attributable to the changing regional composition of populations in the sample. The increasing representation of non-Western populations in the sample, combined with their excessive diarrheal mortality, is largely responsible for the apparent trend in the contribution of this cause. This effect is apparent in the comparison of the two types of partial correlations in columns (a) and (b) (Table 2.10). However, this does not render spurious the partial correlations without the regional variables, since the increased prevalence of non-Western populations in the sample reflects in some measure their increased importance in the world as a whole. Moreover, these diseases have been relatively intransigent in the non-Western region itself, as Moore's comment illustrates.

Cardiovascular Diseases and Neoplasms. These display substantial sex differentials with respect to trends in their contribution to a particular level of mortality. Each of the causes has significantly increased its contribution for males, while for females, neoplasms display no such tendency and the trend for cardiovascular diseases is much weaker. The possibility that a portion of this sex differential in trends is attributable to a greater inflow of deaths from "other and unknown" causes for males than for females is suggested by the larger negative coefficients for this cause among males.

However, there are reasons to suspect that the sex differential is largely real. Almost all the sex difference in trends from cancer in many countries can be ascribed to cancer of the lung, with an obvious environmental correlate.[9] Death rates for cancer of all other sites combined have typically been falling, perhaps in part as a result of reduced ingestion of carbohydrates in certain countries and a consequent reduction in gastric cancer, as well as of improved methods of detection and treatment.[10] Chapter 6 contains a more detailed analysis of sex mortality differentials and suggests that in a broad sense economic modernization and particularly urbanization is a principal source of variability, operating largely through cardiovascular disease. In general, when attention shifts from mortality level to its sex structure, a corresponding analytic shift is provoked from the infectious to the degenerative diseases.

Certain Chronic Diseases. Death rates from "certain chronic diseases" have fallen below expected values in the postwar period. This deficit is primarily attributable to a change in methods of assigning underlying cause when multiple causes are listed on the death certificate, instituted on the occasion of the Sixth Revision of the *International Lists of Diseases, Injuries, and Deaths* (in 1948). Both diabetes and nephritis lost a substantial fraction of their deaths at this time, with the principal recipient being cardiovascular diseases (World Health Organization, 1952 and U.S. Department of Health,

---

[9] For England, see Case (1956). For international figures, see Preston (1970, pp. 59–60).

[10] A dietary argument has been put forth by Wynder and Hoffman (1966). But in a more recent review article, the linkage between diet and stomach cancer was termed "conjectural" by Shils (1968). A new dietary explanation in relation to American trends is the increased consumption of cereals rich in antioxidants according to Shamberger *et al.* (1972).

Education, and Welfare, 1963). Thus, the particular tendency is plausibly ascribed to statistical practices rather than to real developments, although the change in practices is not significant enough to influence substantially the death rate from cardiovascular disease.

Summary

The cause of death typically making the largest contribution to declines in mortality is influenza/pneumonia/bronchitis, which accounts on average for about 25% of mortality change. The figure is somewhat higher for movements that occur at higher mortality levels and lower elsewhere. "Other infectious and parasitic diseases" typically account for about 15% of mortality change, and respiratory tuberculosis and diarrheal diseases for about 10% apiece. These figures are much different from those pertaining to the classically cited case, England and Wales in the late 19th century.

A majority of the remaining decline is attributable to "other and unknown causes." However, there is consistent and compelling statistical evidence suggesting that most of the decline from this cause should be attributed to cardiovascular disease, but that poor diagnostic and coding practices have often obscured the importance of declines from this cause. After making adjustment for the recorded level of mortality from other and unknown causes, cardiovascular disease attains an importance in mortality decline equal to that of influenza/pneumonia/bronchitis.

Differences in habits of life, personal health practices, climate, and economic level probably account for observed regional differences in the cause structure of mortality at a particular level. Non-Western and Southern/Eastern European populations share unusually high death rates from diarrheal disease. When matched with nations from other regions at equivalent mortality levels, non-Western populations invariably display higher death rates from diarrheal diseases. Overseas European populations show abnormally high death rates from cardiovascular diseases and violence, especially among males. The latter tendency is ascribable in more recent years to their high death rates from automobile accidents. Northern/Western European populations display higher than expected death rates from respiratory tuberculosis and from influenza/pneumonia/bronchitis. Surprisingly, the specific infectious diseases of childhood (other infectious and parasitic diseases) do not display significant regional variations.

Over time, the specific infectious diseases have made a smaller and smaller contribution to a particular level of mortality, undoubtedly reflecting an accelerated rate of medical progress against these diseases relative to the rate pertaining to other causes normally implicated in mortality decline. The changes are not confined to the postwar period or to non-Western populations. Diarrheal diseases, on the other hand, have tended to gain prominence in mortality structures over time, particularly in non-Western populations.

CHAPTER 3

Effect of Various Causes
on the Chances
of Death and Longevity

The different causes enter additively into the death rate (crude, age-specific, or age-standardized) from all causes combined. The previous chapter took advantage of this property to attribute mortality variation uniquely to causes. Interrelations among causes are not nearly so simple in the determination of survival chances or longevity. Given a certain set of age-specific death rates from a particular cause, a person is more likely to die from that cause the lower are death rates from other causes. Because this interaction among causes is often awkward to interpret, we have chosen to focus throughout most of this volume on death rates.

Nevertheless, because of the familiarity and appeal of life table measures of mortality, it seems worthwhile to translate some of the basic descriptive results of the previous chapter into life table equivalents. The aim of this chapter is to demonstrate the typical amount by which life is shortened as a consequence of an individual cause of death, and the likelihood that a person will die from a particular underlying cause. As noted, both quantities are affected by the prevalence of other causes. But relatively simple statistical procedures are available to estimate these amounts for an individual population; it is interpopulation *comparisons* that are rendered awkward by the inescapable interactions. In order to estimate the influence of a cause of death on survivorship in an individual population, we rely here upon an iterative technique developed largely by Nathan Keyfitz and described in *Causes of Death: Life Tables for National Populations* (Preston *et al.*, 1972, Chapter II). The basic assumption on which computation is based is that the underlying causes are independent of one another. Operationally, independence means that a change in the death rate at any age x from cause i, $\Delta\mu_x^i$, is assumed to leave unaltered the set of death rates from all other causes of death combined, $\mu_x^{(-i)}$. In computing the chances of death, the assumption of independence means that death can always be ascribed to a particular cause and never need be assigned to a combination of causes. In this sense we have already assumed independence in Chapter 2; indeed, it is virtually forced upon us by the prevailing registration practice of ascribing death to one of a set of mutually exclusive underlying causes.

The chance of dying from a certain cause and the contribution of that cause to the shortening of life obviously varies systematically with level of life expectancy, and a major focus of this chapter is on describing this variation within the 165 populations. Motor vehicle accidents and other forms of violence are grouped in this chapter into a single category, "violence," so that 11 rather than 12 categories will be examined.

The Chances of Dying from a Particular Cause of Death

We begin by examining scatter plots of the relationship between $l_0^{(i)}$, the chance that a randomly drawn person of a particular sex aged zero in the period life table will eventually die from cause i, and e_0^0, the period life expectancy at birth for that sex in that population. For example, someone subject for all of his life to the set of age-cause-specific death rates of United States nonwhite males in 1920 had a 10% chance of dying from respiratory tuberculosis and could expect to live 44.2 years (Preston *et al.*, 1972, pp. 740–41). The chances of death sum over the 11 causes of death to 1 in every population. Everyone must die and the death must be attributed to one or another category of cause. Figures 3.1–3.3 show examples of such scatter plots for the female populations. All observations are pooled; we do not consider in detail in this chapter how relationships might vary with time or space. If data were available for a country at two points in time separated by less than five years, the plotting of the later observation was suppressed, although its value is incorporated in all calculations. As in Chapter 2, the figures are computer-drawn from punched output produced simultaneously with the final run of tables appearing in *Causes of Death: Life Tables for National Populations;* consequently, there is minimal chance of manual or transcription error.

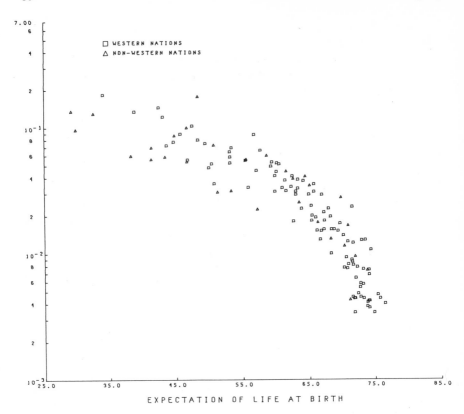

Figure 3.1 Probability of eventual death from other infectious and parasitic diseases for females aged 0.

The three figures presented exhibit the major types of relationships that are to be found in the data for any cause. First, the probability of dying from "other infectious and parasitic diseases" (excluding respiratory tuberculosis) declines quite regularly as life expectancy advances (Figure 3.1). Second, the chance of dying from cardiovascular diseases rises spectacularly, from about 10% to about 60% over the observed range of mortality. This rise is completely caused by the more rapid disappearance of other causes of death, since we have shown in Chapter 2 that female death rates from cardiovascular disease tend themselves to decline as overall mortality level declines. Finally, the chances of dying from violence (suicide, homicide, and accidents) are relatively invariant with the level of life expectancy. When death rates decline from all causes combined, they also decline from violence, and by an amount sufficient to alter the chances of eventual death from this cause by only moderate amounts.

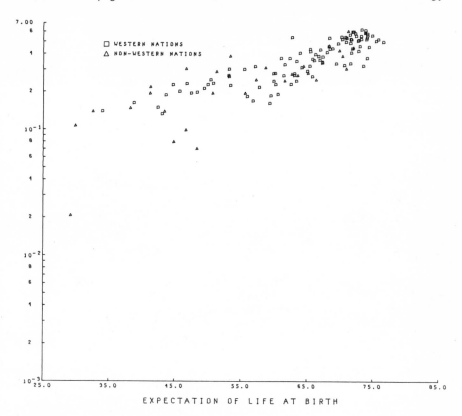

Figure 3.2 Probability of eventual death from cardiovascular disease for females aged 0.

Note that observations for non-Western countries—Africa (except South African whites), Asia, and Latin America—are scattered more or less randomly through the more numerous observations for Western countries. This is also true in general for other diseases and for males, although a newborn in non-Western areas has a somewhat higher risk of eventually dying from diarrheal disease at a particular mortality level, and a smaller risk of death from respiratory tuberculosis or cardiovascular diseases.

A more precise way of expressing these relationships is to fit curves to the scatter plots and use the coefficients of those curves to predict the chances of death from various causes at different levels of life expectancy. Curve fitting seems preferable to averaging observations within a certain range for two reasons: it adds stability by permitting estimates at a particular level to be based partly upon observations at neighboring levels; and it does not disregard variability within an arbitrarily chosen range. The added stability

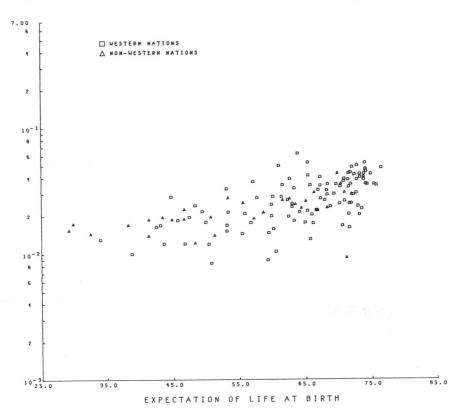

Figure 3.3   Probability of eventual death from all accidents and violence for females aged 0.

becomes quite important for the lower life expectancies, where fewer observations are available. Second-degree polynomials have been computed for
each relationship, fitted by classical least-squares regression. The coefficients of these relationships are such that the predicted values of $l_0^{(i)}$ always
sum to 1, a necessary feature of such a system of equations (Espenshade,
1973). At very high life expectancies for minor causes of death the predictions were occasionally negative, in which case values from a logarithmic
regression are shown and other values adjusted proportionally to sum to 1.
A modest extrapolation of the relationships back to life expectancy of 25
years and forward to one of 75 for males and 80 for females permits some
educated guesses regarding the past and future probabilities of dying from
various causes.

Table 3.1

Probability (× 100) that a person aged 0 will eventually die from a particular cause at various levels of life expectancy

Life Expectancy at Birth	Respiratory Tuberculosis (1)	Other Infectious and Parasitic Diseases (2)	Neoplasms (3)	Cardiovascular Disease (4)	Influenza, Pneumonia, Bronchitis (5)	Diarrheal Diseases (6)	Diabetes, Cirrhosis of Liver, Nephritis, Stomach Ulcer (7)	Maternal Mortality (8)	Certain Diseases of Infancy (9)	Violence (10)	All Other and Unknown Causes (11)	(1)+(2)+ (5)+(6)+ (8) (12)
Females												
25.00	8.24	14.60	0.80	16.57	24.92	8.62	0.93	1.49	5.91	2.03	15.89	57.87
30.00	8.40	13.20	1.53	14.53	22.88	8.51	1.09	1.54	5.50	1.82	21.00	54.53
35.00	8.35	11.75	2.47	13.72	20.82	8.21	1.28	1.55	5.07	1.71	25.07	50.68
40.00	8.00	10.17	3.60	14.09	18.56	7.66	2.42	1.49	4.56	1.67	27.78	45.88
45.00	7.43	8.60	4.92	15.78	16.36	6.94	3.52	1.39	4.06	1.73	29.62	40.72
50.00	6.66	7.07	6.43	18.83	14.27	6.08	4.33	1.24	3.57	1.90	29.63	35.32
55.00	5.70	5.59	8.14	23.25	12.28	5.07	4.83	1.04	3.09	2.18	28.83	29.68
60.00	4.55	4.16	10.04	29.03	10.41	3.92	5.03	0.80	2.61	2.55	26.90	23.84
65.00	3.20	2.77	12.13	36.15	8.65	2.62	4.94	0.52	2.15	3.04	23.83	17.76
70.00	1.65	1.42	14.42	44.60	6.99	1.18	4.55	0.26*	1.70	3.63	19.60	11.50
75.00	0.67*	0.66*	16.48	53.09	5.31	0.52*	3.75	0.18*	1.23	4.21	13.90	7.34
80.00	0.44*	0.42*	18.26	61.23	3.75	0.34*	2.66	0.12*	0.76	4.77	7.25	5.07
Males												
25.00	7.99	14.06	2.04	13.47	26.11	7.93	1.36	....	6.26	2.13	18.65	56.09
30.00	8.55	12.79	1.70	12.00	23.56	8.00	1.56	....	5.93	3.32	22.59	52.90
35.00	8.79	11.41	1.91	11.86	20.99	7.79	1.87	....	5.53	4.34	25.51	48.98
40.00	8.58	9.81	2.64	12.94	18.25	7.26	3.32	....	5.02	5.15	27.03	43.90
45.00	8.08	8.24	3.92	15.42	15.69	6.51	4.38	....	4.48	5.78	27.50	38.52
50.00	7.27	6.65	5.77	19.33	13.33	5.55	5.04	....	3.91	6.24	26.91	32.80
55.00	6.15	5.07	8.17	24.66	11.16	4.37	5.30	....	3.32	6.33	25.27	26.75
60.00	4.73	3.48	11.12	31.41	9.18	2.98	5.18	....	2.70	6.63	22.59	30.37
65.00	2.99	1.90	14.64	39.57	7.39	1.38	4.65	....	2.06	6.56	18.86	13.66
70.00	1.40*	0.83*	18.36	48.25	5.68	0.45*	3.66	....	1.37	6.20	13.80	8.36
75.00	0.98*	0.53*	21.81	56.20	4.09	0.28*	2.25	....	0.66	5.52	7.68	5.88

* Value predicted from logarithmic regression: $\log l_0^i = a_0^i + b_0^i \dot{e}_0$. All others are predicted from polynomial regression: $l_0^i = A_0^i + B_0^i \dot{e}_0 + C_2^i (\dot{e}_0)^2$.

The results, shown in Table 3.1, suggest that, at a life expectancy of 25, approximately 60% of those born will ultimately succumb to an infectious or parasitic disease, when the group is broadened to include influenza, pneumonia, bronchitis, diarrheal diseases, and maternal mortality. Only one-tenth of that fraction die from this group of causes at a life expectancy of 75 or 80. Over the same range, the chance of dying from the combination of neoplasms and cardiovascular disease increases fivefold, from 15% to 75%. These tendencies are not unfamiliar, of course, but Table 3.1 assigns more exact dimensions to them than it was previously possible to do. It also permits an assessment of the degree of abnormality in the recorded cause-of-death structures of individual populations. For example, United States males in 1964 had a life expectancy of approximately 66.9 (Preston et al., 1972, pp. 768–769). Interpolating in Table 3.1, we find that this figure yields an expected probability of dying from cardiovascular disease of .429, in contrast to the actual probability of .569. Thus, United States males had a 33% greater chance of dying from cardiovascular disease than would be expected at their level of life expectancy. On the other hand, their probability of dying from the aggregate of infectious diseases was only .051, compared to an expected .104. Obviously, the United States male population achieved its life expectancy through an unusual and atypical cause of death structure, one with important social and demographic implications. Results for American females are in the same direction but are not quite so striking.

Infectious diseases are often thought to afflict children much more than adults and to modify life expectancy primarily through their activity during childhood years. However, the calculations show that in high-mortality populations a person aged 15 has about the same chance of eventually dying from an infectious disease as a child aged 0. Table 3.2 presents information equivalent to that in Table 3.1, derived in an identical manner, but referring to the chances of dying for a person who has survived to age 15. At a life expectancy of 25, the chances of ultimate death from an infectious disease, broadly defined, are virtually identical (.56 versus .57) for persons aged 15 and for infants. As populations achieve higher life expectancies, both series decline, the one for age 15 declining somewhat faster. The equivalence between the series at low life expectancies results from the counterveiling influences of tuberculosis, primarily a disease of young adults, and "other infectious and parasitic diseases," consisting primarily of well-defined childhood diseases. In a population with a life expectancy of 35.0, a newborn female has an 8.35% chance of eventually dying from tuberculosis (Table 3.1), but if she survives to age 15 that chance increases to 12.30% (Table 3.2). Obviously, the relative incidence of tuberculosis is higher above age 15 than below.

Table 3.2

Probability (× 100) that a person aged 15 will eventually die from a particular cause at various levels of life expectancy

Life Expectancy at Birth	Respiratory Tuberculosis (1)	Other Infectious and Parasitic Diseases (2)	Neoplasms (3)	Cardiovascular Disease (4)	Influenza, Pneumonia, Bronchitis (5)	Diarrheal Diseases (6)	Diabetes, Cirrhosis of Liver, Nephritis, Stomach Ulcer (7)	Maternal Mortality (8)	Certain Diseases of Infancy (9)	Violence (10)	All Other and Unknown Causes (11)	(1)+(2)+ (5)+(6)+ (8) (12)
Females												
25.00	14.33	9.53	2.13	23.21	25.30	4.79	1.42	3.14	......	1.98	14.17	57.09
30.00	13.37	8.52	3.09	20.99	22.60	4.55	1.60	2.91	......	1.73	20.64	51.95
35.00	12.30	7.51	4.18	19.92	20.05	4.25	1.70	2.67	......	1.55	25.87	46.78
40.00	10.97	6.41	5.37	19.79	17.36	3.84	3.13	2.37	......	1.46	29.30	40.95
45.00	9.60	5.37	6.69	20.95	14.96	3.38	4.22	2.07	......	1.47	31.29	35.38
50.00	8.18	4.40	8.14	23.41	12.82	2.89	4.98	1.76	......	1.56	31.86	30.05
55.00	6.72	3.48	9.72	27.16	10.96	2.36	5.42	1.44	......	1.77	30.97	24.96
60.00	5.22	2.62	11.44	32.22	9.36	1.78	5.53	1.12	......	2.08	28.63	20.10
65.00	3.68	1.83	13.30	38.59	8.02	1.17	5.31	0.79	......	2.47	24.84	15.49
70.00	2.09	1.08	15.30	46.28	6.96	0.51	4.75	0.45	......	2.99	19.59	11.09
75.00	0.68*	0.51*	17.26	54.78	6.11	0.36*	3.81	0.18*	......	3.56	12.75	7.84
80.00	0.42*	0.34*	18.98	63.26	5.45	0.26*	2.53	0.12*	......	4.14	4.50	6.59
Males												
25.00	14.40	10.02	2.69	18.74	27.47	4.25	2.19	......	......	4.33	15.91	56.14
30.00	13.82	8.94	2.73	17.66	24.03	3.93	2.38	......	......	5.22	21.29	50.72
35.00	12.97	7.80	3.20	17.67	20.69	3.56	2.79	......	......	5.95	25.37	45.02
40.00	11.74	6.58	4.10	18.62	17.37	3.10	4.28	......	......	6.45	27.76	38.79
45.00	10.34	5.43	5.47	20.82	14.46	2.62	5.31	......	......	6.73	28.82	32.85
50.00	8.76	4.33	7.29	24.22	11.94	2.13	5.88	......	......	6.98	28.47	27.16
55.00	7.03	3.30	9.59	28.86	9.84	1.61	5.99	......	......	7.00	26.78	21.78
60.00	5.13	2.32	12.35	34.73	8.14	1.08	5.65	......	......	6.88	23.72	16.67
65.00	3.08	1.40	15.56	41.82	6.84	0.52	4.86	......	......	6.60	19.32	11.84
70.00	1.41*	0.64*	19.06	49.64	5.89	0.26*	3.58	......	......	6.11	13.41	8.20
75.00	0.94*	0.44*	22.48	57.30	5.25	0.18*	1.85	......	......	5.37	6.19	6.81

* Value predicted from logarithmic regression: $\log l_{15}^i = a_{15}^i + b_{15}^i \dot{e}_0$. All others are predicted from polynomial regression: $l_{15}^i = A_{15}^i + B_{15}^i \dot{e}_0 + C_{15}^i (\dot{e}_0)^2$.

55

At low life expectancies, the probability of dying from cardiovascular disease or cancer is increased considerably if one survives to age 15. But at the highest levels of life expectancy, the chance of ultimately dying from one of these diseases is largely unaffected by survival to age 15, since almost no one dies before this age. The chance that a male aged 15 will eventually die from violence is largely invariant with respect to level of life expectancy (a range of 5.95–7.00% from life expectancy of 35 to one of 70), but the chance that a newborn male will die a violent death increases steadily as his chances of survival to ages of highest violent mortality improve.

Effect of Various Causes on the Length of Life

The amount by which a cause of death shortens life can be defined as being equal to the gain in life expectancy that would result from the complete elimination of that cause, holding age-specific death rates from other causes constant. Such calculations were carried out for each of the 165 populations with respect to each cause of death and to certain combinations of causes, under the assumption of independence that was defined above. The results are summarized in Table 3.3 for populations located at varying levels of life expectancy. Like the preceding two tables, it is developed by fitting second-degree polynomials to the 165 observations on life expectancy and on the gain in life expectancy from eliminating a cause of death.

As shown in Chapter 2, death rates from the large majority of causes tend to be higher in high mortality populations. This covariance among causes has two partially counterveiling effects on the gain in length of life from eliminating a cause. In high mortality populations, the cause being eliminated itself tends to have higher death rates, producing *ceteris paribus* a larger gain in life from its hypothetical elimination; but persons "saved" from dying from that cause tend to live shorter lives than in a lower mortality population, since death rates from the other causes of death are also in general higher. Table 3.3 shows, for example, that these effects nearly offset one another for maternal mortality over a wide range of life expectancy. It is responsible for little more loss of life in a population with a life expectancy of 30 than in one with a life expectancy of 55, despite what are in general much higher death rates from the cause in the former case (Chapter 2). The same result applies for "certain diseases of early infancy." But the gain in years of life from eliminating most of the infectious-type diseases is clearly much higher in high mortality populations. For causes that tend to be loosely associated with overall mortality level, such as neoplasms, cardiovascular disease, and

Table 3.3

Expected gain in average length of life from eliminating various causes of death or combinations of causes

Life Expectancy at Birth	Respiratory Tuberculosis (1)	Other Infectious and Parasitic Diseases (2)	Neo-plasms (3)	Cardio-vascular Disease (4)	Influenza, Pneumonia, Bronchitis (5)	Diarrheal Diseases (6)	Diabetes, Cirrhosis of Liver, Nephritis, Stomach Ulcer (7)	Maternal Mortality (8)	Certain Diseases of Infancy (9)	Violence (10)	All Other and Unknown Causes (11)	(1)+(2)+ (5)+(6)+ (8) (12)	Life Expectancy Eliminating All Causes in Col. 12 plus Ascribed Infectious Diseases (13)
Females													
30.00	2.53	5.05	0.25	3.38	7.62	3.00	0.04	0.46	1.94	0.45	7.69	23.98	73.59
35.00	2.58	4.57	0.41	2.63	6.64	3.04	0.23	0.50	2.00	0.46	7.84	21.52	72.99
40.00	2.55	4.06	0.60	2.24	5.71	2.98	0.45	0.52	2.02	0.48	7.79	19.02	72.61
45.00	2.43	3.54	0.80	2.21	4.83	2.82	0.62	0.52	1.99	0.51	7.55	16.48	72.47
50.00	2.22	2.99	1.04	2.54	4.00	2.56	0.73	0.49	1.91	0.54	7.10	13.89	72.56
55.00	1.94	2.42	1.31	3.23	3.23	2.20	0.79	0.44	1.78	0.57	6.46	11.26	72.87
60.00	1.56	1.83	1.60	4.28	2.50	1.74	0.79	0.37	1.61	0.61	5.63	8.58	73.42
65.00	1.10	1.22	1.92	5.70	1.82	1.17	0.74	0.28	1.39	0.65	4.59	5.86	74.20
70.00	0.56	0.59	2.28	7.47	1.20	0.51	0.63	0.17	1.13	0.70	3.36	3.09	75.21
72.50	0.26	0.27	2.46	8.49	0.91	0.14	0.56	0.10	0.98	0.73	2.67	1.69	75.81
Males													
30.00	2.25	4.68	0.26	2.46	7.28	2.79	0.06	.....	2.13	0.89	7.51	21.61	70.23
35.00	2.36	4.23	0.27	2.01	6.31	2.90	0.34	.....	2.25	1.22	7.51	19.36	69.86
40.00	2.36	3.73	0.36	1.89	5.38	2.87	0.56	.....	2.29	1.48	7.31	17.00	69.65
45.00	2.25	3.20	0.53	2.09	4.49	2.70	0.72	.....	2.27	1.67	6.92	14.52	69.60
50.00	2.03	2.63	0.78	2.63	3.65	2.38	0.81	.....	2.16	1.81	6.33	11.93	69.70
55.00	1.70	2.02	1.11	3.49	2.84	1.93	0.83	.....	1.99	1.89	5.55	9.22	69.97
60.00	1.27	1.38	1.53	4.68	2.07	1.33	0.79	.....	1.74	1.89	4.57	6.39	70.40
65.00	0.73	0.70	2.02	6.20	1.34	0.59	0.69	.....	1.42	1.85	3.40	3.46	70.99
67.50	0.41	0.34	2.29	7.09	1.00	0.17	0.61	.....	1.24	1.80	2.75	1.95	72.34

violence, the second effect should dominate. Table 3.3 shows clearly that in fact these causes shorten life by larger amounts in low mortality populations.[1]

The gain in years of life from eliminating two diseases must on purely formal grounds exceed the sum of gains that would occur if each were eliminated individually and separately. This proposition is made intuitively obvious by considering a population in which there are only two causes of death altogether; eliminating both produces immortality, but eliminating one at a time produces only finite gains which sum to a finite amount. In general, the gain from eliminating, say, cancer, is greater the lower is the death rate from heart disease. The causes of death are necessarily synergistic in their effect on longevity.

Table 3.3 demonstrates the hypothetical gains that would occur if respiratory tuberculosis, "other infectious and parasitic diseases," influenza/pneumonia/bronchitis, diarrheal diseases, and maternal mortality were simultaneously eliminated. In female populations with a life expectancy of 30, the gain in years of life would be 23.98 years, on average, exceeding the sum of gains from elimination of these diseases one at a time by 5.32 years. The resulting life expectancy of 53.98 years is still far below what has been achieved in contemporary western countries, suggesting again that noninfectious causes bear some of the responsibility when mortality exceeds what is the current low standard. Ambiguity is added to the conclusion by the "other and unknown" category, which tends to have higher death rates in high mortality populations, and to some extent by "certain diseases of early infancy" which can also include ill-defined infectious conditions. In order to estimate what would happen if deaths from these causes were assigned to other causes, *Causes of Death: Life Tables for National Populations* simply distributed deaths in these two categories in every population to infectious diseases (those listed in Col. 12) and noninfectious diseases (all others) in proportion to the recorded rates of death from these two groups. This was done separately for each of the 19 age groups. The surprising results are summarized in Col. 13. Regardless of initial level of mortality, the elimination of deaths from infectious diseases plus those distributed

---

[1] It should be noted that the estimated gain from eliminating cardiovascular disease in populations at high levels of life expectancy is unreliable. The procedure employed assumed that death rates from remaining causes were constant after age 85. This assumption is of little consequence when cardiovascular disease is present among the remaining causes because few survive to 85 and death rates thereafter are so high that almost none survive to 95. But when cardiovascular disease itself is eliminated in a population that has already achieved a long average life, these conditions no longer apply and the assumption of constancy—undoubtedly inaccurate—comes to play a more central role. The effect of assuming constancy is an overestimation of the gain from eliminating cardiovascular disease. Revised estimates for the U.S. 1964 population are presented in Chapter 7.

to them in the way described produces a life expectancy between 72 and 76 for females and between 69 and 72.5 for males. A "modern" life expectancy is achieved in virtually every population by this process, complete with a modern sex differential.

This result does not appear consistent with the contention of the previous chapter that cardiovascular diseases have in general made an important contribution to mortality decline. A combination of three observations would appear to reconcile these results. First, there is still a gain of 2.22 years for females and 2.11 years for males in years of life in going from lowest to highest life expectancy even after all of the actual and ascribed infectious diseases are hypothetically eliminated; this unexplained gain could well be ascribed to declines in cardiovascular diseases. Second, changes in death rates from cardiovascular disease tend to have a larger impact on age-standardized death rates (the subject of Chapter 2) than on life expectancy (the subject here). This follows from the heavy concentration of these diseases at older ages where death rates rise steeply. Third, it seems likely that the procedure used to distribute the ill-defined conditions has overascribed them to the infectious group. Senility, the major factor in this category in high mortality populations, seems disproportionately to consist of degenerative causes; this was clearly the case when death certification was reviewed in the 10 Latin American cities (Puffer and Griffith, 1967) and seems in general to be prevailing wisdom (Pascua, 1952). Nevertheless, there is no way of verifying that a misappropriation has occurred; and the age-specific nature of the allocation should reduce the bias from this source. Since only the third of these factors suggests that an error has occurred and that factor is itself none too securely established, it seems wisest at this stage to conclude that indications in column 13 are largely correct: the mortality profile of an advanced country is typically present in every population, awaiting only a successful attack on infectious diseases before emerging.

Effect of Various Causes on Expected Years of Productive Life

The social value of an extra year of life depends upon the age at which it will be lived. The prime years of economic and familial contribution occur between ages 15 and 65 in most societies, and it seems natural that deaths in this interval should occasion greater social concern. In this section we compute the impact of various causes on average years lived in this interval for someone who survives to its beginning, that is, for someone who has absorbed many resources and is just at the stage where he or she is expected to begin making a return.

Table 3.4 displays the causes that are most likely to interfere with that return. In life table notation, it displays

$$\Delta EPL = \frac{T_{15}^{(-i)} - T_{65}^{(-i)}}{l_{15}^{(-i)}} - \frac{T_{15} - T_{65}}{l_{15}},$$

where ΔEPL is the gain in expected years of productive life from elimination of cause i, T_x the person years lived by hypothetical life table cohort above age x, l_{15} the number of survivors to age 15 in hypothetical life table cohort, and $(-i)$ refers to the life table computed with cause of death i eliminated.

This table is another reminder that infectious diseases take a heavy toll of lives during the productive years as well as in childhood. At a life expectancy of 30 years, an average of 8–10 years of potential life during the productive span are lost to mortality from the aggregated infectious diseases alone (Column 11). Respiratory diseases are responsible for the largest foreshortening of productive life at the lowest levels of life expectancy. In the long range of life expectancies from 35–60, tuberculosis is preeminent, largely by virtue of its unique age incidence. While tuberculosis never ranks above third in years lost at birth, it is first over a majority of mortality levels for both sexes in terms of loss of productive life. Tuberculosis ultimately gives way to cancer for women and violence for men. This occurs despite the fact that violence displays a striking invariance as source of lost productive years, varying only from .22 to .23 years for females and from .96 years to 1.21 years for males. Although the loss is nearly constant over mortality level, the rank of violence increases as other diseases decline.

Despite the major and well-publicized role of cardiovascular disease in the modern mortality structure, its effects are so heavily concentrated above age 65 that it is not an important source of lost productive years. In fact, productive years lost to cardiovascular disease tend to decline as mortality levels improve, reflecting substantial reductions in mortality from the cause below age 65, as will be demonstrated in Chapter 5. In the United States in 1964, cardiovascular disease held a slight margin over cancer and violence as the leading source of loss of productive life (.643 versus .637 years for females and 1.385 versus 1.270 years for males). Even in this atypical population, the margin seems unexpectedly small. Combined with the probable sensitivity of the several death rates to public expenditures, the results suggest that public health moneys are probably most appropriately directed toward the elimination or reduction of cancer and violent deaths. The ranking of diseases as a threat to public health depends upon the index chosen, however. The less heavily discounted are the "unproductive" ages, the more serious a public health problem cardiovascular disease becomes.

Table 3.4

Expected gain in average length of productive life from eliminating various causes of death or combinations of causes

Life Expectancy at Birth	Respiratory Tuberculosis (1)	Other Infectious and Parasitic Diseases (2)	Neoplasms (3)	Cardiovascular Diseases (4)	Influenza, Pneumonia, Bronchitis (5)	Diarrheal Diseases (6)	Diabetes, Cirrhosis of Liver, Nephritis, Stomach Ulcer (7)	Maternal Mortality (8)	Violence (9)	All Other and Unknown Causes (10)	(1)+(2)+ (5)+(6)+ (8) (11)	All in Col. 11 plus Ascribed Infectious Diseases (12)
Females												
30.00	2.76	1.38	0.23	0.99	2.91	0.36	0.12	0.74	0.22	2.02	9.17	11.56
35.00	2.57	1.19	0.32	1.04	2.24	0.30	0.20	0.69	0.22	1.88	7.76	9.76
40.00	2.34	1.01	0.39	1.07	1.67	0.25	0.26	0.63	0.22	1.73	6.45	8.08
45.00	2.09	0.84	0.46	1.06	1.18	0.21	0.30	0.56	0.22	1.56	5.24	6.54
50.00	1.80	0.68	0.51	1.03	0.78	0.16	0.31	0.49	0.23	1.37	4.13	5.13
55.00	1.49	0.53	0.55	0.97	0.47	0.12	0.31	0.40	0.23	1.17	3.12	3.86
60.00	1.14	0.38	0.59	0.88	0.25	0.08	0.29	0.32	0.23	0.95	2.21	2.71
65.00	0.77	0.25	0.61	0.76	0.11	0.04	0.24	0.22	0.23	0.72	1.41	1.70
70.00	0.36	0.13	0.62	0.61	0.06	0.01	0.18	0.12	0.23	0.47	0.70	0.83
72.50	0.15	0.07	0.63	0.52	0.07	0.00	0.14	0.07	0.23	0.34	0.38	0.44
Males												
30.00	2.54	1.49	0.14	1.00	2.95	0.31	0.15	. . . . . .	1.00	2.09	8.19	10.57
35.00	2.39	1.27	0.18	1.00	2.24	0.26	0.24	. . . . . .	1.10	1.91	6.80	8.69
40.00	2.20	1.05	0.23	0.99	1.64	0.21	0.31	. . . . . .	1.17	1.72	5.51	6.97
45.00	1.95	0.85	0.28	0.97	1.14	0.17	0.35	. . . . . .	1.21	1.52	4.34	5.42
50.00	1.65	0.66	0.33	0.95	0.74	0.13	0.36	. . . . . .	1.21	1.30	3.28	4.04
55.00	1.31	0.49	0.39	0.93	0.44	0.09	0.35	. . . . . .	1.18	1.07	2.33	2.82
60.00	0.91	0.32	0.45	0.90	0.25	0.06	0.31	. . . . . .	1.12	0.83	1.48	1.77
65.00	0.46	0.17	0.52	0.86	0.15	0.02	0.24	. . . . . .	1.02	0.57	0.75	0.88
67.50	0.19	0.09	0.55	0.84	0.12	0.01	0.20	. . . . . .	0.96	0.43	0.42	0.50

CHAPTER 4

Contribution of Economic Factors
to Declines in Mortality
during the Twentieth Century

The influence of economic conditions on mortality has been recognized at least since biblical times. Empiricism of the most causal sort was sufficient to establish the link between food supply and mortality. Other components of living standards, such as shelter and living space, awaited a revolution in scientific method before their influence was finally acknowledged. But recent years have witnessed a movement away from economic determinism in mortality analysis. It is widely believed that mortality has become increasingly dissociated from economic level because of an international diffusion of medical and health technologies, facilities, and personnel that occurred, in large part, independently of economic level. This position has its critics (Frederiksen, 1961, 1966a, 1966b) who have proven relatively persuasive (Heer, 1968, p. 69). This chapter utilizes readily available evidence in a new but obvious way to estimate the relative contribution of economic factors to increases in life expectancy during the twentieth century. The evidence consists of cross-sectional relationships between national life expectancy and national income per capita during three different decades of the twentieth century. These relationships are further used to assess the realism of certain economic-demographic models and to re-examine what have become classical distinctions regarding sources of mortality in Western and non-Western areas.

There are several reasons for focusing on national income rather than on another socioeconomic variable. First, national income is probably the best single indicator of living standards in a country since it comprises the value of all final products (goods and services) produced in a certain period. A wide range of these products can be expected to influence mortality, and expenditures on all of them are represented, with varying weights, in national income. It is the indicator more comprehensive of these multiple factors. Second, as the leading index of level of economic development, per capita income is the focus of growth models from which policy measures are derived. Several of these models incorporate a relationship between mortality and level of economic development. For example, Leibenstein (1954) and Nelson (1956) argue that a small gain in per capita income in low income countries will tend to produce a decline in mortality and hence a more rapid rate of population growth that will propel the population back to its initial level of income. Partly on this basis, they argue for the necessity of a "big push" in economic development in order to project the economy past the point where increments in income can be dissipated in this fashion. Hagen (1962, pp. 38, 48) and Demeny (1965), on the other hand, attack this type of big push theory on the grounds that mortality has not been responsive to income but rather to public health factors. Which view prevails obviously should have a decided impact on the policies pursued. Indeed, Taylor and Hall (1967) assert that, because of a fear that public health programs would be reduced in scope because of the blame they were receiving for large increases in rates of population growth during the postwar period, international health specialists undertook to discredit their own role in mortality decline and to emphasize that of economic development.

Models attempting to simulate the future course of demographic and economic development must also address the question of the responsiveness of mortality to economic change. The International Labour Office (1973, p. 18), in its simulation model of world employment/population relationships, plans to incorporate an assumption that life expectancy increases gradually with average household incomes. *The Limits to Growth* already includes a similar feature, although the parameter values appear to have been chosen in a somewhat arbitrary fashion (see the discussion of the mortality submodel in Bongaarts, 1973).

Types of Relationships

National income per capita in constant dollars is an index of the total value of final products produced per inhabitant during a defined period, exclusive of goods which merely replace losses from depreciation of capital equipment. There is no reason to expect a direct influence of national income per capita on mortality; it measures simply the rate of entry of new goods and services into the household and business sectors. Its influence is instead indirect; a higher income implies and facilitates, though it does not necessarily entail, larger real consumption of items affecting health, such as food, housing, medical and public health services, education, leisure, health-related research, and on the negative side, automobiles, cigarettes, animal fats, and physical inertia.

Levels of mortality and economic development can be related to one another, conceptually and substantively, in a variety of ways. It is useful at the outset to distinguish among at least three different types of relationships that have been proposed by various analysts, although the exact formulation is often only implicit in their work. We disregard here the few works (e.g., Barlow, 1968) which deal with the relatively minor effect of mortality on economic processes and concentrate instead on income as it causally affects mortality level. In order to simplify the task, we confine the review to international studies.

A. Level of Income Influences Level of Mortality at a Moment in Time

Attempts at empirical estimation have focused on the cross-sectional relationship between mortality and economic level. Most commonly, the relationship between national infant mortality rates and levels of income has been examined (Adelman, 1963; Corsa and Oakley, 1971; United Nations, 1961). Coefficients of correlation between the variables have been found to be consistently high, on the order of $-.8$. The relationship is sufficiently strong that infant mortality rates have on occasion been used as an indicator of income levels when the requisite data are missing for computing the latter (United Nations, 1970). Gordon, Wyon, and Ascoli (1967) have suggested that the death rate of children in their second year of life may be a better indicator of general health levels than is infant mortality, which responds to a number of influences not present at other ages. Frederiksen (1966a,b) provides partial support by showing that death rates at ages 1–4 are more closely correlated with per capita GNP in 15 countries than are death rates at ages 0–1, 20–24, or 65–69.

One study, confined to less developed countries, has demonstrated a close cross-national relationship between an index of mortality at all ages and from all causes, life expectancy at birth, and the level of national income. Vallin (1968) suggests that no country can attain a life expectancy of more than 60 years without having made very substantial progress out of the category, "less developed." At the same time, he stresses that the relationship is not deterministic and that a nation can, within limits, modify its life expectancy independently of its level of income. We shall reexamine the type of relationship studied by Vallin in a subsequent section.

On several occasions the United Nations Population Division has expressed the opinion that the cross-sectional relationship between mortality and level of economic development has become progressively weaker over time (United Nations, 1963b, p. 11; United Nations, 1965). Others have echoed this claim and referred to a "dissociation" of the two types of variables. However, data to support the claim has not been presented, and the present analysis fails to support the contention.

B. Level of Income Influences Rate of Change in Mortality

Arriga and Davis (1969) suggest that the rate of improvement of mortality can be expected to be a direct function of the existing level of mortality in a country. They make it clear that they intend the existing level of mortality to be a proxy variable for a nation's level of income, so that the rate of change of mortality is considered to be a function of level of income. Their pathbreaking analysis of developments in Latin America shows that the expected relationships applies prior to 1920 or 1930 but that thereafter the rate of change in life expectancy became independent of levels of income. A lack of relationship was also suggested by Stolnitz (1965, p. 117) in his review of postwar mortality trends in less developed regions.

It is difficult to devise a plausible model in which the rate of change of mortality is a direct function of the level of income. One mechanism that conceivably could produce such a relationship occurs when a positive fraction of additions to current income becomes invested in various enterprises (such as housing, hospitals and training programs for medical personnel) that exert an effect on subsequent mortality. When the assumption is made that these investments continue to cumulate at a given level of income (rather than simply to replace depreciating facilities and withdrawing personnel), it becomes plausible that higher incomes will produce larger gains in life expectancy. The assumption is treacherous, however, and lacks an empirical basis. It implies that a country at a constant level of income will experience continuous increments in its stock of health-related capital, which it can do in reality only if the proportion of income invested in such capital is constantly rising or if the rate of depreciation of such capital is constantly falling.

A second mechanism that could produce a relationship between the level of income and the rate of change of mortality is dependent upon an association between the level of income and the rate of change of income. If low income countries typically have slowly growing economies, and if the growth of income is positively associated with the gain in life expectancy, then one would observe larger gains in richer countries. This is probably the mechanism that Arriga and Davis have in mind. However, the resulting relationship between level of income and change in mortality is clearly dependent upon the more fundamental (and logically separable) relationship between changes in income and changes in mortality.

We could continue to list possible reasons for expecting a relationship between level of income and change in mortality: for example, by assuming that a particular level of income is associated with a particular time-sequence of "tastes" for health-related services or health technology. But these mechanisms become increasingly speculative and groundless. There is no persuasive reason for expecting an association between income level and mortality change independently of their joint association with other variables such as income change.

C. Rate of Change of Income Influences Rate of Change of Mortality

A cross-sectional relationship between income and mortality, firmly established in the references cited above, also implies a dynamic relationship between the two. If the relationship is indeed causal, then a certain change in income should be associated with a particular change in mortality, with relative magnitudes of change determined by coefficients of the relationship. Additional elements may figure into the dynamic relationship, however. In particular, the cross-sectional relationship between mortality and income may itself be changing in response to new influences.

Malthus, of course, made a negative dynamic relationship between mortality and income level a central tenet of his dismal theory. Those who have recently examined the relationship fail to uncover support for the postulated relationship. Stolnitz (1965, p. 117) states that recent mortality trends in Asia, Latin America, and Africa have been "remarkably neutral" with respect to economic events. Demeny (1965, p. 210) states that "the large amount of statistical material on underdeveloped countries which is available for the past two or three decades reveals the almost complete absence of such a relationship. . . . There is a high degree of uniformity between mortality trends through time and in different countries—a uniformity not existent as far as trends in per capita income are concerned." Although perhaps obvious, it may be worth emphasizing that such a pattern is not inconsistent with a tight cross-sectional relationship between mortality and economic level throughout the period under consideration, providing that the structure of the cross-sectional relationship is changing.

The Relations Reexamined

It is a straightforward matter to indicate what has happened to the cross-sectional relationship between income and mortality during the twentieth century. Figure 4.1 presents a scatter plot of the relationship between level of life expectancy (average, male and female) and per capita national income (1963 United States dollars) in the 1900's, 1930's, and 1960's. The criterion for inclusion was simply the availability of measures of the two variables; however, in the 1960's countries under 2 million in population were excluded in order to reduce sampling variability. The data on which the figure is based are presented in Appendix 4A. Life expectancy is computed by standard direct methods with a few exceptions noted in the Appendix. Income figures are derived from Kuznets (1956) for the 1900's, from Kuznets and the United Nations *Statistical Yearbook* for the 1930's, and primarily from the United Nations *Statistical Yearbook* for the 1960's. A country's income in a particular year is first converted to United States dollars in that year by official exchange rates, and then converted to 1963 United States dollars by the series of official United States consumer price indexes. This is only one possible way of proceeding, and it is well known that any choice of prices for weighting output intertemporally or interspatially is arbitrary. The

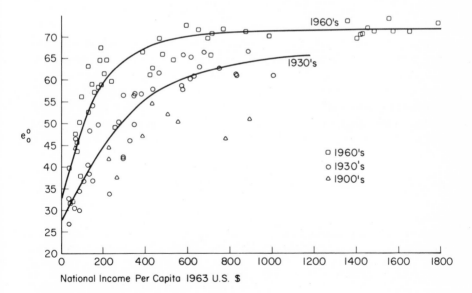

Figure 4.1 Scatter plots of relations between life expectancy at birth (e_0^0) and per capita national income for nations in the 1900's, 1930's, and 1960's.

present procedure is the only one capable of yielding as much data as is utilized here. As noted below, it seems virtually certain that an alternate procedure would not change the fundamental conclusions.

Attention is focused on the relationships in the 1930's and 1960's, for which most data are available. A logistic curve, plotted on the figure, was fitted to each set of data. The equations of the curves are[1]

$$1930\text{'s:}\quad e_0^{\,0} = \frac{80}{1 + \exp\{-1.6251 + 2.0768(.9317)^{Y'}\}}$$

$$1960\text{'s:}\quad e_0^{\,0} = \frac{80}{1 + \exp\{-2.1354 + 2.1697(.7672)^{Y'}\}}$$

Placing all three sets of data on the same graph may obscure the fact that a curve fits the data for a particular period quite well at every portion of the range. The simple correlation between life expectancy and the log of per capita income is .885 in the 1930's and .889 in the 1960's; however, the simple logarithmic curves consistently overestimated life expectancy at lower levels of income, hence a more flexible curve was adopted. Despite the simplicity of approach, the following points can be made with some degree of assurance:

(1)   The relationship between life expectancy and per capita national income has shifted upward during the twentieth century.

The point can be made with greatest certainty for the period from the 1930's to the 1960's. There are relatively few data points at incomes less than $100 but such information as exists is broadly consistent with the conclusion. At higher income levels the shift is unmistakable. It amounts to some 10–12 years of life expectancy at incomes between $100 and $500 and progressively less thereafter. The upper asymptotes differ by 4.7 years, suggesting that the maximum average length of life to be attained by gains in income alone was some 66.8 years in the 1930's and 71.5 years in the 1960's.

---

[1] Y' is a linear transformation of per capita national income in 1963 United States dollars (Y). Income is transformed to a scale ranging from 0 to the number of observations minus one.

$$1930\text{'s:}\quad Y' = \frac{Y - 37}{1012 - 37}(37). \qquad 1960\text{'s:}\quad Y' = \frac{Y - 39.81}{2995 - 39.81}(49).$$

The value of 80 in the numerator was specified *a priori;* other parameters are derived by least-squares techniques. We experimented with values other than 80 in the numerator but the highest amount of variance was explained when 80 was used, although differences were small. Data for Soviet bloc countries in the 1960's are not represented on the graph or used to compute the coefficients of the line because of the high degree of uncertainty attached to their income estimates. This bloc will be considered in greater detail below. Income for Canada, Sweden, Switzerland, and the United States fell above the defined plotting range for the 1960's, although the data for these countries were used in the computation of the logistic equation.

The upper asymptote of 73.9 years assumed by the official United Nations projections (1966) can be attained on a broad scale only if the curve continues to shift upward.[2]

The curves can be compared horizontally as well as vertically. Such a comparison suggests that, in order to attain a particular value of life expectancy between 40 and 60, a range that includes a large majority of the current world population, a nation required an income level approximately 2.6 times higher in the 1930's than in the 1960's (the constancy of this factor is one of the more intriguing features of the curves). No error in intertemporal income comparisons seems capable of accounting for a change of anywhere near this magnitude.

There are too few observations in the 1900's to make curve fitting worthwhile. But evidence that a shift occurred during the earlier period as well is persuasive. Of the 10 observations for the decade of the 1900's, 9 lie below the line computed for the 1930's.[3] There is some suggestion that the shift during the earlier period as compared to the later may have been somewhat smaller at low levels of income and somewhat larger at higher levels, but firm conclusions are not warranted. In any case, there is little reason to think that factors exogenous to a country's level of economic development began to affect significantly mortality levels only after the 1930's. While postwar antimalarial campaigns are perhaps the most dramatic example of noneconomic factors influencing mortality, they were often preceded by smaller, more persistent campaigns against specific diseases. For example, Balfour, Evans, Notestein, and Taeuber (1950, pp. 92, 104) report that colonial administrations achieved through specific public health measures the elimination of mortality from smallpox and cholera in Indonesia during the 1920's and major reductions from smallpox and plague in the Philippines by 1922. Mandle (1970) cites similar developments in British Guiana during the 1920's with respect to malaria and respiratory and diarrheal diseases. In these instances, the mortality reductions were not accompanied by substantial economic progress and Mandle indicates that the 1920's was a period of economic stagnation in British Guiana. Petersen (1967) demonstrates that, by 1920,

---

[2] There is mounting evidence that the United Nations mortality projections are overly optimistic, at least for countries at higher levels of life expectancy. For example, the projection assumed that the United States would achieve the life expectancy of 73.9 years by 1970. However, the actual life expectancy for the total population of the United States in 1970 was only 70.9 years (U.S. National Center for Health Statistics, n.d.). The rate of improvement in Canada, Australia, and New Zealand is also behind schedule.

[3] The only exception is Japan. The unusually high life expectancy in Japan relative to per capita income has also been noted by Taeuber (1958, p. 284). She cites personal cleanliness and the assumption of health responsibility by government organizations as important factors in counteracting the adverse effects of poverty in Japan.

Japanese colonial administrators in Taiwan had succeeded in bringing the plague, cholera, and smallpox under effective control through a variety of public health activities. Similar developments were unquestionably occurring in western countries, as indicated below.

Since a country has attained a certain life expectancy in the 1960's at what is generally a much lower level of income than a country achieving that mortality level earlier, one should expect to observe certain differences in the structure of mortality by cause of death in the two populations. In particular, diseases most closely associated with standards of living, and least amenable to attack by specific medical and public health measures, ought to be relatively more prominent in the later population. Diarrheal diseases, highly influenced by nutritional adequacy and level of personal sanitation, represent such a group. The analysis in Chapter 2 leaves little doubt that countries achieving a certain level of mortality at a later point in time typically do so with a higher incidence of death from diarrheal diseases (and a lower incidence of death from respiratory tuberculosis), than countries achieving that level earlier. Thus, data on causes of death tend to confirm the shift in the income/mortality relationship that has been described.

An estimate of the causes of death responsible for the shift in the relationship can be made by performing a similar analysis that is cause specific. However, because of failures to record causes of death in many populations, the number of cases declines considerably, and so must the precision of results. Table 4.1 displays the death rates from four groups of causes for populations that fall into one of five ranges of per capita income in the 1930's and in the 1960's. In every case but one, the average cause-specific death rates decline between the 1930's and 1960's for populations falling into a particular range. Between 17% and 35% of the decline within any range is attributable to declining mortality from specific infectious diseases. Approximately one quarter is attributable to changing death rates from respiratory diseases. Diarrheal diseases contribute more than 5% to the decline within only one income range, and they actually increase in one other; their contribution to the shift is minimal, far less than their average contribution to a change in mortality level identified in Chapter 2. The intransigence of diarrheal diseases compared to, for example, respiratory diseases, is consistent with the finding of Puffer and Serrano (1973, p. 184) that nutritional disorders are implicated much more frequently in diarrheal than in respiratory deaths in childhood in Latin America. To repeat a refrain of Chapter 2, diarrheal disease is more closely associated with general living standards than most other causes, hence should not have exhibited the same degree of shift in their relation to those standards.

Approximately half of the shift in the mortality/income relationship is attributable to other causes of death, of which the most important is cardio-

Table 4.1

Comparative levels of mortality from various groups of causes in populations at equivalent levels of per capita income in the 1930's and 1960's[a]

Level of per capita income (1963$)	Populations with age-cause-specific death rates and national income estimates available in		Average of male and female age-standardized death rates per 1000 from								Proportion of differences in all cause rate due to			
			Resp. TB. and other infect. and parasitic		Influenza/ pneumonia/ bronchitis		Diarrheal diseases		All other causes		TB. and infect. & para	Infl./ pneu./ bronch.	Diar- rheal	All other
	1930's	1960's	1930's	1960's	1930's	1960's	1930's	1960,s	1930's	1960's				
50–199	Czechoslovakia, Greece, Japan (3)	Ceylon, Philippines, Taiwan (3)	3.14	1.20	2.28	1.03	1.28	.42	12.21	8.30	.244	.157	.108	.491
200–399	Chile, Italy (2)	Colombia, Guatemala, Portugal (3)	3.06	1.70	4.82	1.73	1.60	1.20	12.82	9.75	.172	.390	.050	.388
400–599	France, Norway (2)	Chile, Greece, Hong Kong, Mexico (4)	1.81	.74	1.25	1.18	.18	.36	10.99	8.85	.345	.022	.058	.690
600–799	Australia, Canada, Denmark Netherlands, Sweden, United Kingdom (6)	Ireland, Japan Puerto Rico, Spain, Venezuela (5)	1.20	.40	1.55	.66	.26	.20	10.29	8.52	.227	.253	.017	.502
800–1199	New Zealand, Switzerland, U.S.A. (3)	Austria, Italy (2)	1.17	.22	1.23	.53	.18	.09	10.12	8.70	.300	.221	.028	.450

[a] Appendix 4A and Preston, Keyfitz, and Schoen (1972).

vascular disease. Thus, while specific infectious diseases and respiratory diseases account for perhaps a half of the shift in the relationship, they are by no means exclusively responsible for it. With the exception of diarrheal diseases, causes seem to have contributed to the shift in approximately the same proportion as they typically contribute to *any* change in mortality level, as described in Chapter 2. The diffuseness of the changes cautions against interpretations of recent mortality history that focus on one or a small set of explanatory factors.

(2) Factors exogenous to a country's current level of income probably account for 75–90% of the growth in life expectancy for the world as a whole between the 1930's and the 1960's. Income growth *per se* accounts for only 10–25%.

Evidence for this assertion is developed in the following way. We first assume that the curves fit to data in the 1930's and 1960's accurately represent the relationship for all countries in those years, including those for which data are unavailable. We then substitute estimates of per capita national income for each region of the world in the 1930's, use the 1930's curve to predict regional life expectancy, and weigh the resulting predictions by population to estimate life expectancy for the world in the 1930's. Repeating the process but with income data for the 1960's, we produce an estimate of what life expectancy would have been in the 1960's with current income but with the 1930's relationship between income and life expectancy still in effect. The difference between the two estimates indicates the gain in life expectancy attributable to income growth *per se* between the 1930's and the 1960's. We repeat the procedure once again, this time using the 30's income data but the 60's relationship; the difference between this estimate and the first indicates the gain in life expectancy attributable to shifts in the curve, or to factors exogenous to a country's contemporary level of economic development. The two differences, when added to the initial estimate, should come close to reproducing actual life expectancy in the 1960's.

Regional income data used in this procedure are presented in Appendix 4B. They are, of course, even less reliable than national figures and can be used to give no more than a crude estimate of the relative importance of different factors.

Results are presented in Table 4.2. If the 1930's relationship had remained in effect, the observed increases in income would have produced a gain in world life expectancy of 2.5 years between 1938 and 1963; the observed income changes combined with the 1960's relationship produces a gain of 1.3 years. These are estimates of the increase in life expectancy due to rising income during the period. The shift in the curve, on the other hand, produces a gain of 10.9 years when combined with the 1938 income distribution, and a

Table 4.2

Life expectancy for world associated with combinations of income distributions and relationships between income and life expectancy

Relationship between income and life expectancy as observed in	Regional income in		Estimated change due to increase in income
	1938	1963	
1930's	44.2	46.7	2.5
			Average 1.9
1960's	55.1	56.4	1.3
Estimated change due to shift in relationship	10.9	9.7	Total Change 12.2
	Average 10.3		

gain of 9.7 years in combination with the 1963 distribution. The total increase estimated through the use of this procedure is 12.2 years during the quarter century. The predicted life expectancy of 56.4 years for the 1960's can be compared with the recent estimate by the United Nations Population Division (1971, p. 32) of 53 for the period 1965–1970 (no comparable estimate is available for the 1930's). The comparison shows reasonable agreement considering the faulty but different data on which both estimates are based. Aggregation of individual countries into regional blocs would tend to produce overestimation of life expectancy, as noted below in section 3a, and could account for the excess in our estimate. However, the need to aggregate should not significantly bias the trends or the relative weighing of factors responsible.

This analysis implies that around 16% of the increase in life expectancy between 1938 and 1963 for the world as a whole is attributable to increases in per capita national income *per se*. A large but unspecifiable margin of error should be attached to this estimate because of faulty data and the simplicity of assumptions. The uncertainty is increased because the estimates are least reliable (based on fewest observations and on observations most susceptible to error) at lowest levels of income where a substantial proportion of the world's population was and is located. Nevertheless, it is almost inconceivable that income could be a factor of no consequence in the trends, in view of the tight cross-sectional relationship between income and mortality and the major improvements in income experienced by most regions during the period; on the other hand, it is implausible that income changes could account for more than a third of the growth in life expectancy during the period, in view of the massive shift that occurred in the relation between income and life expectancy. The amount of change attributable to income growth varies, of course, from region to region and country to country; our calculations indicate that in Japan, for example, a majority of the expected increase in life expectancy was caused by rapid income growth. But it is doubtful that a sufficient number of rigorous studies of mortality decline in different countries will soon be available to permit estimates based on a cumulation of microlevel observations. The more aggregative approach pursued here may serve to provide interim estimates of the magnitude of broad international developments.

Analysis of the 30 countries for which data on both income and life expectancy are available during both periods confirms that income changes were of minor importance in mortality trends. The zero-order correlation between the absolute change in life expectancy and the absolute change in income was strongly *negative* at $-.497$; between the absolute change in life expectancy and the percentage change in income, it was weakly positive at .164. Both figures are highly influenced by the tendency noted above for life expectancy gains to be largest for countries starting out at low income levels, irrespective of income trends. The additive multiple regression equation containing all three terms (which are logically present when the underlying relation is logistic) is

$$Z = 21.364 - .01883X_1 + .00128X_2 + .38756X_3, \qquad R^2 = .441,$$
$$(.00990) \quad (.00588) \quad (1.68985)$$

where Z is the absolute change in life expectancy (1930's to 1960's), X_1 the level of income per capita (1930's). X_2 the absolute change in income per capita, 1930's to 1960's, X_3 the ratio, per capita income, 1960's to 1930's (all income figures in 1963 United States dollars). According to this equation, higher absolute and percentage growth in income contributed to a larger increase in life expectancy during the period, but both coefficients are insignificant ($\alpha = .10$). Only the initial level of income is significant (with a sign that is opposite to that postulated by Arriaga and Davis).

This equation can also be used to estimate the contribution of income change to trends in life expectancy for this sample of countries. In particular, assume that no income growth occurs, i.e., that X_2 and X_3 had mean values of zero and one for the period, rather than their actual (unweighted) mean values of $631 and 1.678. According to the equation, zero economic growth would have reduced the mean gain in life expectancy by 1.07 years during the period. This represents 7.0% of the actual mean growth. These figures are in reasonable agreement with those presented earlier. The earlier estimate is more reliable and useful because the relationship at a moment of time is less influenced by measurement error, is based on larger sample sizes, and is specifically aimed at world-wide coverage incorporating information on the relative size of different regions.

"Factors exogenous to a country's current level of income" are identified as being responsible for some 84% of the increase in life expectancy during the period. The phrase is cumbersome because the analysis does not account for the possibility that the shift in the curve itself may be partly a product of growth in income. If medical research in country A is facilitated by a larger national income and leads to mortality reductions in country B, income has influenced mortality. But neither country's mortality has been directly affected by its own income; the effect shows up as a shift in the curve. Even if country A were to enjoy the fruits of its own research, as long as those fruits were rapidly diffused to others, the originating country would be impossible to identify cross-sectionally; the situation would also find expression as a shift in the curve. In this case the change in mortality would also have been independent, for the vast majority of countries, of individual levels of current income. The curves do not adequately reflect factors associated with income in a small subset of countries that operate on mortality in a larger set. The major factors likely to operate in this fashion are a diffusion of technological advances and to a lesser extent of international transfer payments that distort the proportion of national income spent on health-related services or affect the efficiency of those services. What the curves do reflect is the influence of a country's *own* level of income on mortality as it operates internally through such factors as nutrition, medical and public health services, and literacy.

We have "explained" only some 16% of the rise in life expectancy during the period. Modest as this achievement is, it might be viewed in the context of statements appearing in numerous places that disentangling the separate effects of economic and social progress, as opposed to those of specific health measures, is impossible (United Nations, 1963a, p. 15). Moreover, the figure is in sharp contrast to that promoted by certain other analysts. H. Frederiksen has been the leading advocate of the importance of economic factors in mortality decline during the period. He argues (1961) that a rise in standards of living was responsible for virtually all of the spectacular postwar mortality decline in Ceylon. In later papers (1966a,b) he implies that this conclusion extends to Mauritius and British Guiana and then to 21 nations. His arguments regarding Ceylon and British Guiana have been convincingly refuted by Newman (1965, 1970) and their international applicability is highly questionable in view of present findings.

Although we cannot account for the remaining increases in life expectancy, we can essentially rule out nutrition and literacy as major contributors. A graph has been prepared showing the relations between national levels of adult literacy and life expectancy around 1940 and in the 1960's. The same has been done for the relation between calorie consumption per capita and life expectancy. There is no question that a vertical shift in the relationship, of a magnitude comparable to that pertaining to income, occurs in both of these cases. If anything, the shift appears larger in the relation between calories and life expectancy. Income, food, and literacy were unquestionably placing limits on levels of life expectancy attained in the 1930's, as they are today. But they are not the only factors operating, and one must look elsewhere to account for the majority of recent trends.

(3)   Mortality has not become progressively dissociated from standards of living at a moment in time.

This conclusion follows directly from our equal success in predicting life expectancy on the basis of national income in the 1930's and 1960's, as measured by the correlation coefficients presented earlier. There is virtually no difference between the log–linear correlation coefficients; the logistic form actually fits the points in the 1960's somewhat better than it does in the 1930's.[4]

More interesting than the correlations is the suggestion that the shape of the relation has changed. The later curve appears to be steeper at incomes less than $400 and flatter at incomes over $600. In other words, for low income countries, a given increment in income tends to be associated with a larger gain in life expectancy in the 1960's than in the 1930's. For from becoming dissociated from income, mortality may have become more responsive to it in low-income countries where economic–demographic interrelations are most critical for economic prospects. Two interpretations are consistent with such a change. First, new health measures may have evolved that are exploitable only by countries past the lowest levels of income. Vaccination against tuberculosis and treatment of infectious diseases by antibiotics and by sulfa drugs are two important examples of technical improvements during the postwar period whose potential can be realized only by fairly costly expenditure. A second interpretation is that international health programs, more vigorous during the postwar period, have focused their efforts on those underdeveloped countries with greatest potential for mortality reduction; in general, these would be the more advanced of the group. There may be nothing callous or sinister about such an agenda. It is easy to demonstrate, for example, that in two countries with identical age schedules of death rates from malaria, its eradication results in more years

---

[4] The proportion of variance in $\ln[80/e_0^0 - 1]$ explained by income is .800 in the 1930's and .847 in the 1960's.

of life gained in the population with lower death rates from other causes. Unfortunately, documentation of the amount and effectiveness of international aid received for health proved to be a task far beyond the author's resources.

To claim on the one hand that income has been a trivial factor in recent mortality trends and on the other that it is still a critical determinant of mortality level is not inconsistent. The point is simply that mortality is subject to multiple influences. The demonstration that income has not been important for recent trends is absolutely no justification for removing the relationship from growth models that aspire to realism. If anything, the data suggest that mortality has become more responsive to income in the range of greatest interest.

The justification for ignoring the mortality effects of income growth is not the nonexistence of a relationship but rather its quantitative weakness in dynamic systems. Although the model of the low level equilibrium trap associated with Nelson and Leibenstein is necessarily dynamic, no attempt has been made to identify the time-frame within which it operates. In order to do this, we assume that the logistic curve estimated for the 1960's represents what life expectancy would be at all possible levels of income for a hypothetical country. We further assume that the country experiences a sudden growth of income of 20%, calculate the expected increment in life expectancy associated with that increase, translate the increase into an increase in growth rates, and calculate how long it takes before the incremental growth results in a 20% larger population. That is, how long will it take before the income-induced growth of population erases the initial growth in income? One fundamental assumption underlying the calculation is that the additional persons produced by the mortality decline will make no contribution to total product. If they do contribute, the actual amount of time required to regain the initial equilibrium will be even longer than estimated here. A second assumption is that the initial population is stable in the demographic sense and that a new stability is immediately established following the mortality change. Results are shown in Table 4.3.

For countries at every initial income level, more than a century is required in order for the population to grow sufficiently large that the initial gain in income is totally dissipated. Experimentation with income growth of 5% and 40%, using the same set of initial incomes, demonstrates that population growth does not match income growth until more than a century has passed in any case. Moreover, these calculations are likely to be underestimates of the length of time required for two reasons: the incremental growth rate is assumed to apply for the entire period, rather than to attenuate as the population reapproaches its initial income level; and added persons almost certainly make some contribution to total product in the country. While the

Table 4.3

**Estimated number of years required before an increase in income is erased by the larger
population resulting from the induced decline in mortality**

Initial level of income ($)	Expected gain in life expectancy from 20% increase in income (years)[a]	Increase in intrinsic growth rate associated with mortality decline[b]	Minimum number of years required before increase in growth rate results in 20% larger population[c]
50	1.78	.00122	149
100	2.61	.00145	126
200	2.53	.00106	172
300	1.89	.00069	264
500	.93	.00030	608

[a] Estimated from logistic relation between national levels of life expectancy and per capita income in the 1960's.

[b] Estimated from Coale and Demeny (1966) "West" female model life tables by relation derived in Preston (1974). Assumes average age at childbearing of 30 years.

[c] Estimated by assuming that incremental growth rate prevails throughout the period until the population has grown by 20%.

Malthusian mechanism should probably not be disregarded altogether, there is convincing evidence that it plays a minor role in contemporary economic–demographic processes. The low level equilibrium trap shuts so slowly that escape seems inevitable.

(3a) Some of the observed scatter in cross-sectional relations is almost certainly caused by differences in national income distributions

The obvious explanation of the nonlinearity of the mortality/income relationship is that it reflects diminishing returns to increases in income. It reflects on a broad scale a wide variety of dose–response relationships at the individual level that themselves exhibit diminishing returns: diarrheal disease and nutrition; respiratory pneumonia and antibiotics; tuberculosis and living space, and so on. Moreover, it reflects aggregate-level relationships between national income and the success of programs of sanitation, insect control, disease surveillance, and so on.

When individual-level factors are pertinent in mortality and when the individual-level dose-response relations are nonlinear, as they almost certainly are in this case, then the distribution of those factors will affect the aggregate life expectancy. If the dose-response relations were all linear, and identical from individual to individual and nation to nation, it is easy to show that a nation with a particular mean income would have the same life expectancy regardless of how income were distributed. Suppose that in a particular country personal income followed some frequency distribution $F(Y)$. With each Y is associated some life expectancy, $e_0^0(Y)$, such that

$$e_0^0(Y) = a + bY$$

Then mean life expectancy for the population as a whole is

$$\bar{e}_0^0 = \int F(Y)e_0^0(Y)\,dY = a\int F(Y)\,dY + b\int F(Y)Y\,dY = a + b\bar{Y}.$$

Life expectancy for a population would be a linear function of mean income in this case.

Now suppose, on the other hand, that life expectancy is an increasing function of personal income but subject to diminishing returns. A simple function of this type is

$$e_0^0(Y) = a + bY - cY^2 \qquad (0 < Y < b/2c).$$

Then

$$e_0^0 = \int F(Y)[a + bY - cY^2]\,dY = a + b\bar{Y} - c\bar{Y}^2 - c\sigma_Y^2.$$

At a certain level of mean national income, life expectancy is lower the higher is the variance in the distribution of income (σ_Y^2). The reason for this outcome is obvious: people below the mean income lose more years of life than is gained by people at the equivalent distance above the mean. The greater the spread, the larger the net loss. The distribution of income is clearly a likely source of variance in the basic relation between national life expectancy and mean national income and accounts for some of the scatter in the observed relationship. Unfortunately, the basic data on income distribution are inadequate to incorporate this factor explicitly in the analysis. Nevertheless, it is instructive to note that a country widely cited for large income equalities, Venezuela, has one of the largest negative deviations of any population. Actual life expectancy in 1965 fell short of that predicted on the basis of its mean income by 4.8 years. Kuznets (1963) provides figures on the percent of income earned by the top 5% of families in 18 selected countries. Mexico and Colombia have the most uneven distributions of income on this index of any countries considered here, ranking 14th and 15th. These countries have life expectancies below levels predicted on the basis of mean incomes by 6.7 and 2.1 years. On the other hand, the Soviet bloc countries, where income inequalities are expected to be smaller than those of other countries at equivalent average income levels, do not have exceptionally high life expectancies. Using the lower income figures for these countries in Appendix 4A, thereby producing lower estimates of expected life expectancy, one finds that the deviations of actual from predicted life expectancy in the 1960's are as follows: Bulgaria, +2.1 years; Czechoslovakia, −.5; East Germany, −.8; Hungary, −2.4; Poland, −1.3; U.S.S.R., −.2; Yugoslavia, −1.6. Actual life expectancy falls short of that predicted in every case but one. These deviations of actual from expected life expectancy may be artificially depressed by virtue of the fact that they refer to the period 1960–1961, whereas the curve was computed on the basis of points observed throughout the 1960's; if the curve continued to shift upward during the period, the earlier points would fall increasingly short of the line. On the other hand, the deviations are probably artificially raised by the use of income figures that are almost certainly too low for comparative purposes. Net material product excludes the monetary value of the greater part of general administrative and social services and falls some 10–20% short of GNP (World Health Organization, 1967a, p. 50). In general, there is no compelling evidence that greater income equality (or better health services) have raised the life expectancy in Soviet bloc countries above that level to be expected on the basis of their mean incomes.

(4)   Factors exogeneous to a nation's per capita income have had a major effect on mortality trends in more developed as well as in less developed countries.

It is traditional wisdom that the mortality decline in more developed areas was intimately dependent upon advances in standards of living, hence proceeded slowly; in less developed areas, it was a result of the importation of medical techniques and personnel and hence was rapid (Omran, 1971; Davis, 1956; United Nations, 1963a,b). As a statement of general tendencies this assertion is probably correct, but it requires important qualification. It has been based on a comparison of rates of mortality decline between two equivalent levels rather than between two equivalent points in time and has focused on the most spectacular declines in less developed areas. But the period-specific influences that operated on mortality in less developed areas after the 1930's also operated on mortality in more developed areas. It is clear from the graph that factors exogeneous to a nation's level of economic development have affected the level of mortality in both groups. The result is that, during the period, the distributions of mortality declines for the two groups overlap, while favoring the lower income group. France gained 13.7 years of life expectancy between 1928–1938 and 1965, while Indonesia gained 13.3 between 1930–1935 and 1961. Austria gained 13.7 years between 1930–1933 and 1966; the Philippines, according to official figures subject to considerable error, gained 10.8 between 1938 and 1960, representing about the same annual rate. Spain, an intermediate case, showed a higher rate of improvement than any of these countries, with a gain of 21.6 years between 1930–1931 and 1967. It is implausible that the tropical African countries with life expectancies in the high 30's or lower 40's during the 1960's (Brass and Coale, 1968) could have gained at a rate as rapid as that in France, Austria, or Spain during the preceding 30 years.

Similarly, the emphasis on the uniqueness of specifically *imported* health technology in less developed countries appears misdirected when equivalent periods rather than stages are considered. To be sure, the nature of imported technologies differed. It seem to have been predominately broad gauged public health programs of insect control, environmental sanitation, health education, and maternal and child health services that transformed the mortality picture in less developed areas, while it was primarily specific vaccines, antibiotics, and sulfonamides in more developed areas. But the technologies were not, for the most part, indigenously developed by countries in either group. Universal values assured that health breakthroughs in any country would spread rapidly to all others where the means for implementation existed.

The importance of exogenous, largely imported, healthy technology in the now-developed countries may have been underestimated for earlier periods as well. The disappearance of the plague during the 17th and 18th centuries was probably the first major event to transform systematically western mortality patterns in three centuries. The reasons for the disappearance are obscure, but it does not appear to have been closely related to a nation's rate or level of economic development. Shrewsbury (1970) suggests that a change in housing patterns may have been responsible in England, but Cipolla (1965) points out that the plague essentially disappeared from Italy in a period when housing patterns were stable and in the face of an economic decline. The decline of the plague was followed by major reductions in mortality from smallpox in many countries, unquestionably a product of innoculation in the latter half of the eighteenth century and vaccination throughout the nineteenth century (Razzell, 1965; Drake, 1969, pp. 41–54). The techniques, once proven effective, spread rapidly from country to country. Innoculation itself appears to have been introduced from China, providing an ironic variation on the theme of transferring health technologies from Western to non-Western areas.

For the period after 1850 the emphasis on endogenous factors appears even less appropriate. As Stolnitz (1955, pp. 32–33) suggests, it is difficult to account for the simultaneity of unprecedentedly rapid mortality declines after 1880 in many western countries except by reference to factors that cut across national boundaries. The most obvious such set of factors was a result of the empirical validation of the germ theory of disease during this time. McKeown has been the most outspoken advocate of improved living standards as the motivating factor in western mortality declines. He argues (1965, p. 38) that a rising standard of living was the principal cause of increased life expectancy in England between 1838 and the present. But his arguments are based principally upon a consideration of the period 1851–1860 to 1891–1900, during which time life expectancy increased by only about 6–7 years. The increase of 24–25 years during the twentieth century is essentially unaccounted for.[5] He may be correct that specific drugs were not a factor until after 1935, but such a result does not require that most of the remaining explanation be advances in living standards. The germ theory of disease stimulated many innovations other than drugs and vaccines, such as improved antiseptic practices, quarantines, and segregation of infectious patients, and it gave impetus to the movements for cleaner food and water, better personal sanitation, and improved infant feeding. The logistic curve for the 1960's suggests that, even if England and Wales had experienced no improvement in living standards between 1901–1910 and the present, its life expectancy could be expected to have increased from 50.4 years to 69.6 years. This is the figure achieved by Hong Kong, 1966, at a lower national income than that of England in the first decade of the century, and is considerably exceeded by Greece 1966–1968, at a slightly higher level. The expected increase in life expectancy on the assumption of no growth accounts for 88% of that which actually occurred. There is no guarantee that such an increase would have taken place, of course, and the estimate merely says that economic advance was not an essential prerequisite to a major increase in life expectancy, rather than assigns weight to the factors actually operative. But it surely adds credibility to the view that economic advance was not a major factor in that increase.

Summary

A very simple technique has been used to shed light on a number of questions about the influence of economic level on national mortality trends and differentials. Scatter plots of the cross-sectional relation between per capita national income and life expectancy are developed for three decades during the twentieth century. The relations established appear to shift systematically during the century. In general, in order to attain a certain life expectancy between 40 and 60, a nation required an income level almost three times greater in the 1930's than in the 1960's. This shift is corroborated

[5] Life expectancy (average, male and female) is estimated to be 41.76 in 1861 and 47.40 in 1901 (Keyfitz and Flieger, 1968); in 1838–1854, 40.8 (Coale and Demeny collection of national life tables); and in 1967, 72.12 (Keyfitz and Flieger, 1971).

by a changing structure of mortality by cause of death for populations at equivalent mortality levels. The magnitude of the shifts, combined with regional income data, suggests that some 75–90% of the growth in life expectancy for the world as a whole over these three decades is attributable to factors exogeneous to a nation's contemporary level of income. Through similar techniques, improved nutrition and higher literacy can also be ruled out as important contributors.

Nevertheless, the cross-sectional relation between income and life expectancy remains strong, and there is some suggestion that mortality is now more responsive to variations in income levels among countries with national incomes below $400 (1963 dollars) than it was in the 1930's. However, population size appears to respond so slowly to the mortality declines that typically result from income growth that these mortality effects present little impediment to the process of economic development. Some of the variability in the cross-sectional mortality–income relation is doubtless due to variation in income distributions. Life expectancy in Venezuela, Mexico, and Colombia, countries with wide disparities in income, falls short of levels expected on the basis of their mean income. On the other hand, life expectancy in Soviet bloc countries, where income equality is expected to be greater than average, also falls short of expected levels.

Western and non-Western countries alike profited from the activity of "exogenous" medical and public health factors. Differences between the two types of countries have been exaggerated by concentration on movements between equivalent mortality levels rather than during equivalent time periods. Recent work in historical demography suggests that the importance in western mortality trends of endogenous factors consequent to rising standards of living has been overstated for earlier periods as well.

Appendix 4A

Estimates of Life Expectancy and Per Capita
National Income in Three Decades of the Twentieth Century

Table A.1

Estimates of life expectancy and per capita income for various countries in the 1900's[a]

Country	Year	Life expectancy at birth		Year	Per capita national income in 1963 U.S. dollars
		Male	Female		
Denmark	1901–05	52.9	54.5	1899–1908	428
France	1898–1903	45.31	47.00	1901–10	383
Germany	1901–10	44.82	46.57	1900–09	447
Hungary	1900–01	37.1	37.5	1899–1901	267
Italy	1901–11	44.24	44.53	1899–1908	226
Japan	1899–1903	43.97	44.41	1898–1907	68
Netherlands	1900–09	51.0	52.2	1900–08	504
Spain	1910	40.92	41.74	1906–13	225
United Kingdom	1901–10	48.53	50.45	1900–09	551
United States	1909–11	49.86	51.55	1904–13	892

[a] Life expectancy compiled from *Demographic Yearbook, 1967*. New York: United Nations, 1968. Per Capita Income compiled from S. Kuznets, Quantitative Aspects of the Economic Growth of Nations. I. *Economic Development and Cultural Change*. Oct. 1956, *V* (No. 1), 5–94; Exchange rates from *Statistical Yearbook, 1949–50*. New York: United Nations, 1951. United States consumer price indexes from United States Bureau of Census. *Statistical Abstract of the United States*. 1965.

Table A.2

Estimates of life expectancy and per capita income for various countries in the 1930's[a]

Country	Year	Life expectancy at birth			Year	Per capita national income in 1963 U.S. dollars	Source
		Male	Female	Source			
Australia	1932–34	63.48	67.14	1	1933	615	7
Austria	1930–33	54.5	58.5	1	1931	296	7
Belgium	1928–32	56.02	59.79	1	1930	432	7
Brazil	1940	36.06	37.25	9	1940	49	10
Canada	1931	59.09	61.58	2	1931	609	7
Chile	1940	40.91	43.16	1	1940	296	7
Colombia	1938	36.04	37.19	9	1938–40	68	10
Czechoslovakia	1937	54.92	58.66	1	1938	159	10
Denmark	1931–35	62.0	63.8	1	1929–38	749	8
Dominican Rep.	1935	29.88	29.95	9	1940	40	10
Finland	1936–40	54.32	59.48	1	1938	380	7
France	1928–38	55.12	60.33	1	1929–38	575	8
Germany	1932–34	59.86	62.81	1	1930–39	825	8
Guatemala	1940	30.25	30.46	9	1940	28	10

Table A.2 (continued)

Country	Year	Life expectancy at birth Male	Female	Source	Year	Per capita national income in 1963 U.S. dollars	Source
Greece	1940	52.94	55.80	1	1938	68	10
Hungary	1930–31	48.27	51.34	1	1925–34	345	8
Iceland	1931–40	60.9	65.6	1	1936	462	7
India	1931	26.9	26.6	3	1931	37	7
Indonesia	1930–35	32.5	32.5	4	1932	39	7
Ireland	1935–37	58.20	59.62	1	1936	570	7
Italy	1935–37	55.25	57.49	1	1929–38	342	8
Japan	1935–36	46.92	49.63	1	1936	134	7
Mexico	1935	38.94	41.89	1	1935	127	7
Netherlands	1931–40	65.5	67.2	1	1929–38	675	8
New Zealand	1934–38	65.04	68.45	1	1936	885	7
Nicaragua	1940	33.88	35.09	9	1940	38	10
Norway	1931–41	64.08	67.55	1	1936	579	7
Panama	1940	41.50	43.26	9	1940	135	10
Philippines	1938	44.80	47.72	1	1938	68	7
Poland	1931–32	48.20	51.40	1	Average 1929 and 1933	174	7
Puerto Rico	1939–41	45.07	47.11	1	1940	325	7
Spain	1930–31	48.74	51.94	1	1929–35	272	8
Sweden	1928–32	62.02	64.11	5	1930	651	7
Switzerland	1929–32	59.17	63.05	1	1931	826	7
United Arab Rep.	1936–38	35.65	41.48	1	1939	60	10
United Kingdom	1930–32	58.74	62.88	1	1925–34	624	8
United States	1929–38	59.2	62.8	6	1929–38	1012	8
Venezuela	1936	33.29	34.47	9	1940	105	10

[a] Sources:

1. United Nations, *Demographic Yearbook, 1967*. New York.
2. S. H. Preston, N. Keyfitz, and R. Schoen. *Causes of Death: Life Tables for National Populations*. New York: Seminar Press, 1972.
3. K. Dandekar. Mortality and longevity in India, 1901–61. In K. E. Vaidyanathan, ed., *Studies on Mortality in India*. Grandhigram Institute of Rural Health, 1972.
4. W. Nitisastro. *Population Trends in Indonesia*. Cornell University Press, 1970.
5. N. Keyfitz and W. Flieger. *World Population*. Chicago: University of Chicago, 1968.
6. Annual average for 1929–1938. United States Department of Health, Education, and Welfare. *Vital Statistics of the United States, 1960*, Vol. II, Section 2.
7. Compiled from figures on national income and exchange rates. United Nations. *Statistical Yearbook, 1949–50*. New York. On population: United Nations *Demographic Yearbook, 1948*. New York. On U.S. Consumer Price Indexes: U.S. Bureau of Census. *Statistical Abstract of the United States, 1965*.
8. Compiled from Simon Kuznets. Quantitative aspects of the economic growth of nations. I. *Economic Development and Cultural Change*, Oct. 1956, *V* (No. 1), 5–94. Exchange rates, population, and price indexes from same sources as in (7).
9. E. E. Arriaga, *New Life Tables for Latin American Populations in the Nineteenth and Twentieth Centuries* (Population Monograph #3). Berkeley, Calif.: Institute of International Studies. University of California, Berkeley, 1968.
10. United States Bureau of the Budget figures cited in: Food, income, and mortality. *Population Index*, April, 1947, *13*(2), 96–103. Price indexes from same source as in (7).

Table A.3

Estimates of life expectancy and per capita national income for various countries in the 1960's[a]

Country	Year of mortality estimate	Life expectancy at birth		Year of income estimate	Per capita national income in 1963 U.S. dollars
		Male	Female		
Algeria	1965[b]	63.02	66.85	1965	184[d]
Argentina	1960–65	63.7	69.5	1963	480
Australia	1967	67.79	74.48	1967	1657
Austria	1966	66.82	73.54	1966	982
Belgium	1966[b]	67.74	73.79	1966	1427
Bulgaria	1960–62	67.82	71.35	1960	402(851)[e]
Burundi	1965	35.0	38.5	1965	40
Cambodia	1958–59	44.2	43.3	1958	74
Canada	1966–68[b]	68.89	75.47	1967	1913
Ceylon	1963[b]	63.04	63.44	1963	128
Chad	1963–64	29.	35.	1963	55
Chile	1967[b]	59.24	66.16	1967	434
Colombia	1965[b]	58.23	61.71	1965	239
Czechoslovakia	1960–61	67.64	73.12	1960	816(1385)[e]
Denmark	1967	70.66	75.41	1967	1794
Dominican Republic	1966[b]	63.61	66.06	1966	217
Ecuador	1965[b]	57.03	60.16	1965	179
El Salvador	1960–61	56.56	60.42	1960	194[d]
Finland	1966[b]	65.98	73.17	1966	1400
France	1965	67.8	75.0	1965	1483
Germany (East)	1960–61	67.31	73.34	1960	919(1395)[e]
Germany (West)	1964–65	67.59	73.45	1965	1420
Greece	1966–68	70.65	74.50	1967	597
Guatemala	1963–65	48.29	49.74	Average, 1963 and 1965	260
Hong Kong	1966[b]	65.90	72.69	1965	468
Hungary	1959–60	65.18	69.57	1960	572(985)[e]
India	1966–70[c]	48.9	46.2	1967	67
Indonesia	1961[b]	44.13	47.53	1960	85[d]
Ireland	1968[b]	68.69	73.21	1968	711
Italy	1966[b]	68.44	74.24	1968	873
Japan	1966	68.35	73.61	1966	774
Korea (South)	1955–60	51.12	53.73	1958	134
Madagascar	1966[b]	37.58	38.49	1966	90
Mexico	1966[b]	59.49	62.82	1966	421
Netherlands	1967[b]	71.20	76.59	1967	1359
New Zealand	1966–68[b]	68.21	74.33	1967	1573
Norway	1967[b]	71.36	76.85	1967	557
Pakistan	1962[b]	53.72	48.80?	1962	82
Peru	1963[b]	60.53	62.78	1963	202
Philippines	1960[b]	55.40	58.68	1960	154

Table A.3 (continued)

Country	Year of mortality estimate	Life expectancy at birth		Year of income estimate	Per capita national income in 1963 U.S. dollars
		Male	Female		
Poland	1960–61	64.80	70.50	1960	504(960)[e]
Portugal	1966–68[b]	63.97	69.73	1967	386
Puerto Rico	1959–61	67.14	71.88	1960	695[d]
Spain	1967[b]	69.24	74.55	1967	650
Sweden	1967[b]	71.87	76.58	1967	2144[f]
Switzerland	1967[b]	69.73	75.88	1967	1987
Taiwan	1966[b]	65.19	69.83	1966	188
Tunisia	1960[b]	55.66	63.23	1960	146
USSR	1960–61	66.	74.	1960	620(1022)[e]
United Arab Republic	1960	51.6	53.8	1960	124
United Kingdom	1966–68[b]	68.72	74.92	1967	1455
United States	1966	66.7	73.8	1966	2995
Upper Volta	1960–61	32.1	31.1	1960	44[d]
Uruguay	1963[b]	61.37	68.16	1963	533
Venezuela	1965[b]	63.90	67.70	1965	712
Yugoslavia	1960–61	62.18	65.27	1960	322(672)[e]
Thailand	1960	53.6	58.7	1960	95

[a] Unless otherwise noted, mortality figures are from United Nations, *Demographic Yearbook*, 1967, and per capita national income figures are from United Nations, *Statistical Yearbook, 1969* (adjusted by the United States Consumer Price Index from United States Bureau of Census, *Statistical Abstract of the United States.* 1965, 1968, and 1970). Note: Countries with fewer than 2 million inhabitants are excluded.

[b] From N. Keyfitz and W. Flieger, *Population: Facts and Methods of Demography.* San Francisco: Freeman, 1971.

[c] Revised estimate of the Indian Expert Committee on Population Projection, cited in India, Vital Statistics Division. *Measures of Fertility and Mortality in India.* SRS Analytical Series No. 2. 1972.

[d] From: World Bank, Economic Program Department, Socio-Economic Data Division. *World Tables IV. Resources, Product, and Income, 1971.* Estimates of GNP per capita in this publication for a particular country were scaled down by the ratio of national income to GNP for that country in a nearby year. These scaling factors (always close to unity) are taken from: United Nations. *Statistical Yearbook, 1969.* New York.

[e] Two estimates are provided for Eastern European countries and the USSR. Both refer to GNP/capita, somewhat higher than national income/capita. The first is taken from World Bank, *op. cit.*, and is based on the concept of net material product. The second figure, in parenthesis, refers to 1965 and is taken from: United Nations. Economic Commission for Europe. *Economic Survey of Europe in 1969. Part I. Structural Trends and Prospects in the European Economy.* New York, 1970. The second estimate is based on the use of physical or nonmonetary indicators of output and/or consumption.

[f] GDP for 1967 scaled down by the average ratio of NI to GDP for Switzerland, Denmark, and Norway in 1967 (.849).

Appendix 4B.   Data Employed to Decompose Change in Life Expectancy from 1930's to 1960's

Region	% of world population	National income per capita (1963 U.S. $)
1938[a]		
United States	6.1	1166
Rest of Overseas Western Europe	1.0	972
Western Europe	10.1	747
Other Europe	8.4	350
U.S.S.R.	7.9	277
Latin America, including Carribean	6.0	193
Asia except Japan	49.8	86
Japan	3.4	142
Africa except Republic of South Africa	6.9	67
Republic of South Africa	.4	439
1963[b]		
North America	6.6	2475
Oceania	.5	1230
Europe, except Eastern Europe	10.1	1070
Eastern Europe	3.7	876
U.S.S.R.	7.2	1022
Latin America, including Caribbean[c]	7.3	300
Middle East	1.8	290
Asia, except Japan and mainland China[c]	28.5	90
Japan	3.1	576
Mainland China	21.7	76
Africa, except Republic of South Africa	8.9	101
Republic of South Africa	.6	399

[a] Derived from Kuznets (1956, Table 4 and Appendix Tables 14, 16, 17).

[b] United Nations. *Statistical Yearbook, 1970*. Tables 18 and 184. New York. China figure derived from International Bank for Reconstruction and Development. Economic Program Department. *World Tables,* January, 1971, 4. GNP estimate scaled down by ratio of National Income to GNP for rest of Asia. Eastern Europe and U.S.S.R. figures derived from: Economic Commission for Europe. Economic Survey of Europe in 1969, *Structural Trends and Prospects in the European Economy,* Appendix Table 4V. Based on physical indicators approach. GNP estimate scaled down to National Income by average ratio, NI/GNP, for Italy, the Netherlands, Austria, Ireland, and Spain.

[c] Value for rest of Latin America assumed for Cuba; value for rest of Asia, excluding Japan and mainland China, assumed for N. Korea, Mongolia, and N. Vietnam.

CHAPTER 5

Causes of Death
and Age Patterns
of Mortality

In this chapter and Chapter 6, attention is turned to the analysis of mortality structure rather than of mortality level. Age variation in mortality is the focus of the present chapter and sex of the next. Sex differentials have their own intrinsic interest because sex is one of the most fundamental biological and social distinctions. But age patterns are probably more important demographically because of the rapid evolution and application of techniques for estimating vital rates from census age distributions. These techniques rely upon the assumption that the age function of mortality in the population at hand is a member of one or another "families" of age functions, and the estimates are quite sensitive to the choice of family (United Nations, 1967). In particular, the estimated birth and death rates depend heavily upon whether the population is assumed to belong to a family having high or low mortality below age 10 relative to mortality above age 10. The basic purpose of this chapter is to identify some common sources of variation in age patterns of mortality and thereby to assist the user in choosing sensibly among the many available "families." However, the chapter begins with a brief description summary of the contribution of the causes of death to age-specific death rates and to changes therein.

Average Age Patterns of Mortality

The age pattern of mortality varies systematically with mortality level. This observation is commonplace and has been well documented in a variety of places (United Nations, 1955, 1963a; Coale and Demeny, 1966; Ledermann, 1969; Carrier and Hobcraft, 1971). In general, as mortality levels improve, the largest absolute declines in mortality occur at ages under 5 and above 65; the largest proportionate declines occur between ages 1 and 20. Assignment of these changes to causes of death is straightforward. The infectious diseases responsible for a large part of the mortality reduction have a U-shaped age pattern that is especially sharply angled for influenza/pneumonia/bronchitis, so that as these diseases are reduced to levels near zero, the age pattern of absolute reduction must also be U-shaped. The proportionate reductions, on the other hand, are largest in the older childhood ages where infectious diseases were the only major killers (i.e., where developmental conditions and degenerative diseases are not prominent).

Table 5.1 shows the average age pattern of mortality for all causes combined and for each individual cause of death in populations falling within five different ranges of life expectancy. The ranges are: 25–44.99 years; 45.00–54.99 years; 55.00–64.99 years; 65.00–69.99 years; and 70.00–74.99 years. The assignment of a particular population is based on the mean of male and female life expectancies; the sexes are not disassociated according to their respective levels because of interest in the comparative position of the two.

Figure 5.1 displays semilogarithmic graphs of the female age-specific death rates in quintiles of female life expectancy for certain of the causes or for combinations of causes. Quintile one refers to the 33 populations with lowest female life expectancy and quintile five to those with the highest. The figures reveal that the causes differ substantially in age pattern, with infectious and parasitic diseases being relatively flat after age 10, especially in high mortality populations, and tuberculosis relatively flat after age 20; influenza/pneumonia/bronchitis sharply U-shaped; the combination of diarrhea and certain diseases of infancy heavily concentrated below age 5; violence peaking locally in the early twenties, and rising again at older ages in a fashion that becomes steeper as mortality levels decline (the order of quintiles in terms of their average violence death rates at ages 5–9 is exactly reversed from their order at 80–84); maternal mortality shaped much like the age curve of fertility but with a tilt to the right; and all other causes being highly regular, virtually linear after age 30, and heavily concentrated at the older ages. The figures also indicate that age patterns of death by cause typically change as the level of mortality changes. If the death rates declined

Table 5.1

Average age-cause-specific death rates (per 1000) in populations grouped according to mean level of male and female life expectancy: populations with life expectancy below 45 years

Chile: 1909, 1920, 1930, 1940; Taiwan: 1920, 1930, 1936; Italy: 1881, 1891, 1901; England and Wales: 1861, 1871, 1891; South Africa (coloured): 1941; U.S. (nonwhite): 1920; Japan: 1908

Females

AGE	ALL CAUSES	RESP. T.B.	OTHER I AND P	CANCER	CARDIO-VASCULAR	INFL. PNUE. BRUNCH.	DIAR-RHEAL	CERTAIN CHRONIC	MATER-NAL	CERTAIN DISEASES OF INF.	AJTO ACCIDENT	OTHER VIOLENCE	OTHER AND UNKNOWN
0	206.384	1.084	25.886	.067	3.360	41.724	29.971*	.295*	0.000	47.224*	0.000	2.145	54.628*
1	36.637*	.813*	9.392*	.040*	.495*	9.734*	6.360*	.257*	.000	0.000	.005	.771	8.770*
5	6.869*	.453*	2.315*	.017	.238	1.408*	.437*	.097*	.000	0.000	.011	.267	1.626*
10	4.562*	.884*	1.192*	.021*	.286*	.866*	.149*	.065*	.014	0.000	.044	.156	.925
15	7.238*	.368*	1.155	.024	.404*	1.227*	.144*	.094*	.416*	0.000	.002	.293	1.111
20	9.611	3.165*	1.185	.068*	.511	1.629	.213*	.134	.928*	0.000	.005	.317	1.456*
25	10.542*	3.164*	1.169	.131*	.721*	1.887	.264*	.194*	1.113	0.000	.005	.354	1.640*
30	11.339	3.015	1.104	.315	.909*	1.988	.280*	.274	1.210	0.000	.003	.241	2.000*
35	12.503	2.818	1.176	.563*	1.340	2.122	.390*	.363	1.179*	0.000	.009	.242	2.301
40	13.247	2.545	1.167	.924*	1.855	2.355	.417	.434	.758*	0.010	.001	.265	2.526
45	15.161	2.454	1.179	1.384*	2.762*	2.769	.529	.599	.212*	0.010	.002	.272	2.999
50	18.575	2.348	1.347	1.833*	3.955	3.389	.672	.790	.028*	0.010	.006	.315	3.892
55	24.519	2.433	1.513	2.423*	5.761	4.431	.984	1.074	.010	0.000	.013	.303	5.574
60	35.783	2.491	1.735	2.730*	9.447	6.934	1.532	1.404	.006	0.000	.006	.502	8.396
65	52.517	2.719	2.208	3.350*	14.737	10.037	2.374	1.828	.000	0.000	.072*	.526	14.636
70	74.491	2.940	2.590	4.123*	20.668	13.864	2.813	1.939	0.000	0.000	.002*	.833	24.719
75	110.852	2.676	3.094	4.493*	30.728*	20.218	4.827	2.727	0.000	0.000	.073*	1.055	40.966
80	176.032	2.538	3.464	4.537*	39.523	26.799	9.155	3.336	0.000	0.000	.006	1.051	84.823
85	297.518	1.729	4.211	4.093*	53.866	41.358	15.613	4.350	0.000	0.010	0.000	2.757	169.541

Males

AGE	ALL CAUSES	RESP. T.B.	OTHER I AND P	CANCER	CARDIO-VASCULAR	INFL. PNUE. BRUNCH.	DIAR-RHEAL	CERTAIN CHRONIC	MATER-NAL	CERTAIN DISEASES OF INF.	AJTO ACCIDENT	OTHER VIOLENCE	OTHER AND UNKNOWN
0	239.824	1.164	29.363	.086	3.872	49.087	33.397	.342	0.000	55.602	.002	2.470	64.439
1	35.613	.787	9.129	.035	.490	9.506	5.909	.240	0.000	0.000	.009	.855	8.653
5	6.527	.327	2.151	.017	.239	1.233	.407	.086	0.000	0.000	.016	.431	1.620
10	4.004	.420	1.017	.018	.249	.704	.147	.060	0.000	0.000	.010	.454	.925
15	6.648	1.657	1.172	.028	.363	1.786	.133	.086	0.000	0.000	.012	.860	1.116
20	9.581	2.712	1.441	.045	.454	2.049	.186	.135	0.000	0.000	.029	1.344	1.449
25	10.465	2.868	1.360	.062	.632	2.387	.225	.176	0.000	0.000	.025	1.421	1.647
30	11.734	3.027	1.470	.115	.893	2.759	.262	.274	0.000	0.000	.026	1.360	1.920
35	13.437	3.138	1.519	.228	1.303	3.455	.345	.386	0.000	0.000	.037	1.314	2.403
40	16.178	3.338	1.624	.477	1.921	4.164	.490	.562	0.000	0.000	.036	1.280	2.995
45	19.649	3.638	1.755	.761	2.755	5.016	.608	.788	0.000	0.000	.047	1.225	3.908
50	24.321	3.791	1.802	1.217	4.171	6.332	.833	1.042	0.000	0.000	.039	1.309	5.101
55	31.568	3.989	1.971	1.899	6.214	8.830	1.208	1.444	0.000	0.000	.037	1.333	7.141
60	43.377	4.118	2.305	2.464	9.655	12.613	1.754	1.698	0.000	0.000	.059	1.504	11.050
65	61.380	4.201	2.831	3.093	14.793	16.336	2.621	2.475	0.000	0.000	.049	1.500	17.174
70	84.242	4.134	3.169	3.815	20.742	23.203	3.274	2.969	0.000	0.000	.041	1.830	27.932
75	120.038	3.661	3.554	4.087	29.393	29.203	5.424	3.754	0.000	0.000	.036	2.041	44.921
80	191.289	3.551	4.239	4.190	39.523	32.450	10.166	4.701	0.000	0.000	.026	2.659	89.784
85	320.989	2.145	4.751	3.880	54.633	51.014	16.933	6.401	0.000	0.010	.019	4.107	177.106

Table 5.1 (continued)   Populations with life expectancy between 45.00 and 54.99 years

Chile: 1950, 1959; Colombia: 1960; Czechoslovakia: 1934; England and Wales: 1881, 1901, 1911; Guatemala: 1961, 1964; Italy: 1910, 1921, 1931; Japan: 1940; Portugal: 1930, 1940; South Africa (coloured): 1951, 1960; Spain: 1930, 1940; U.S.: 1900, 1910

Females

AGE	ALL CAUSES	RESP. T.B.	OTHER I AND P	CANCER	CARDIO-VASCULAR	INFL. PNUE. BRONCH.	DIAR-RHEAL	CERTAIN CHRONIC	MATER-NAL	CERTAIN DISEASES OF INF.	AUTO ACCIDENT	OTHER VIOLENCE	OTHER AND UNKNOWN
0	35.202	.044	1.513	.086	.167	5.298	3.025	.057	0.000	16.480	.020	.272	7.940
1	2.281	.020	.441*	.092	.036	.497*	.252	.032	0.000	.001	.056	.228	.626
5	.659	.010*	.123*	.060	.036	.058*	.017	.022	0.000	.000	.058	.000	.169
10	.473	.018*	.064*	.049	.056	.034*	.006*	.029*	.001*	.000	.027	.063	.126
15	.730	.084*	.060	.064	.079	.035	.005	.038	.026*	.030	.050	.123	.166
20	1.019	.187*	.067	.084	.109	.039	.008*	.047	.096*	.000	.084	.151	.167
25	1.293	.244*	.068	.144*	.156	.048*	.009*	.068	.140*	.000	.033	.142	.241*
30	1.567	.243	.064	.263*	.238	.052	.011	.093	.161*	.000	.033	.146	.263
35	2.151	.245	.069	.514*	.388	.076	.013	.131	.160*	.000	.035	.164	.356
40	2.923	.237	.076	.876*	.657	.103	.016	.191	.088*	.000	.037	.175	.467
45	4.322	.231	.082	1.453	1.189	.153	.024*	.289	.014	0.000	.047	.218	.622
50	6.593	.242	.110	2.111	2.181	.239	.032*	.463	.021*	0.000	.054	.294	.966
55	9.792	.289	.140	2.845	3.806	.360	.040	.693	.001*	0.000	.061	.273	1.284
60	16.354	.380	.179	4.067	7.269	.687	.075	1.105	.001*	0.000	.092	.352	2.147
65	26.198	.437	.220	5.432	12.987	1.273	.131	1.680	.000	0.000	.093	.486	3.457
70	44.542	.531	.289	7.446	23.545	2.607	.239*	2.363	.000	0.000	.127	.791	6.604
75	75.183	.579	.361	9.454	41.252	5.106	.428	3.208	.000	0.000	.165	1.534*	13.096
80	125.078	.588	.410	11.462	66.793	9.573	.850*	3.845	.000	0.000	.166	3.044*	28.347
85	220.563	.488	.625	12.644	111.282	19.179	1.383	4.401	.000	0.000	.165	6.628	63.763

Males

AGE	ALL CAUSES	RESP. T.B.	OTHER I AND P	CANCER	CARDIO-VASCULAR	INFL. PNUE. BRONCH.	DIAR-RHEAL	CERTAIN CHRONIC	MATER-NAL	CERTAIN DISEASES OF INF.	AUTO ACCIDENT	OTHER VIOLENCE	OTHER AND UNKNOWN
0	43.750	.000	1.673	.110	.205	6.208	3.534	.088	0.000	21.600	.044	.736	9.492
1	2.489	.023	.429*	.114	.039	.488	.254	.039	0.000	.001	.093	.345	.664
5	.855	.009	.126	.078	.041	.063	.018	.024	0.000	.000	.104	.194	.198
10	.666	.011	.061	.068	.097	.031	.005	.022	0.000	.000	.069	.196	.146
15	1.245	.059	.073	.094	.113	.046	.007	.042	0.000	.000	.204	.437	.195
20	1.846	.154	.070	.111	.167	.046	.008	.067	0.000	.000	.329	.717	.226
25	1.924	.233	.070	.150	.281	.047	.009	.091	0.000	.000	.252	.673	.233
30	2.199	.287	.074	.216	.563	.068	.013	.136	0.000	.000	.204	.631	.294
35	2.939	.361	.095	.347	.793	.103	.016	.211	0.000	.000	.191	.654	.398
40	4.253	.441	.113	.635	1.106	.164	.022	.314	0.000	.000	.207	.714	.556
45	6.543	.554	.150	1.181	2.020	.273	.031	.504	0.000	.000	.216	.808	.824
50	10.650	.754	.204	2.166	3.883	.489	.052	.761	0.000	.000	.239	.918	1.229
55	16.738	.981	.268	3.726	6.689	.811	.098	1.092	0.000	.000	.266	.950	1.933
60	27.005	1.046	.384	5.804	11.733	1.503	.139	1.602	0.000	.000	.315	1.046	3.339
65	40.750	1.342	.415	8.257	19.143	2.445	.238	2.224	0.000	.000	.459	1.098	5.367
70	62.791	1.425	.467	10.936	30.781	4.139	.440	2.965	0.000	.000	.499	1.334	10.047
75	97.075	1.383	.521	13.688	49.084	7.226	.611	3.862	0.000	.000	.750	1.846	18.526
80	151.069	1.323	.542	15.499	75.231	12.064	.834	4.780	0.000	.000	.855	3.007	37.033
85	249.780	.965	.766	16.267	117.373	23.589	1.614	6.204	0.000	.000	.855	5.395	76.746

Table 5.1 (continued) Populations with life expectancy between 55.00 and 64.99 years

Australia: 1911, 1921; Canada: 1921, 1931, 1941; Chile: 1964; Colombia: 1964; Costa Rica: 1960, 1964; Denmark: 1921, 1930; England and Wales: 1921, 1931, 1940; Ireland: 1951; Italy: 1910, 1920, 1930; Japan: 1951; Mexico: 1960, 1964; Netherlands: 1931; New Zealand: 1881, 1891, 1901, 1911, 1921; 1926; Panama: 1960; Portugal: 1960; South Africa (white): 1941; Sweden: 1911, 1920, 1930; Switzerland: 1930, 1941; Taiwan: 1960; U.S.: 1930, 1940; U.S. (white): 1920; U.S. (nonwhite): 1950; Venezuela: 1960

Females

AGE	ALL CAUSES	RESP. T.B.	OTHER I AND P	CANCER	CARDIO-VASCULAR	INFL. PNUE. BRONCH.	DIAR-RHEAL	CERTAIN CHRONIC	MATER-NAL	CERTAIN DISEASES OF INF.	AUTO ACCIDENT	OTHER VIOLENCE	OTHER AND UNKNOWN
0	135.149	.698	10.882	.073*	.766	24.526	35.503	.285	0.000	38.935*	.002	.950	22.529
1	20.842	.444	5.192*	.052	.181	4.720	5.054*	.236	0.000	.109*	.014	.510	4.330
5	3.842	.194*	1.319*	.024	.164*	.533*	.344*	.088	0.000*	.000	.018	.105	.973
10	2.432*	.386*	.626*	.024	.242*	.260*	.113	.063*	.001*	0.000	.009	.106	.602
15	3.757	1.261*	.642	.041	.284*	.330	.097	.087*	.135*	0.000	.007	.172	.704
20	4.965	1.816*	.628	.064	.333*	.387	.120*	.127*	.415*	0.000	.011	.192	.072*
25	5.494	1.325	.609	.130*	.427*	.446	.141*	.159	.541*	0.000	.012	.189	1.015*
30	6.146	1.630	.596	.281*	.629*	.549	.159*	.250	.635*	0.000	.024	.174	1.199
35	6.826	1.455	.572	.545*	.903	.637	.176*	.319	.636*	0.000	.027	.200	1.356
40	7.882	1.291	.558	.962*	1.369	.753	.213	.441	.410*	0.000	.010	.232	1.643
45	9.485	1.154	.589	1.463*	2.153	.919	.268	.627	.081*	0.000	.018	.238	1.974
50	12.701	1.123	.697	1.995*	3.430	1.334	.374	.853	.014*	0.000	.030	.274	2.577
55	17.649	1.065	.823	2.809*	5.296	2.074	.570	1.179	.003*	0.000	.036	.299	3.495
60	26.690	1.053	1.035	3.563	8.784	3.447	.887	1.605	.002*	0.000	.033	.397	5.084
65	41.192	1.153	1.268	4.720	14.810	5.436	1.429*	2.222	.004*	0.000	.027	.509	9.614
70	64.057	1.063	1.486	5.694	23.432	8.758	2.032	2.875	.000	0.000	.035	.790	17.914
75	97.758	1.100	1.712	6.785	35.436	12.923	3.032	3.528	.001	0.000	.045	1.230	32.056
80	152.321	.829	2.407	6.752	46.904	19.578	4.387*	4.115	.000	0.010	.019	2.047	65.283
85	247.219	.562	2.594	7.286	62.174	29.093	6.402	4.899	.006	0.000	.041	3.365	130.803

Males

AGE	ALL CAUSES	RESP. T.B.	OTHER I AND P	CANCER	CARDIO-VASCULAR	INFL. PNUE. BRONCH.	DIAR-RHEAL	CERTAIN CHRONIC	MATER-NAL	CERTAIN DISEASES OF INF.	AUTO ACCIDENT	OTHER VIOLENCE	OTHER AND UNKNOWN
0	158.745	.789	11.690	.069	.959	28.642	40.290	.375	0.000	47.720	.011	1.011	27.189
1	21.060	.455	5.075	.059	.204*	4.744	4.960	.262	0.000	.107	.025	.646	4.523
5	3.870	.160	1.251	.037	.158	.505	.311	.092	0.000	.000	.024	.324	1.003
10	2.420	.196	.577	.031	.199	.243	.102	.060	0.000	0.000	.029	.337	.648
15	3.932	.915	.645	.045	.270	.355	.102	.083	0.000	0.000	.044	.693	.780
20	5.637	1.807	.665	.069	.313	.437	.098	.118	0.000	0.000	.078	1.167	.880
25	6.252	1.941	.612	.095	.405	.498	.136	.176	0.000	0.000	.088	1.315	1.003
30	7.102	1.995	.649	.170	.614	.622	.163	.261	0.000	0.000	.107	1.303	1.245
35	8.247	2.045	.693	.281	.917	.829	.163	.382	0.000	0.000	.103	1.278	1.556
40	10.054	2.039	.798	.530	1.450	1.087	.221	.577	0.000	0.000	.107	1.268	1.977
45	12.963	2.187	.927	.954	2.314	1.428	.285	.825	0.000	0.000	.098	1.361	2.584
50	16.998	2.154	1.002	1.612	3.754	1.999	.388	1.206	0.000	0.000	.109	1.359	3.415
55	24.072	2.263	1.181	2.035	6.223	2.999	.591	1.696	0.000	0.000	.095	1.502	4.802
60	34.851	2.297	1.387	3.729	10.493	4.483	.932	2.338	0.000	0.000	.112	1.509	7.571
65	50.243	2.112	1.612	4.992	16.844	6.657	1.342	3.150	0.000	0.000	.113	1.536	11.885
70	76.805	1.857	1.955	6.369	26.290	10.573	2.035	4.083	0.000	0.000	.106	1.851	21.686
75	111.754	1.663	2.228	7.208	38.510	14.857	3.024	5.041	0.000	0.000	.148	2.225	36.850
80	166.856	1.359	2.847	7.315	50.083	21.632	4.297	5.622	0.000	0.000	.065	2.555	71.081
85	263.799	1.158	2.818	7.468	67.002	31.963	6.677	7.446	0.000	0.000	.173	3.844	135.250

Table 5.1 (continued) Populations with life expectancy between 65.00 and 69.99 years

Australia: 1933, 1940, 1951; Austria: 1961; Belgium: 1960; Canada: 1951; Denmark: 1940; England and Wales: 1951; Finland: 1951, 1960, 1964; France: 1951; West Germany: 1960, 1964; Hong Kong: 1961, 1964; Hungary: 1960, 1964; Ireland: 1961; Israel (Jewish): 1951; Italy: 1960; Japan: 1960; Malta and Gozo: 1964; Netherlands: 1940; New Zealand: 1936, 1945; Northern Ireland: 1960; Norway: 1946; Panama: 1964; Poland: 1960, 1964; Portugal: 1964; Puerto Rico: 1960, 1964; Scotland: 1951, 1960, 1964; South Africa (White): 1951, 1960, 1964; Spain: 1960; Sweden: 1940; Switzerland: 1951; Taiwan: 1964; Trinidad and Tobago: 1963; U.S.: 1960; U.S. (White): 1950; Venezuela: 1964; Yugoslavia: 1961, 1964.

Females

AGE	ALL CAUSES	RESP. T.B.	OTHER I AND P	CANCER	CARDIO-VASCULAR	INFL. PNUE. BRONCH.	DIAR-RHEAL	CERTAIN CHRONIC	MATER-NAL	CERTAIN DISEASES OF INF.	AUTO ACCIDENT	OTHER VIOLENCE	OTHER AND UNKNOWN
0	63.299	.190	5.191	.074	.298	11.098	9.747	.094	0.000	23.771*	.011	.859	11.966
1	6.440	.089	1.851*	.063	.084	1.446	.915	.071	0.000	0.000	.031	.424	1.466
5	1.850	.067	.638	.033	.118	.199	.078*	.054	.004*	0.000	.032	.178	.473
10	1.387	.181	.332	.035	.159*	.106*	.027	.070*	.104*	0.000	.015	.115	.343
15	2.276	.755	.333	.050	.200*	.145	.023	.083	.310*	0.000	.024	.162	.397
20	3.067	1.091*	.284	.076	.235*	.199	.031*	.114	.447	0.000	.023	.179	.482
25	3.551	1.180*	.270	.138*	.306*	.244	.039*	.142	.507*	0.000	.018	.180	.573*
30	3.943	1.004*	.275	.288*	.442	.315	.044	.200	.553*	0.000	.020	.179	.674*
35	4.745	.931	.290	.567*	.655*	.355	.064*	.292	.296*	0.000	.019	.195	.639*
40	5.476	.776	.297	1.022*	.976	.384	.060	.394	.067	0.000	.024	.201	1.653
45	7.073	.705	.297	1.657*	1.621	.465	.080	.586	.003*	0.000	.028	.245	1.322
50	9.793	.671	.331	2.419*	2.675	.633	.121*	.882	.000	0.000	.031	.257	1.770
55	13.875	.712	.432	3.249*	4.404	1.035	.153	1.334	.000	0.000	.046	.311	2.193
60	20.891	.728	.475	4.370	7.486	1.738	.245	1.918	.000	0.000	.047	.386	3.498
65	31.782	.784	.526	5.890	12.499	3.009	.449	2.590	.000	0.000	.055	.490	5.490
70	52.032	.792	.695	7.353	21.164	5.415	.724	3.495	.001	0.000	.066	.852	11.475
75	83.127	.822	.926	8.970	32.746	9.302	.954*	4.514	.000	0.000	.082	1.522	23.289
80	127.798	.737	.916	9.800	46.026	13.419	1.724*	5.262	.000	0.010	.097	2.800	47.017
85	244.399	.409	1.503	12.758	76.827	25.399	2.896	7.159	.000	0.000	.064	6.053	111.331

Males

AGE	ALL CAUSES	RESP. T.B.	OTHER I AND P	CANCER	CARDIO-VASCULAR	INFL. PNUE. BRONCH.	DIAR-RHEAL	CERTAIN CHRONIC	MATER-NAL	CERTAIN DISEASES OF INF.	AUTO ACCIDENT	OTHER VIOLENCE	OTHER AND UNKNOWN
0	78.876	.197	5.677	.082	.444	13.520	11.888	.153	0.000	30.520	.011	1.024	15.360
1	6.850	.097	1.821	.074	.095	1.479	.947	.076	0.000	0.000	.049	.609	1.603
5	2.112	.049	.653	.051	.120	.202	.077	.054	0.000	0.000	.063	.328	.515
10	1.548	.085	.333	.042	.137	.102	.029	.059	0.000	0.000	.041	.334	.386
15	2.504	.455	.347	.067	.183	.185	.027	.088	0.000	0.000	.085	.619	.448
20	3.636	.951	.346	.082	.214	.245	.027	.121	0.000	0.000	.127	.986	.537
25	3.862	1.051	.324	.113	.271	.269	.033	.166	0.000	0.000	.115	.969	.551
30	4.282	1.002	.325	.171	.380	.333	.044	.238	0.000	0.000	.104	1.029	.656
35	5.147	.991	.356	.317	.633	.443	.044	.365	0.000	0.000	.105	1.061	.832
40	6.529	1.016	.434	.574	1.067	.578	.066	.530	0.000	0.000	.115	1.074	1.075
45	8.898	1.069	.524	1.026	1.822	.774	.080	.832	0.000	0.007	.124	1.219	1.428
50	12.483	1.137	.608	1.872	3.174	1.042	.105	1.170	0.000	0.000	.130	1.252	1.993
55	18.200	1.265	.696	3.022	5.428	1.483	.180	1.679	0.000	0.000	.136	1.399	2.912
60	27.013	1.312	.747	4.790	9.087	2.209	.265	2.256	0.000	0.000	.162	1.502	4.681
65	40.642	1.334	.849	6.933	14.983	3.571	.356	3.206	0.000	0.000	.168	1.608	7.639
70	62.263	1.157	.830	8.945	24.095	5.714	.686	4.186	0.000	0.000	.181	1.783	14.686
75	95.750	1.085	.973	10.842	36.754	9.641	.922	5.567	0.000	0.000	.258	2.130	27.578
80	146.375	.871	1.035	10.856	51.024	15.030	1.497	6.959	0.000	0.000	.342	3.138	55.623
85	245.436	.642	1.295	11.626	73.765	26.399	2.702	8.598	0.000	0.000	.282	4.845	115.281

Table 5.1 (continued) Populations with life expectancy above 70 years

Australia: 1960, 1964; Austria: 1964; Belgium: 1964; Bulgaria: 1964; Canada: 1960, 1964; Czechoslovakia: 1960, 1964; Denmark: 1960, 1964; England and Wales: 1960, 1964; France: 1960, 1964; Greece: 1960, 1964; Iceland: 1964; Israel (Jewish): 1960, 1964; Italy: 1964; Japan: 1964; Netherlands: 1950, 1960, 1964; New Zealand: 1951, 1964; Northern Ireland: 1964; Norway: 1951, 1964; Sweden: 1951, 1960, 1964; Switzerland: 1960, 1964; U. S.: 1964

Females

AGE	ALL CAUSES	RESP. T.B.	OTHER I AND P	CANCER	CARDIO-VASCULAR	INFL. PNEU. BRONCH.	DIAR-RHEAL	CERTAIN CHRONIC	MATER-NAL	CERTAIN DISEASES OF INF.	AUTO ACCIDENT	OTHER VIOLENCE	OTHER AND UNKNOWN
0	20.808	.008	.509	.096	.101	2.323	.675	.026	0.000	11.011	.020	.484	5.555
1	1.053	.003	.104*	.111	.024	.153	.040	.011	0.000	.001	.089	.186	.331
5	.388	.001	.031	.072	.015*	.026*	.004	.010	0.000	.000	.073	.053	.103
10	.282	.003*	.015	.060	.028*	.014	.002*	.013	.000	.000	.033	.038	.076
15	.433	.009*	.020	.064	.039	.013	.004*	.026	.007*	.000	.078	.079	.094
20	.586	.024*	.021*	.087	.057	.014	.003	.036	.042*	.000	.076	.114	.112
25	.698	.041	.022*	.136	.091	.017	.005	.040	.058*	0.000	.042	.115	.131
30	.938	.060	.019	.264*	.138	.023	.005	.057	.058*	0.000	.040	.111	.163
35	1.380	.054	.029	.484*	.233	.027	.005	.077	.067*	0.000	.043	.142	.219
40	2.046	.060	.029	.839*	.419	.049	.010	.108	.031*	0.000	.053	.154	.294
45	3.300	.062	.041	1.411*	.813	.074	.010	.173	.005*	0.000	.060	.195	.456
50	4.929	.067	.054	2.039	1.496	.098	.020	.254	.001*	0.000	.080	.224	.596
55	7.809	.080	.064	2.936	2.791	.222	.027	.424	.000	0.000	.086	.275	.904
60	12.673	.102	.069	3.974	5.529	.389	.045	.698	.000	0.000	.116	.311	1.420
65	21.516	.140	.133	5.413	10.954	.783	.082	1.141	.000	.010	.132	.444	2.294
70	37.431	.199	.165	7.408	20.919	1.736	.165	1.763	.000	.000	.198	.812	4.066
75	65.605	.275	.228	10.023	39.010	3.797	.331	2.361	0.000	.000	.273	1.633*	7.674
80	112.010	.317	.291	12.385	68.771	7.662	.557	2.950	.000	.000	.259	3.469*	15.349
85	208.114	.301	.415	15.184	122.175	17.411	1.054	3.525	.000	.000	.204	7.816*	40.029

Males

AGE	ALL CAUSES	RESP. T.B.	OTHER I AND P	CANCER	CARDIO-VASCULAR	INFL. PNEU. BRONCH.	DIAR-RHEAL	CERTAIN CHRONIC	MATER-NAL	CERTAIN DISEASES OF INF.	AUTO ACCIDENT	OTHER VIOLENCE	OTHER AND UNKNOWN
0	26.549	.008	.540	.109	.113	2.744	.781	.031	0.000	14.956	.022	.643	6.596
1	1.269	.004	.098	.129	.026	.154	.052	.011	0.000	.002	.118	.299	.376
5	.595	.001	.033	.100	.014	.023	.004	.010	0.000	.000	.119	.157	.134
10	.477	.001	.018	.087	.023	.015	.003	.014	0.000	.000	.073	.141	.102
15	1.016	.007	.022	.102	.050	.021	.002	.028	0.000	.000	.307	.346	.131
20	1.378	.017	.021	.127	.070	.023	.004	.037	0.000	.000	.419	.514	.146
25	1.353	.040	.019	.161	.122	.017	.005	.064	0.000	.000	.285	.478	.162
30	1.549	.070	.028	.216	.220	.024	.007	.089	0.000	.000	.224	.482	.189
35	2.077	.096	.033	.345	.436	.044	.008	.135	0.000	.000	.202	.517	.261
40	3.136	.116	.045	.602	.914	.079	.010	.199	0.000	.000	.206	.568	.397
45	5.091	.162	.055	1.123	1.816	.129	.014	.330	0.000	.000	.238	.650	.574
50	8.363	.216	.084	2.134	3.341	.250	.022	.496	0.000	.000	.250	.701	.869
55	13.996	.304	.118	3.722	6.022	.518	.031	.758	0.000	.000	.284	.828	1.411
60	22.533	.417	.157	5.975	10.361	.987	.048	1.137	0.000	.000	.316	.838	2.297
65	35.450	.504	.233	8.781	17.385	1.817	.087	1.569	0.000	.000	.400	.968	3.706
70	54.333	.618	.281	11.638	28.512	3.191	.148	2.137	0.000	.000	.444	1.195	6.169
75	85.161	.670	.364	15.061	46.882	5.970	.273	2.810	0.000	.000	.584	1.747	10.800
80	134.776	.616	.388	18.126	76.403	10.707	.592	3.434	0.000	.000	.677	3.034	20.799
85	230.560	.611	.406	20.105	126.907	22.517	1.144	4.029	0.000	.000	.672	6.207	47.962

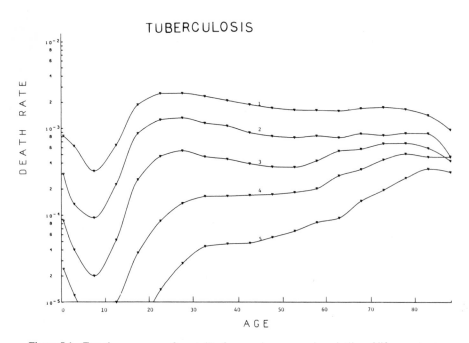

Figure 5.1   Female age curves of mortality from various causes in quintiles of life expectancy.

Figure 5.1 (continued)

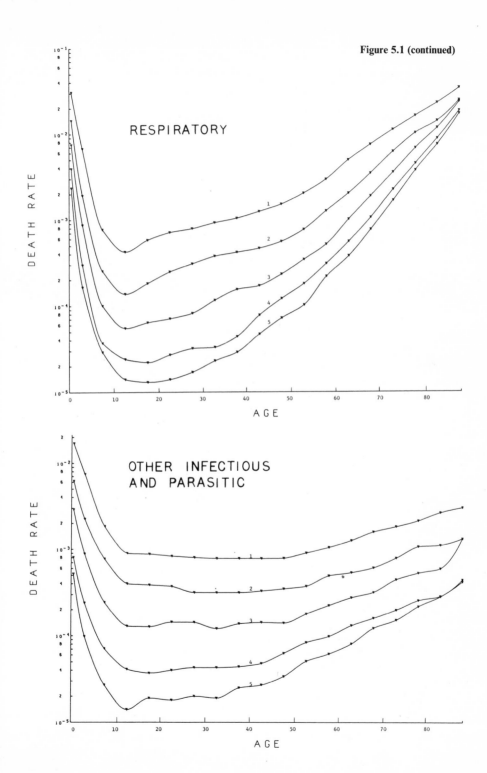

Figure 5.1 (continued)

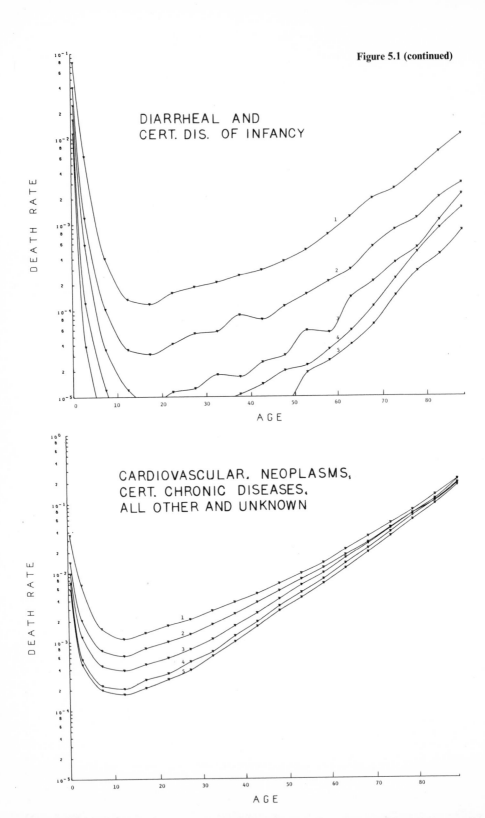

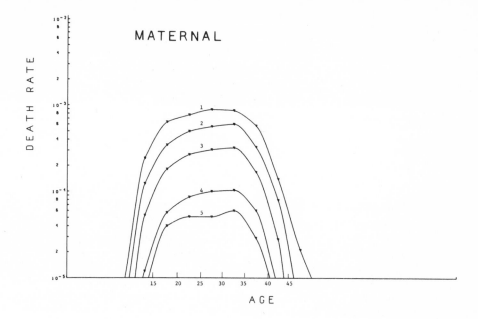

MATERNAL

Figure 5.1 (continued)

VIOLENCE

99

by a factor constant with age, the age-curves would appear to be parallel on a semilog graph. But parallelism is not even a remote tendency except for "other infectious and parasitic diseases."

The cause of death making the largest contribution to declines in mortality at a particular age can be directly inferred by comparing populations at the lowest and highest levels of mortality in Table 5.1. A convenient index is

$$\text{Percentage contribution of cause } i \atop \text{to mortality decline at age } x = \frac{\begin{array}{l}\text{(Average Death Rate, cause } i, \text{ age } x \text{ in}\\ \text{group 1 minus Average Death Rate,}\\ \text{cause } i, \text{ age } x, \text{ in group 5)}\end{array}}{\begin{array}{l}\text{(Average Death Rate, all causes, age } x\\ \text{in group 1 minus Average Death}\\ \text{Rate, all causes, age } x, \text{ in group 5)}\end{array}}$$

where group 1 are populations with average life expectancy less than 45 and group 2 are populations with average life expectancy above 70. Table 5.2 presents the two causes of death that are the largest contributors to mortality reduction at each age, exclusive of other and unknown causes whose contribution is difficult to interpret.

This table reveals the preeminent importance of influenza/pneumonia/bronchitis on an age-by-age basis. It is the first or second most influential cause for mortality reduction in every age interval except 10–19. Its contribution never falls below 17.8% of the total decline and reaches a peak of 36.3% at ages 75–79. The relative constancy of its contribution suggests that the age pattern of absolute decline in mortality from influenza/pneumonia/bronchitis is quite similar in form to that for all causes combined, though its angle is somewhat sharper.

Other causes that are influential at various ages are infectious and parasitic diseases at ages 1–19, respiratory tuberculosis at ages 10–49, cardiovascular disease at ages 50–59, and diarrheal disease at ages 75 and over. The importance of diarrheal and respiratory diseases at the extremes of life probably reflects both the great vulnerability of persons at these ages to chronic digestive and respiratory problems in populations with poor health levels and the tendency to assign deaths to symptomatic causes in such populations. Two causes of death with special social significance are moderately important causes of decline in certain age intervals. Maternal mortality is the third or fourth largest contributor to female declines at ages 25–39, accounting for between 10.0% and 11.1% of the total change, and "other violence" is the fourth leading source of male declines at ages 10–34, contributing between 8.6% and 10.3% of the total decline.

The leading cause of decline for males is identical to that for females at every age, and separate enumeration seems unnecessary. The list of second

Table 5.2

Causes of death making the largest contribution to declines in death rates by age for females

Age	Proportion of total decline when e_0^0 improves from <45 to >70 accounted for by		Proportion of total decline when e_0^0 improves from 45–54.99 to >70 accounted for by	
	Most important cause	Next most important cause	Most important cause	Next most important cause
0	Influ./pneu./bronch. (.212)	Cert. dis. inf. (.195)	Diarrheal (.304)	Cert. dis. inf. (.244)
1–4	(.269)	Infec. & para. (.261)	Infec. & para. (.257)	Diarrheal (.253)
5–9	Infec. & para. (.352)	Influ./pneu./bronch. (.213)	(.373)	Influ./pneu./bronch. (.147)
10–14	(.275)	Resp. T.B. (.206)	(.284)	Resp. T.B. (.178)
15–19	Resp. T.B. (.346)	Infec. & para. (.166)	Resp. T.B. (.376)	Infec. & para. (.187)
20–24	(.348)	Influ./pneu./bronch. (.179)	(.409)	(.138)
25–29	(.317)	(.190)	(.372)	(.122)
30–34	(.284)	(.189)	(.301)	(.111)
35–39	(.248)	(.188)	(.257)	Cardiovascular (.125)
40–44	(.222)	(.206)	(.211)	(.163)
45–49	Influ./pneu./bronch. (.227)	Resp. T.B. (.202)	Cardiovascular (.216)	Resp. T.B. (.176)
50–54	(.241)	Cardiovascular (.180)	(.248)	Influ./pneu./bronch. (.158)
55–59	(.252)	(.178)	(.254)	(.188)
60–64	(.283)	(.169)	(.232)	(.218)
65–69	(.298)	(.122)	Influ./pneu./bronch. (.236)	Cardiovascular (.195)
70–74	(.327)	Resp. T.B. (.074)	(.264)	(.093)
75–79	(.363)	Diarrheal (.099)	(.284)	Diarrheal (.084)
80–84	(.299)	(.134)	(.296)	(.095)
85+	(.267)	(.162)	(.299)	(.137)

most important contributors is also identical except that for males influenza/
pneumonia/bronchitis appear at ages 10–19, and respiratory tuberculosis at
ages 50–69.

The list of important causes does change substantially, however, when
declines are measured from the next higher level of life expectancy. The two
rightmost columns in Table 5.2 identify the causes most influential in mortality declines when mortality improves from a life expectancy in the range
of 45.–54.99 to one of above 70. In general, the importance of influenza/
pneumonia/bronchitis declines. Its appearance as the leading cause of mortality decline is now confined to ages over 65, and there it typically makes a
smaller percentage contribution than before. These results are congruent
with the indication in Chapter 2 that the relation between age-standardized
death rates from this cause and from all causes combined is nonlinear.
Causes that emerge as more important in the truncated mortality transition
are diarrheal diseases at ages 0–4 and cardiovascular diseases at ages 45–64,
where there are now the leading source of mortality change. Indications
from Chapter 2 are that they would also emerge as influential at higher ages
if the disturbing role of "other and unknown" could be effectively eliminated.
In general, the figures presented in Table 5.2 are probably all seriously
affected by the presence of deaths to which no precise cause has been assigned, and the values must be considered suggestive rather than definitive.

Variations in Age Patterns of Mortality

Not all populations falling into a certain mortality range have age patterns similar to the average for that range, even when the range is very
narrow. The considerable variability is a source of much uncertainty when
estimating vital rates from age distributions. The variability cannot be
attributed to random error. For example, Coale and Demeny (1966) have
identified four distinct and persistent regional age patterns of mortality in
Europe, and Brass (1968) has identified a distinctive tropical African pattern.
The purpose of the remainder of this chapter is to show that much of the
variability in age patterns of mortality for populations at the same mortality
level can be ascribed to differences in their underlying cause-of-death
structure.

The question with which it is concerned can be rephrased in the following
way: "How much more accurately can age curves of mortality be predicted
on the basis of rates of death rates from various causes than on the basis of
death rates from all causes combined?" Causes of death rates would offer
no additional information if age curves of mortality from the various causes
were identical in shape, varying only in level, or if the level of mortality

from each cause were perfectly correlated with the level of mortality from every other cause. (These conditions will be made more precise momentarily.) The values in Table 5.1 indicate clearly that age patterns vary among the causes. Table 2.3 showed that, while death rates from many causes are highly correlated with one another, the correlation is far from perfect, and is nearly zero for some combinations. Taken together, these tables suggest the value of introducing information on cause.

In order to measure the added predictive value of cause of death structure, it is first necessary to see how well age patterns can be predicted in the absence of such information. Here we will adopt the purely empirical, atheoretical approach pursued by previous authors and attempt to construct an empirical model of age patterns. The original United Nations (1955) model mortality patterns used second-degree polynomial regressions to summarize the relationship between death rates in adjacent age intervals, but the contribution of the second-degree term was typically quite small. In their reformulation of the U.N. models, Gabriel and Ronen (1958) ignored the second-degree term altogether, and Ledermann's (1969) later revision assumed linearity except for those relationships involving $_4q_1$, the probability of dying between ages 1 and 5. Even here the nonlinearity is virtually invisible to the naked eye (Ledermann, 1969, p. 20).

If the death rate at each age is linearly related to the death rate at every other age, then it is linearly related to a linear combination of death rates at all ages. We will measure mortality "level" by such a linear combination of age-specific death rates, in particular by an age-standardized crude death rate:

$$\text{ASCDR} = \sum_i c_i^s \cdot M_i,$$

where c_i^s is the proportion of the standard population in the ith age interval and M_i the death rate in the ith age interval. Any linear combination in principle will do; in practice we choose the one introduced in Chapter 2. Note that the expectation of life is *not* a linear combination of age-specific death rates. Instead, the e_0^0 implicitly assigns to death rates at the several ages weights which vary from population to population, depending on the mortality function itself. Since mortality rises with age over most of its range, a reduction in mortality produces more survivors to ages of higher mortality and thus is partially offset in its effect on life expectancy.[1] As a result, the relation between death rates at a particular age and *life expectancy* is curvilinear, as noted empirically by Ledermann (1969: Section 2–10).

---

[1] This proposition is formally demonstrated for the linear case in Preston (1972, p. 207).

We can therefore expect the relationship between death rates at a particular age and overall mortality level to be satisfactorily represented by a linear function on the age-standardized crude death rate. Linear correlation and regression is a convenient means of deriving the coefficients of the relationships and measuring their goodness-of-fit. Examination of residuals from the regressions indicates that the error assumptions of classical least squares regression are not severely violated in our data.

Before proceeding to the calculations, we modify the dependent variable slightly by first noting that the probability of survival between age x and age $x + n$, $_np_x$, can be written as

$$_np_x = \exp\left(-\int_x^{x+n} \mu_t\, dt\right),$$

where μ_t is the annual death rate at exact age t. Thus,

$$-\log {_np_x} = \int_x^{x+n} \mu_t\, dt.$$

Since mortality at all ages is assumed to be a linear function of the age-standardized crude death rate, and since the natural logarithm of the probability of survival is simply a sum of age-specific death rates, the logarithm should also be a linear function of the age-standardized crude death rate:

$$\log {_np_x} = {_nA_x} + {_nB_x} \cdot \text{ASCDR}. \tag{5.1}$$

Equation 5.1 provides a convenient means of relating the index of mortality ASCDR to life table parameters and will be utilized throughout this chapter.

Coefficients of the relationships between $\log {_np_x}$ in various age intervals and the age-standardized crude death rate are displayed in Table 5.3. These coefficients are calculated by classical least squares methods applied to 163 observations.[2] For convenience, we deal throughout with six age intervals. It should be noted that the values of mortality parameters for one of these age intervals are based upon mortality rates in intervals of 5 years or less. Regardless of the width of the interval displayed, the estimated parameters for an interval are not subject to age distributional disturbances.

The model of mortality relationships contained in Table 5.3 is very similar to that of the United Nations' model life tables and that of the Coale–Demeny "West" pattern. Both of these represent "average" patterns, the former based upon all populations examined and the latter upon all populations remaining after anomalous cases had been removed. Table 5.4 com-

---

[2] Chile (1909) and Taiwan (1920) were excluded from the analysis in the remainder of this chapter because of serious questions about the accuracy of their age reporting. Hence the number of populations in the data set declines from 165 to 163.

Table 5.3

Regression equations relating life table functions to level of mortality:

$\log(l_{x+n}/l_x) = a_x + b_x \cdot \text{ASCDR} + \epsilon$

Dependent variable	a_x	b_x	R^2	Cause of death having highest partial correlation with $\log(l_{x+n}/l_x)$ holding constant ASCDR	
FEMALES					
$\log(l_1/l_0)$	.05356	-9.8722	.874	Cert. dis. of infancy	$(-.606)$
		(.2947)			
$\log(l_5/l_1)$	.05977	-7.7134	.880	Diarrheal diseases	$(-.582)$
		(.2243)			
$\log(l_{20}/l_5)$	.02982	-4.5684	.906	Infec. and para.	$(-.499)$
		(.1162)			
$\log(l_{40}/l_{20})$	.05411	-9.9101	.897	Tuberculosis	$(-.661)$
		(.2642)			
$\log(l_{60}/l_{40})$	.00036	-13.5567	.848	Cert. chronic dis.	$(-.506)$
		(.4520)			
$\log(l_{80}/l_{60})$	$-.44342$	-40.0032	.867	Cardiovascular	$(-.434)$
		(1.2358)			
MALES					
$\log(l_1/l_0)$	.09451	-11.5953	.872	Cert. dis. of infancy	$(-.609)$
		(.3482)			
$\log(l_5/l_1)$	.07836	-7.5193	.826	Infec. and para.	$(-.624)$
		(.2717)			
$\log(l_{20}/l_5)$	.03007	-3.8824	.814	Infec. and para.	$(-.694)$
		(.1467)			
$\log(l_{40}/l_{20})$	.06562	-9.5712	.856	Tuberculosis	$(-.475)$
		(.3104)			
$\log(l_{60}/l_{40})$	.00675	-15.8733	.872	Violence	$(-.422)$
		(.4794)			
$\log(l_{80}/l_{60})$	$-.67160$	-34.2633	.676	Cardiovascular	$(-.610)$
		(1.8687)			

pares the female survivorship columns of the three models at four different levels of mortality. The three models are in close correspondence, especially when contrasted with other regional families. They are virtually identical at the lowest level of mortality. At the next lowest level, the present model's survivorship column is always intermediate between the other two, even though they themselves cross. At higher levels, a slight tendency emerges for the present pattern to display lower death rates at older ages, and the U.N. pattern slightly higher rates at those ages. In short, the equations of Table 5.3 produce models of mortality relationships quite similar to those

of two other "average" patterns, despite differences in the sample of populations and in the specification of the relationships. We can be confident that
neither our sample nor our specification substantially misrepresents average
mortality relationships.

Table 5.3 also shows that 80–90% of the variance in the death rate at a
particular age could be "explained" by variation in the death rate at all ages
combined. For some purposes, this is an acceptable degree of predictability.
For use in inferring vital rates from census data, however, one seeks greater
accuracy. Even relatively minor variations among model age curves of mortality can produce major differences in estimates of demographic parameters.
Their sensitivity results in large part from the fact that, in census age distributions, a recent infant death is indistinguishable from a birth that never
occurred. For example, United Nations Manual IV (1967, p. 42) shows that
stable estimates of birth rate in a hypothetical population vary from 44.5
to 50.1/1000, depending upon whether the "West" or "South" model mortality patterns are used.

How much of the unexplained variance in age specific death rates is
caused by differences in the cause-structure of mortality at a particular
level? Table 5.3 permits some initial observations on this point. Partial
correlation coefficients between $\log {_n}p_x$ and age-standardized death rates
from particular causes ($ASCDR_i$) are displayed, with ASCDR held constant. The causes of death that are most closely associated with age-specific
death rates for both sexes are, starting at the lowest ages: certain diseases
of early infancy; infectious and parasitic diseases; tuberculosis; and cardiovascular disease. It is clear that a disease proves to be significant at an age
where one expects its relative incidence to be greatest. This result offers the
first indication of the importance of cause of death structure for age curves
of mortality.

Variation in Model Age Patterns Attributed to Varying
Causes of Death Structures

In order to introduce causes of death into model age patterns of mortality, we require information on the manner in which age-specific death
rates *from a particular cause* are related to one another among populations.
In this matter there are no previous studies available for reference, and we
must rely upon the cause of death data forming the basis of this study.
Unfortunately, there are 3672 individual relationships between cause-
specific death rates at two different ages to be examined, with 163 observations on each. As a result, it was necessary to draw samples both from the

Table 5.4

Proportions surviving from birth to age x in various model female life tables at four levels of mortality[a]

Age (x)	Coale–Demeny "West", $e_0^0 = 72.5$	Computed from Table 5.3 ASCDR = .00806	U.N., $e_0^0 = 73.09$	Coale–Demeny "West", $e_0^0 = 60.0$	Computed from Table 5.3 ASCDR = .0133	U.N., $e_0^0 = 60.17$
0	1.000	1.000	1.000	1.000	1.000	1.000
1	.977	.974	.978	.929	.926	.918
5	.973	.972	.973	.899	.886	.886
20	.966	.966	.965	.870	.860	.858
40	.943	.941	.939	.800	.795	.793
60	.849	.844	.846	.656	.664	.669
80	.392	.392	.399	.230	.250	.253

Age (x)	Coale–Demeny "West", $e_0^0 = 47.5$	Computed from Table 5.3 ASCDR = .0205	U.N., $e_0^0 = 47.63$	Coale–Demeny "West", $e_0^0 = 35.0$	Computed from Table 5.3 ASCDR = .0300	U.N., $e_0^0 = 34.31$
0	1.000	1.000	1.000	1.000	1.000	1.000
1	.868	.862	.860	.786	.784	.791
5	.797	.781	.795	.672	.661	.681
20	.743	.733	.743	.597	.594	.601
40	.634	.631	.635	.459	.465	.449
60	.469	.478	.478	.292	.310	.274
80	.125	.135	.131	.050	.060	.046

[a] A. Coale and P. Demeny (1966, pp. 8, 13, 18, 23); United Nations Department of Social Affairs (1955, Table I).

total number of possible relationships and from the number of observations available on each. In the process of plotting these relationships, it quickly became apparent that linearity continued to be a good approximation of the shape of these relationships. For several causes of death, most notably other infectious and parasitic diseases, the constant terms were typically quite close to zero.

It follows as before that if death rates from a particular cause at various ages are linearly related to one another, then they are each linearly related to a linear combination of such rates. Since the death rate from all causes combined is a summation of death rates from the individual causes, it is a summation of such linear combinations:

$$\log {}_nP_x = A'_x + \sum B_x{}^i \cdot \text{ASCDR}^i, \tag{5.2}$$

where

$$A'_x = \sum_i A_x{}^i$$

is the sum of constants in the cause-specific regression. Equation 5.2 is the form in which model patterns that incorporate information on causes of death will be developed. Equation 5.2 must explain variance in $\log {}_nP_x$ at least as well as Equation 5.1. It would do no better if

(a) The $B_x{}^i$'s were always equal for the different causes; in effect, if the age curve of mortality variation were the same from cause to cause. The age curves themselves could differ radically as long as the difference did not vary with mortality level but was contained exclusively within the $A_x{}^i$ terms. Or if

(b) Causes of death were always found in linear combination with one another, in which case $\text{ASCDR}^i = m^i + n^i \cdot \text{ASCDR}$ for all i and Equation (2) would again reduce to Equation (1).

We have already seen evidence that neither of these conditions strictly applies. However, there are certain combinations of causes of death wherein one of the conditions is met sufficiently well that separate enumeration of the causes adds little explanatory power, while subtracting considerable economy from the presentation. In short, it is not necessary to deal with all twelve causes of death in order to demonstrate the importance of cause-structure for age-structure. Consideration of a and b, together with additional information about coding practices, led to the following choice of categories

    I.   Tuberculosis
   II.   Other infectious and parasitic diseases
  III.   Respiratory disease (influenza/pneumonia/bronchitis)

    IV.   Diarrheal disease and certain diseases of infancy
    V.   All violence
    VI.   Maternal complications (females only)
    VII. All other and unknown

Diarrheal diseases are combined with certain diseases of early infancy not simply because of the similarity of their age patterns of influence. Under the 6th and 7th Revisions of the International List of Causes of Death, deaths from diarrhea in the first four weeks of life are assigned to CDEI, an assignment not operative in other Revisions. Moreover, deaths from "toxicosis" under age 1 are assigned to CDEI, although the principal cause of this condition is diarrhea. According to Verhoestraete and Puffer (1958, p. 27), this important coding peculiarity in Latin America frequently prevents diarrhea from emerging as the leading cause of death in infancy, and improperly projects CDEI into this position.

Table 5.5 presents the regression equations that relate age-specific death rates, in the form of $(-\log {}_np_x)$, to age-standardized death rates from these 6 or 7 causes. The final column displays the proportion of variance left unexplained by the regression equation using all causes combined (from Table 5.3) that is explained when information on these 6–7 causes is introduced. On average, 49% of the unexplained variance can be accounted for by cause of death structure. The figure rises to 59.9% if all twelve causes are separately included. Thus, it is justifiable to conclude that roughly half of the variance in age-curves of mortality at a particular mortality level can be accounted for by variance in relative importance of 6–7 cause of death categories among populations at that level. This is the principal result of this chapter, and it suggests that causes of death have substantial value in accounting for disparities in age patterns of mortality.

Since the dependent variables in Table 5.5 are negative cumulations of death rates, it should be the case that higher mortality from a particular cause is associated with lower values of the dependent variables; that is, the coefficients should be negative. In fact, 59 out of the 75 coefficients presented are negative, or 79%. The causes whose variation is most significant for mortality at a particular age can best be gauged by the standardized beta coefficient: the coefficients presented in Table 5.5 multiplied by (σ^i/σ_x), where σ^i is the standard deviation of the age standardized death rate from cause i and σ_x is the standard deviation of the dependent variable. The standardized beta coefficient indicates the change in the dependent variable (expressed in standard deviation units) produced by a one-standard-deviation change in the independent variable.

Table 5.6 lists the causes of death having the largest standardized beta coefficients in the various age intervals. At ages 0–1 and 1–4 for both sexes, a one standard deviation change in the combination, diarrhea and certain

Table 5.5 Coefficients of regression equations relating age-specific death rates from all causes combined to age standardized death rates for particular causes, $N = 163$

Dependent variable	Constant	Coefficient of tuberculosis	Coefficient of infectious and paras.	Coefficient of respiratory	Coefficient of diarrheal and cert. dis. of infancy	Coefficient of violence	Coefficient of other & unknown	Coefficient of maternal	R^2	Proportionate reduction in unexplained variance from introduction of information on causes of death
FEMALES										
$\log(l_1/l_0)$	.00866	-9.9285 (3.3306)	10.8098 (2.7983)	-14.9013 (2.0959)	-30.5294 (2.4384)	8.4661 (11.8654)	-2.5468 (1.1025)	-58.7727 (21.2818)	.937	.500
$\log(l_5/l_1)$	.02004	-6.1873 (2.3737)	-20.3757 (1.9943)	-4.2076 (1.4937)	-20.0184 (1.7378)	4.3736 (8.4561)	-2.0869 (.7858)	31.3303 (15.1670)	.947	.558
$\log(l_{20}/l_5)$	.01265	-14.0136 (1.1926)	-13.8533 (1.0540)	.5256 (.7608)	-2.3515 (.9293)	2.9396 (4.4175)	-2.5863 (.4138)		.955	.521
$\log(l_{40}/l_{20})$	.02142	-34.1307 (2.4470)	-10.0233 (2.6321)		-3.0013 (1.7830)	-8.2513 (9.2271)	-4.9133 (.8587)	-132.1588 (15.7858)	.960	.621
$\log(l_{60}/l_{40})$	.00902	-15.1575 (5.5709)	-15.0771 (4.6805)	-11.0574 (3.5057)	7.1795 (4.0784)	-79.2064 (19.8461)	-11.5012 (1.8441)	-217.8493 (35.5961)	.908	.394
$\log(l_{80}/l_{60})$	-.21010	25.3880 (15.9044)	-47.3659 (13.3625)	-81.5535 (10.0084)	10.0419 (11.6435)	-113.3955 (56.6589)	-74.5970 (5.2648)	331.710 (101.6238)	.912	.338
								Mean		.489
MALES										
$\log(l_1/l_0)$	.02454	-10.7699 (3.1820)	-1.6411 (2.9641)	-13.5127 (2.0318)	-31.9127 (2.6373)	-17.4076 (4.5058)	-1.8465 (1.1565)		.929	.445
$\log(l_5/l_1)$	.02610	-.9512 (2.1811)	-22.3760 (2.0317)	-2.6001 (1.3927)	-16.8333 (1.8078)	6.0128 (3.0885)	-2.6772 (.7927)		.925	.570
$\log(l_{20}/l_5)$	.00579	-5.3421 (1.2358)	-16.6080 (1.1511)	-.3039 (.7891)	-1.8474 (1.0242)	-4.9403 (1.7499)	-1.1097 (.4491)		.910	.516
$\log(l_{40}/l_{20})$	.02524	-31.6330 (2.5301)	-18.0716 (2.3569)	-2.5905 (1.6156)	-4.8679 (2.0971)	-37.5044 (3.5827)	-2.0634 (.9196)		.935	.549
$\log(l_{60}/l_{40})$	.03922	-36.1242 (4.7289)	-10.8434 (3.8911)	-15.5975 (2.8852)		-56.8239 (6.7189)	-15.8312 (1.7143)		.916	.344
$\log(l_{80}/l_{60})$	-.18828	37.1778 (15.6107)	19.9587 (14.5417)	-65.3533 (9.9678)	8.9527 (12.9386)	20.0802 (22.1050)	-98.5621 (5.6738)		.848	.531
								Mean		.493

Table 5.6

Causes of death with largest standardized beta coefficients at a particular age

Age	Females	Males
0–1	Diarrhea/cert. dis. of infancy	Diarrhea/cert. dis. of infancy
1–4	Diarrhea/cert. dis. of infancy	Diarrhea/cert. dis. of infancy
5–20	Infectious and parasitic	Infectious and parasitic
20–40	Tuberculosis	Tuberculosis
40–60	Maternal	Tuberculosis
60–80	Other and unknown	Other and unknown

diseases of early infancy, has the largest effect on death rates. This combination consists almost exclusively of diarrhea at age 1–4. Infectious and parasitic, tuberculosis, and other and unknown emerge as the most important sources of variation at progressively higher ages. It is important to note that these are not necessarily the most important causes at these ages but rather the causes that are most likely to act independently to create variation in age-specific death rates. If a nation exhibits an unusual death rate in a particular age interval, Table 5.6 identifies the cause of death most likely to be responsible.

The one unexpected finding in the table is that maternal mortality variation is more influential than variation in any other cause of death for female death rates in the age interval 40–60. This is unexpected because maternal mortality has by far the lowest mean and variance of any causes under consideration; moreover, the large majority of deaths from the cause are recorded in the age interval 20–40 rather than 40–60. It is clear that recorded deaths from maternal mortality are acting as an indicator of a more general health disadvantage suffered by middleaged women in some populations. It may be the case that a heavy burden of childbearing combined with poor health standards continues to exert an effect on mortality well past the end of the childbearing period itself. Kitagawa and Hauser (1973) find support for this contention in United States data. Or it may be that the same factors producing high death rates from maternal mortality (e.g., low status of women leading to poor access to nutrition and medical care, high rates of childbearing) influence mortality from many causes, of which maternal mortality is the best proxy for the underlying factor.[3] In either case, the indirect approach pursued here has revealed a tendency that would not have been suggested by a more direct, decompositional approach to the raw data.

[3] These issues are considered in more detail in Chapter 6.

Illustration of the Importance of Cause-of-Death Structure
for Divergencies in Age Patterns of Mortality:
The Coale–Demeny Models

If the age pattern of mortality in a population at a certain level of life expectancy is influenced by its cause of death structure, then one should be able to attribute differences in age patterns of mortality in two or more populations at the same level at least partially to differences in their cause structures. Systematic and persistent regional differences in age patterns have been identified by Coale and Demeny (1966) on the basis of an exhaustive review of published life tables. They identified four distinct regional patterns in European populations: the "North," with low infant mortality and low mortality above age 50 and high mortality in the middle adult years; the "South," with high infant mortality and even higher relative mortality in the range of 1–5 years; the "East," with high infant mortality and high mortality above age 60; and the "West," which showed no systematic pattern of deviations from the average when all regions were com-

Table 5.7

Age-standardized crude death rates from all causes and specific causes in five populations[a]

	Males		Females		
Disease	England & Wales, 1871, $e_0^0 = 39.16$	Italy, 1891, $e_0^0 = 38.48$	U. S., 1940, $e_0^0 = 65.43$	Norway, 1930, $e_0^0 = 65.78$	Portugal, 1960, $e_0^0 = 66.72$
Respiratory tuberculosis	.00260	.00091	.00033	.00120	.00024
Other infectious and parasitic	.00389	.00355	.00028	.00055	.00021
Influenza/ pneumonia/ bronchitis	.00400	.00338	.00083	.00095	.00096
Diarrheal and cert. dis. of infancy	.00232	.00449[b]	.00057	.00047	.00134[c]
Violence	.00125	.00067	.00063	.00017	.00027
Maternal	—	—	.00012	.00009	.00005
All other	.01335	.01436	.00883	.00702	.00695
All causes	.02741	.02736	.01159	.01045	.01002

[a] S. Preston, N. Keyfitz, and R. Schoen (1972).
[b] Diarrheal = .00313; Cert. dis. of infancy = .00136.
[c] Diarrheal = .00067; Cert. dis. of infancy = .00067.

bined. It will be recalled from Chapter 2 that members of the West pattern were highly disproportionately represented among populations with the most "normal" cause of death structures. Because of the heavy use which the Coale–Demeny patterns have received in demographic applications, our illustrations will focus on comparison of representatives of these regional patterns.

England and Wales and Italy provide the earliest data on causes of death of any populations in these regional groups. England and Wales belong to the "West" regional group and Italy to the "South." Table 5.7 presents the male age-standardized crude death rates from the six causes for England and Wales in 1871 and for Italy in 1891. The life expectancies of the two populations are quite close at 39.16 and 38.48. The cause-of-death structure differs substantially in the two cases, however, with England and Wales exhibiting higher death rates from tuberculosis and "other infectious and parasitic diseases." Italy's death rate is much higher from diarrheal diseases/certain diseases of infancy, of which the former entity is the more important.

The age sequence of death probabilities in the two populations (Preston *et al.*, 1972) are presented graphically in Figure 5.2. The pattern of deviations agrees with that noted by Coale and Demeny. In order to determine whether this pattern of differences could have been predicted on the basis

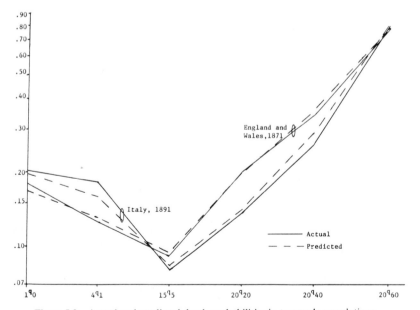

Figure 5.2 Actual and predicted death probabilities in two male populations

of the causes of death structure prevailing in the two populations, we can enter the standardized death rates by cause in the two populations (Table 5.7) into the male regression equations of Table 5.5. The sequences of death rates predicted in this fashion should differ for the two populations in the same manner as do the sequences of actual death rates. The predicted death rates are also plotted in Figure 5.2.

Figure 5.2 demonstrates strikingly that the actual age patterns of mortality are accurately predicted by the regression equations in combination with recorded cause-specific mortality in both England and Italy. Hence, the discrepancy in their age patterns is also accurately predicted. Knowledge of the cause-of-death structures proves to be of great value in understanding the source of disparity in the two age curves.

A similar comparison can be made among representatives of three of the regional patterns at a higher level of life expectancy. Table 5.7 presents the female age-standardized death rates from the seven causes in the United States, 1940, Norway, 1930, and Portugal, 1960. The life expectancies in these populations are, respectively, 65.43, 65.78, and 66.72. The Northern representative, Norway, displays the highest death rate from tuberculosis and other infectious and parasitic diseases. The Southern country again displays the highest death rate from diarrheal/certain diseases of infancy. The United States, from the "West," is intermediate in these important causes.

Probabilities of dying in the three countries are plotted in Figure 5.3 and compared to the probabilities predicted on the basis of a country's cause structure in combination with the "female" equations on Table 5.5. Once, again, divergencies are predicted rather well on the basis of the respective cause-of-death structures. The ranking of the three countries is predicted correctly at all ages except infancy, where the order of the United States and Norway is reversed. Thus seventeen of the eighteen rankings of death probabilities in any pair of these three countries are preserved in the predictions.

Many other examples of such comparisons could be presented. Czechoslovakia in 1934 is the only available representative of the "East" pattern before World War II. When compared to New Zealand, 1881, at the same general level of mortality, Czechoslovakia had higher death rates in infancy and ages 60–80 (typical of the East group) and much higher death rates from respiratory and diarrheal diseases. Consequently, their differences in cause-of-death structure are predicted quite accurately. In more recent years, however, members of the "East" family show infant mortality rates substantially higher than predicted levels, suggesting that the unusually high infant mortality in this bloc is a product of unusually high infant mortality from particular causes of death, rather than of the cause-of-death structure itself.

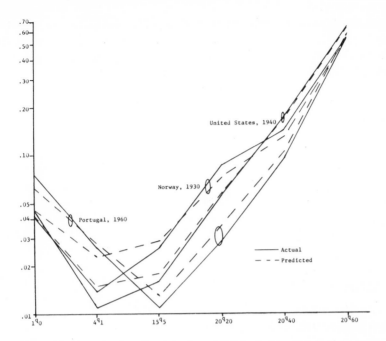

Figure 5.3 Actual and predicted death probabilities in three female populations.

The age structure of mortality in many non-Western nations can be predicted as accurately as that of western countries at the same level of life expectancy. For recent years, the male populations of Chile, Colombia, Costa Rica, Mexico, Panama, Trinidad and Tobago, Venezuela, and the Republic of South Africa (coloured) all show predictions in close accord with reality. One important exception is Guatemala, where predicted death rates in infancy exceed the actual death rate, itself quite high, by about 50%. The reason may be an overrecording of deaths to diarrheal diseases, or gastroenteritis. A review of coding accuracy determined that the number of deaths returned in this category was about three times higher than it should have been among adults in Guatemala City in 1962–64 (Puffer and Griffith, 1967, pp. 238, 327). Predictions of infant mortality are also substantially too high in Taiwan, perhaps because of problems in reporting ages of infants.

As demonstrated in Chapter 2, cause-of-death structures in the non-Western nations contained in this analysis are, as a group, highly similar to those of western nations at equivalent levels of mortality. The two persistent differences are relatively high death rates from diarrheal diseases in the non-Western areas and low death rates from cardiovascular diseases. It was argued that the relatively high death rates for diarrheal diseases in non-Western areas probably represent a slower improvement in nutritional standards and sanitation, of central importance in the etiology of deaths from these diseases, than in medical technology, principally influential against the infectious diseases caused by specific and identifiable micro-organisms. Since southern European countries share abnormally high rates of death from diarrheal diseases, they will typically provide a more accurate model of mortality relations for non-Western areas than will other European regions. United Nations Manual IV (1967, p. 72) notes that Mexico, with virtually complete vital registration, has a mortality pattern much closer to the "South" than to the "West." Sullivan (1973) confirms the importance of diarrheal disease for age patterns of mortality by tracing changes in the Taiwanese pattern between 1957 and 1968 to a rapid reduction in diarrheal death rates.

Turning the Problem on Its Head: Causes of Death and the "African Standard"

Just as the cause-structure of mortality can be used to predict the age pattern, the age pattern implies a special cause of death structure. We illustrate the usefulness of this reversal by reference to the Brass "African standard" mortality schedule (Brass and Coale, 1968). This standard incorporated what were considered characteristic features of tropical African mortality. In particular, the pattern exhibits relatively high death rates between ages 5 and 20 relative to those at ages below 5, and exceedingly high death rates above age 20 relative to those below 20. Brass and Coale cautiously state that "Whether these common features are a characteristic bias in African data or a characteristic feature of African mortality is a matter of conjecture" (p. 133). In any case, it was clear that use of one of the existing European models would have been suspect.

One gauge of the authenticity of the "African standard" is the plausibility of the cause of death structure which it implies. Since Table 5.5 provides six equations for age-specific rates and there are six cause-specific death rates that enter as variable into each equation, once we are presented with a set of $\log {}_np_x$'s we could solve directly for the level of the six unknowns, ASCDR^i ($k = 1, \ldots, 6$). This is the least arbitrary approach to the question but the most risky since it uses no information on the typical level of mortality from various causes; moreover, nothing prevents negative values of ASCDR^i from emerging in the process. Here we use a simpler technique that is more likely to yield reasonable and interpretable numbers, although it is admittedly quite arbitrary. We begin with the cause of death structure typical of a population at the level of mortality under consideration and see how its cause of death structure might reasonably be modified in order to reproduce approximately the recorded age-structure of mortality.

A portion of the African standard $p(x)$ function is presented in Table 5.8. $p(1)$ (for both sexes) is .880, which corresponds approximately to the $p(1)$ for ASCDR = .0205 in Table 5.3. The typical cause of death structure corresponding to an ASCDR = .0205 is determined by use of the linear regressions relating $ASCDR_i$ to ASCDR that were presented in Chapter 2, substituting ASCDR = .0205 into the equations. Predicted death rates for males are as follows: Tuberculosis, .00127; Other Infectious and Parasitic, .00142; Respiratory, .00306; Diarrheal and Certain Diseases of Infancy, .00189; Violence, .00106; Other and Unknown, .01130. The age-curve implied by this combination of causes, when substituted into male equations of Table 5.5, is also shown in Table 5.8. In order to reproduce very closely the "African standard" $p(x)$ function, we multiply the "average" death rate from tuberculosis by 2.00, from infectious and parasitic diseases by 2.75, and from diarrheal and certain diseases of infancy by .6, and once again apply equations in Table 5.5. The resulting $p(x)$ column, shown in Table 5.8, does not differ from the African standard by more than .006 through age 60.

In other words, the African standard age-pattern is consistent with death rates from tuberculosis and infectious and parasitic diseases which are

Table 5.8

Comparison of three survivorship functions (probability of surviving from birth to age x)

Age (x)	Cause-of-death regressions, average structure of causes corresponding to ASCDR = .0205. Males[a] (1)	Cause of death regressions, structure of causes same as (1) but death rate from tuberculosis multiplied by 2.00, infectious and parasitic 2.75, and diarrheal and cert. dis. of inf. by .6. Males[a] (2)	African standard (both sexes)[b] (3)
0	1.000	1.000	1.000
1	.876	.882	.880
5	.816	.786	.786
20	.779	.715	.713
40	.690	.584	.590
60	.506	.398	.398
80	.127	.109	.076

[a] Tables 5.3, 5.5, and text.
[b] W. Brass and A. Coale (1968).

approximately 2–3 times higher than normal for a population at that approximate level of mortality. In view of the overriding importance of malaria in tropical Africa, this implication seems quite acceptable. In fact, malaria has an age curve of mortality intermediate between that of tuberculosis and other infectious and parasitic diseases, excluding both malaria and tuberculosis. For example, of these three categories in Thailand, 1964—the country with highest malarial death rates in World Health Organization statistics of that year—"other infectious and parasitic" has the highest death rate under age 15, malaria between ages 15 and 25, and tuberculosis thereafter.[4] Except at ages 15–25, malaria's rates are always intermediate. The lower than normal death rates from diarrheal diseases implied by this procedure seems consistent with a below average density of living conditions in tropical Africa.

By the same token, unusually high death rates from infectious diseases cannot account for the African standard's exceptionally high death rate at ages 60–80. This feature could be produced by an increment in the "other and unknown" death rate (which, in Table 5.5, has an impact on death rates six times greater in this age interval than in any other). On the other hand, it could easily be bogus. There is surely very little solid information upon which to base estimates of death rates for this group in Africa, in light of pervasive misreporting of age and relatively small numbers of persons. That this feature of the standard age pattern is far out of line with a plausible cause of death structure that accounts quite well for age patterns up to age 60 is some reason to doubt its validity.

Model Mortality Patterns Based on Causes of Death

Model mortality patterns are typically required for demographic estimation only if death registration is incomplete. But if the degree of incompleteness is largely invariant with respect to cause of death, then the cause-structure of mortality can be reliably estimated. In such a case the age pattern of mortality should be largely recoverable without reference to any external models. The level of mortality can then be estimated through conventional stable population or census survival techniques. Two situations can be distinguished in which knowledge of causes of death may provide useful guidelines for model construction.

---

[4] World Health Organization (1964, pp. 126–7, 260–61). While malaria is nominally a member of the "other infectious and parasitic" category, its death rates in the sample are typically too low to have influenced the characteristics of this aggregate.

Situation 1: Age-specific death rates are available by cause of death. Deaths are underrecorded but not differentially by cause. Deaths are assumed to be differentially underrecorded by age.

In this situation, the age-cause specific death rates could be converted into age standardized crude death rates by cause through direct application of the standard population's age distribution (Chapter 1). This set of age-standardized death rates could then be inserted into regression equations presented in Table 5.5, yielding a first approximation to the age curve of mortality. This approximation presumably results in too low a level of mortality, one that is inconsistent with recorded age distributions. In order to adjust the level of mortality, one must simply solve for the level of a multiplier K of all estimated $ASCDR^i$'s that is in best agreement with external evidence. The multiplication of each $ASCDR^i$ by the same constant is consistent with the assumption that there is no differential omission of deaths by cause. This procedure makes little use of the recorded *age* structure of mortality; there is often good reason to ignore such information, since differential omission by age is probably more frequent than differential omission by cause of death.

Situation 2: No information exists on ages at death. Total deaths are available by cause, together with a recorded age distribution. Deaths are underrecorded but not differentially by cause.

In this situation the availability of cause of death information is potentially more valuable than in the prior case because no information at all exists on ages of death. Since the age distribution is known, together with the crude death rate by cause, conventional indirect standardization can be used to make an initial estimate of the level of $ASCDR^i$ for all i. Since the "standard" age curve of mortality from a particular cause often varies with the level of mortality from that cause, the standard should be selected from among the age curves (available in Table 5.1) on the basis of the best initial guess regarding probable mortality level. Once these estimates are available, the procedure is identical to that of Situation 1: use equations in Table 5.5 and solve for the level of that set of $ASCDR^i$'s that is most consistent with external evidence.

In both cases the series of age-specific death rates could be estimated directly and converted by conventional actuarial means into a life table. By use of the regression equations, however, this tedious intervening step can be averted and the set of death rates readily converted into life table parameters.

CHAPTER 6

Causes of Death
Responsible for Variation
in Sex Mortality Differentials

The difference between male and female death rates directly affects the sex ratio of the population at a particular age, the chances of marriage, the expected length of widowhood, and a host of other social and demographic variables. These effects alone provide sufficient reason for studying sex mortality differentials and their determinants. In addition, the differentials are valuable as indicators of the special health problems faced by members of one sex. Since the sexes in a particular country coexist within the same economic, social, and medical environment, persistent differences in their mortality rates are plausibly interpreted as reflecting either differences in the way that environment impinges on the sexes or innate biological differences. In either case the differentials suggest the existence and help to define the extent of health advantages or disadvantages that disproportionately affect members of one sex.

In the first section of this chapter, populations are grouped according to their level of mortality, and the direction of age-cause specific mortality differentials by sex within these groups is briefly described. In the remainder of the chapter, age groups are collapsed by means of age standardization and attention is focused on establishing "normal" patterns of sex mortality differentials, measuring the deviation of individual populations about these normal patterns, attributing their abnormality to particular causes of death, and identifying environmental correlates of the size and direction of the differentials.

Comparative Mortality of the Sexes by Age and Cause as a Function of Mortality Level

The classic international summary of sex mortality differentials was made by Stolnitz (1956, pp. 22–32). Stolnitz demonstrated that higher male mortality was not nearly so pervasive as commonly believed, nor were instances of reversal confined to ages of childbearing. It is now possible to supplement Stolnitz' observations with data on mortality rates by cause of death.

Table 5.1 in the previous chapter presented average levels of age-cause specific death rates by sex in populations falling into one of five ranges of life expectancy. Instances of higher female than male mortality were denoted with an asterisk. The relative frequency of higher female than male mortality by age is indicated in Table 6.1. Maternal mortality is considered to be a separate cause of death in these comparisons, so that the maximum number of instances of higher female than male mortality for any age is 12.

It is clear that the frequency of systematically higher female mortality is greatest in populations at lower levels of mortality and declines monotonically as mortality levels improve. The percentage of all age-cause combinations for which females have higher mortality declines from 29 in populations at the lowest level of mortality to 10 in populations at the highest level. It is generally the case that males suffer higher age-cause specific death rates, but the exceptions are numerous in populations at every mortality level.

The male disadvantage is most pervasive in infancy, where the only instance of higher female mortality is an exceedingly minor one: neoplasms in populations with life expectancy between 45.00 and 54.99. In view of the greater emphasis on son than daughter survival exhibited in many societies, and the virtual absence of the reverse situation (Williamson, 1973), the compelling interpretation is that a male baby has, on average, a serious innate biological disadvantage in survival through the first year of life, a disadvantage that manifests itself in every major cause of death.

As a child ages, this disadvantage either becomes quickly inoperative or is readily obscured by offsetting factors when health conditions are poor. From ages 1 through 30, females in the group of populations with lowest life expectancy have higher average death rates from all causes combined, and this tendency extends to a majority of causes. Only the violent causes of death are a consistent exception to this pattern. Female death rates at ages 1–30 in high mortality populations are consistently higher than male

Table 6.1

Relative frequency of higher female than male cause-specific death rates, by age

Age	Number of causes (out of 12) from which females have higher average death rates than males in populations with life expectancies at birth of				
	Less than 45 years	45.00– 54.99	55.00– 64.99	65.00– 69.99	Greater than 70 years
0	0	1	0	0	0
1	8	3	1	2	1
5	6	5	1	1	2
10	8	7	4	6	2
15	6	4	2	2	3
20	6	5	4	3	2
25	6	5	6	5	3
30	5	4	5	3	2
35	4	3	5	2	2
40	2	2	2	2	2
45	3	2	2	3	2
50	2	2	3	2	0
55	1	2	1	1	0
60	1	1	1	1	0
65	2	2	1	0	0
70	1	0	1	1	1
75	3	1	1	0	1
80	1	1	0	2	1
85+	1	0	3	1	1
Total	66	50	43	37	23
Percentage of all possible instances	28.9	21.9	18.9	16.2	10.1

rates for the infectious diseases, although the magnitude of the differential tends to be minor except for respiratory tuberculosis.

At higher ages in high mortality populations the female disadvantage is largely confined to neoplasms (very incompletely reported) and to maternal mortality. The death rates from infectious diseases all favor females above age 40. Thus, the age-specific death rate curves for the two sexes cross for the various types of infectious diseases somewhere between ages 15 and 40 in high mortality populations. This crossing might be attributed to the greater social value of wives and mothers than of younger females, leading to improvements in female's relative health environment with age. An alternative explanation would ascribe the crossing to changing physical differences between the sexes during the process of maturation and senescence.

The latter hypothesis receives support from two additional pieces of evidence: that the sex differential favoring females is generally maintained above age 60, despite the reduced reproductive and social significance of women above this age; and that such a crossing is still evident (although much attenuated and more irregular) in populations with life expectancies above 70, wherein prevailing equalitarian standards would be unlikely to permit overtly discriminatory health practices by sex.[1]

This is not to say that sex discriminatory practices are not reflected in Table 6.1, only that they are not a likely source of the crossing of male and female age curves of mortality from infectious disease. The general importance of discrimination is in fact suggested by relative mortality from diarrheal diseases, the cause most likely to reflect nutritional difficulties. In all ranges of life expectancy below the highest, this cause exhibits more instances of female disadvantage (50% altogether) than any other predominantly infectious cause.

As mortality levels improve, instances of female disadvantage become increasingly concentrated in the reproductive ages and among three causes of death: neoplasms, maternal mortality, and respiratory tuberculosis. The latter two causes have death rates so low in low mortality populations as to be inconsequential for overall differentials. Thus, the increasing male disadvantage that emerges as mortality improves is accompanied by increasing disadvantages for most causes of death at most ages. It is not a mere artifact of the changing composition of causes. Males do not become increasingly disadvantaged exclusively as a result of the disappearance of the relatively sex-neutral infectious diseases, which unmasks a marked "innate" survival disadvantage from certain degenerative diseases. Instead, their disadvantage *from particular causes of death* increases, especially from infectious diseases at the younger ages and, more importantly, from degenerative diseases at the older. Enterline (1961) has described this process for the United States.

In populations with life expectancy below 45, the average cardiovascular death rates for males and females above age 30 never differ by as much as 8%, and the female rate is either higher or within 2% of the male rate in 9 age intervals out of 12. This suggests that the rate of cardiovascular degeneration with age is virtually identical for the two sexes in these populations. In the same age range in these populations, average death rates from neoplasms are always higher for females than for males. These rates in high mortality populations are undoubtedly depressed by imprecise coding of cause of death, but there is no apparent tendency for the proportion of

---

[1] In these populations it is more accurate to say that mortality from the infectious causes is largely independent of sex at younger ages and diverges increasingly in favor of females at older ages.

deaths assigned to "other and unknown" causes to vary with sex. In the lowest mortality group, on the other hand, male cardiovascular death rates are always higher than female above age 30 and are more than double the female rates from ages 40 to 60. Male death rates from neoplasms are higher than female above age 50 and are more than 50% higher between ages 60 and 80. If there is an *innate* male survival disadvantage for these causes of death, it is a disadvantage that seems to become operative only in combination with factors that emerge in the course of socioeconomic modernization.

One cause of death that manifests a consistent male disadvantage at all mortality levels is violence. Male death rates both from auto accidents and from other forms of violence are higher than female at virtually every age in populations at every mortality level. For both causes combined in the 165 populations, the male death rate from violence exceeds the female by a factor of 2.83 (from Table 2.1). It is striking that substantial differentials are already apparent in infancy, where the vast majority of exposure to violent death is preambulatory. Within the two lowest mortality groups, infant male death rates from "other violence" exceed infant female rates by 29–32%. Since social customs in the advanced western countries that constitute the group with life expectancy above 70 seem unlikely to result in differential exposure of preambulatory children to the risk of violent death, the most plausible interpretation of the large sex differential is that male babies are less well able to recover from such traumas as occur. By age, the sex differentials in accidental deaths among infants in the U.S. are largest not toward the end of the first year of life where walking may begin but in the age interval 1–5 months (United States National Center for Health Statistics, 1974, pp. 2–52 through 2–55).

Measuring Sex Mortality Differentials for Individual Populations

The rest of this chapter will attempt to measure the size of sex mortality differentials in particular populations, identify the contribution of various causes of death to those differentials, and estimate the contribution of various environmental factors to variation in sex mortality differentials from all causes and each specific cause.

A. *All Causes Combined*

There is no conceptual problem in determining whether a male death rate is higher than an equivalent death rate for females. The problematic element is introduced when one attempts to make statements about how *much* higher the male death rate is than the female. Consider two populations, one with a male death rate of 20 and a female of 15, and another with a male death rate of 4 and a female of 2. The absolute difference is larger in the former case but the ratio is larger in the latter. This type of situation is encountered *most of the time* when comparisons are made between a high mortality population and a low mortality population. The ambiguity results from the absence of an appropriate theory that would indicate what sex mortality differentials should be. There are many biological differences between the sexes that should influence their relative mortality. The fact that females have two X chromosomes and males one probably confers a survival advantage on females (Naeye *et al.*, 1971); greater average levels of estrogen in premenopausal women than in men of the same age almost certainly protects them against the development of coronary heart disease (Epstein, 1965, p. 758); women adjust more readily to changes in environmental temperature, they have a higher index of cephalization (relative brain weight), and a number of other specific physiological advantages (Shettles, 1958; Sacher, 1960). Male generative organs are more visible and accessible than female, permitting more rapid detection and superior treatment of this type of cancer. But the translation of these differences into predictions of sex mortality differentials has not been undertaken and appears premature at this stage. Likewise, the exact manner in which differentials in access to, say, medical care of a certain type should translate into mortality differentials is unclear.

In the absence of compelling theory suggesting what sex differentials should be, and in view of the hazards of adopting a ratio or difference expression, we have chosen to construct an empirical "model" of relations between the sexes' death rates and to focus the rest of the chapter on deviations about that model relation. Our procedure is exactly analogous to that used in the construction of model age-patterns of mortality, which has eschewed the abundant but unverified "laws" of human mortality. We do not attempt to study and account for the statistically "normal" relations between the sexes' mortality but rather the peculiar position of populations relative to the standard that is established.

Male and female mortality will once again be expressed by the age-standardized crude death rate. This index is preferred to its most obvious competitor, life expectancy at birth, because of the straightforward manner in which it aggregates the several causes of death and our special interest in the role of various causes. The age standardized crude death rates from individual causes sum to the age standardized crude death rates from all causes combined. No comparable relation is available for life expectancy, in the determination of which causes of death necessarily interact.

Figure 6.1 is a scatter diagram of the relation between male and female

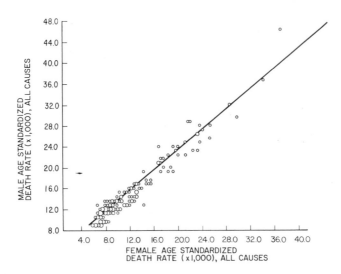

Figure 6.1   Relation between male and female death rates in 165 populations.

age-standardized death rates from all causes combined for the 165 populations. The size of a circle is roughly proportional to the number of populations that fall into that area of the plotting range. The relation is obviously
highly linear, with a simple zero-order correlation of .968. This linearity of
the relation between male and female mortality rates drawn from different
nations or periods has been noted on previous occasions (Martin, 1951;
Coale and Demeny, 1966; Preston, 1970), and we will assume that it is an
adequate representation of the underlying male/female relation. This
assumption greatly simplifies the analysis to follow.

We have chosen to fit the relation between male and female death rates
by orthogonal regression, which minimizes the sum of squared deviations
perpendicular to the line. Unlike ordinary least-squares regression, orthogonal regression does not require the specification of a "dependent" variable,
a specification that in this case would clearly be inappropriate. Orthogonal
regression treats the sexes symmetrically. It can be shown that the slope of
the orthogonal regression is the geometric mean of the two slopes, both
expressed with reference to the same axis, resulting from the minimization
of squared vertical and horizontal deviations. The formula for orthogonal
regression is

$$M = \frac{\sigma_M}{\sigma_F}(F - \bar{F}) + \bar{M}, \tag{6.1}$$

where M, F are the age-standardized crude death rates from all causes combined for males and females, $\overline{M}, \overline{F}$ the mean value of M and F in the sample, and σ_M, σ_F the standard deviation of M and F in the sample. It is clear from (6.1) that, at any point on the regression line, the deviations of male and female death rates from their respective means are equal in standard deviation units.

When applied to our 165 observations, the orthogonal regression is

$$\hat{M} = 1.0112F + 2.8137, \tag{6.1a}$$

with M and F expressed in units of annual deaths per 1000 population. The slope of this regression line is very close to unity, implying that the vertical and horizontal distance between any observation and the line will be very nearly identical in absolute value; thus, excess of actual over expected male mortality for any population is nearly identical to the deficit of actual as compared to expected female mortality (they would be exactly equal if the slope were 1.00). In practice, we will measure all deviations in terms of differences between actual and expected male mortality, with expected male mortality M based upon the actual level of female mortality in conjunction with Equation (6.1a). Thus, the amount of excess in male mortality in population j, D_j is defined to be

$$D_j = M_j - \hat{M}_j = M_j - \left[\frac{\sigma_M}{\sigma_F}(F_j - \overline{F}) + \overline{M} \right], \tag{6.2}$$

where M_j, F_j are the actual male and female death rates from all causes combined in population j.

The expectation implicit in (6.2) is that, when female mortality deviates from its mean by n standard deviation units, male mortality should also deviate from its mean by n standard deviation units in the same direction. Hereafter, D_j will be referred to as the sex mortality differential for population j. Obviously, it can take on both positive and negative values. The fact that the slope is slightly larger than unity implies that male death rates tend to fall slightly more in absolute amount than female rates as mortality levels decline, and thus that sex *differences* tend to *contract*. On the other hand, the existence of a large positive intercept implies that the *ratio* of male to female mortality tends to *rise* as mortality level falls. Thus, the two most common measures of differentials both display "level" effects, a property that would pervade all relations in an analysis focused on one of these measures. More troublesome is the fact that the level effects operate in different directions. Low mortality countries tend to have low sex differences but high sex ratios, and the choice of either measure would clearly influence all subsequent analysis.

B. Individual Causes of Death

The method for measuring a population's sex mortality differential from cause of death i is identical to that used for all causes combined. Relations between male and female death rates from particular causes of death in the 165 populations prove again to be highly linear, as shown in Table 6.2 and in graphs not presented. Orthogonal regressions have been fitted to each of the twelve cause-specific relations between male and female death rates. These regressions are of the form

$$M_i = \frac{\sigma_{M_i}}{\sigma_{F_i}} (F_i - \bar{F}_i) + \bar{M}_i \qquad (6.3)$$

where M_i, F_i are the age-standardized crude death rates from cause i for males and females, $\bar{M}_i$, $\bar{F}_i$ the mean value of M_i and F_i in the sample, and σ_{M_i}, σ_{F_i} the standard deviation of M_i and F_i in the sample.

Coefficients of these regressions are presented in Table 6.2. Analogously to the previous procedure, the amount of deviation j of actual from expected male mortality from cause i in population j, D_{ij} is defined as

$$D_{ij} = M_{ij} - \left[\frac{M_i}{F_i} (F_{ij} - \bar{F}_i) + \bar{M}_i \right], \qquad (6.4)$$

where M_{ij}, F_{ij} are the actual male and female death rates from cause i in population j.

Table 6.2

Coefficients of orthogonal regressions of male mortality from particular causes on female mortality from that cause in 165 populations (deaths per 1000 population)[a]

Cause of death	Constant, $[\bar{M}_i - (\sigma_{M_i}/\sigma_{F_i})\bar{F}_i]$	Slope, $(\sigma_{M_i}/\sigma_{F_i})$	Correlation coef.
Respiratory T.B.	.1035	1.1252	.950
Other infect. and paras.	.0343	1.0833	.996
Neoplasms	−.6929	1.6909	.733
Cardiovascular	−.3603	1.3180	.830
Influ./pneu./bronch.	.0982	1.1606	.988
Diarrheal	.0090	1.0494	.994
Certain chronic	.0576	1.1941	.954
Maternal	0	0	0
Cert. dis. of infancy	.0693	1.1169	.993
Automobile accidents	.0066	3.3884	.951
Other violence	−.2796	3.6047	.570
Other and unknown causes	.3147	1.0870	.984
All causes	2.8130	1.0112	.968

[a] $M_i = (\sigma_{M_i}/\sigma_{F_i})F_i + [\bar{M}_i - (\sigma_{M_i}/\sigma_{F_i})\bar{F}_i]$.

Hereafter, D_{ij} will be referred to as the sex mortality differential for cause i in population j.

It would be convenient if the cause-specific differentials for population j (from (6.4)) added up to the differential for all causes combined (from (6.2)) for that population. But it is clear that such a simple relationship cannot obtain because the overall differential D_j is also influenced by the composition of mortality by cause. Even if there were no cause-specific differentials in a particular population, a large positive differential for all causes combined could result if causes where male mortality is conventionally quite high relative to female were exceptionally prominent. For example, female deaths could be reallocated from infectious and parasitic diseases, a cause that is relatively neutral with respect to sex, to violence, a heavily masculine cause, and the differential from all causes combined would clearly be expected to increase even if all cause-specific differentials were zero before and after the reallocation.

The exact amount of this remainder, which will be denoted D_{cj} and will be termed "the amount of D_j attributable to the composition of causes in j", is

$$D_{cj} = D_j - \sum_i D_{ij},$$

which, after substituting from (6.2) and (6.4) and simplifying, becomes

$$D_{cj} = \sum_i \frac{\sigma_{M_i}}{\sigma_{F_i}} (F_{ij} - \bar{F}_i) - \frac{\sigma_M}{\sigma_F} (F_j - \bar{F}). \tag{6.5}$$

Given a certain level of female mortality from all causes combined in j, F_j, the differential will be higher the higher is female mortality from a cause in which male deviations from mean tend to be quite large relative to female deviation from mean (i.e., where $\sigma_{M_i}/\sigma_{F_i}$ is high). If the ratio of male–female standard deviations for each cause were equal to the ratio for all causes combined (1.0112), then the composition of causes could in no case contribute to the overall deviation and $D_{cj} = 0$. Reallocation of female mortality from one cause to another would be associated with zero net increment in expected male mortality. But given disparate cause-specific relations, the relative level of female mortality from the causes clearly influences the expected level of the differential from all causes combined.

By summing equations (6.2) and (6.4) over all 165 populations, it is obvious that, for the sample as a whole, the average deviation for all causes combined and for each individual cause must be zero. Likewise, from (6.5) it is clear that the average deviation attributable to the composition of causes in a population must be zero.

One disadvantage of this procedure is that the deviation attributable to maternal mortality, from (6.4), will always be zero. Male mortality from the cause will always be zero but so will expected male mortality. Even though death rates from this cause are never very large, it is preferable not to bury them in the composition term of equation (6.5). Therefore, the term for maternal mortality has been extricated from equation (6.5). Rewriting this equation in terms of individual causes of death, the deviation attributable to maternal mortality in population j, D_{mj} is defined as

$$D_{mj} = \frac{\sigma_M}{\sigma_F}(\bar{F}_m - F_{mj}), \qquad (6.6)$$

where F_{mj} is the female death rate from maternal mortality in population j and $\bar{F}_m$ the mean female death rate from maternal mortality in the sample. The logic of (6.6) is obvious. A unit change in female mortality is typically associated with a change in male mortality of σ_M/σ_F units; but since male mortality from maternal causes is always zero, a unit change in maternal mortality of ΔF_{mj} must change the measured differential by $-(\sigma_M/\sigma_F)\cdot\Delta F_{mj}$. Since σ_M/σ_F is approximately unity, D_{mj} is approximately the difference between death rates from maternal mortality in population j and the mean death rate from the cause in the sample. The contribution of the composition of mortality by cause to the overall differential is redefined after the exclusion of maternal mortality as

$$D'_{cj} = \sum_i \frac{\sigma_{M_i}}{\sigma_{F_i}}(F_{ij} - \bar{F}_i) - \frac{\sigma_M}{\sigma_F}\left[\sum_{i \neq m}(F_{ij} - \bar{F}_{ij})\right]. \qquad (6.7)$$

It may seem curious that each of the cause-specific slopes (except for a minor cause, maternal mortality) is greater than the slope for all causes combined. This property is a product of differing relations among specific causes in the male as opposed to the female populations. In particular, the female death rate from cardiovascular disease is positively related to female death rates from respiratory T.B. ($r = .094$), to rates from influenza/ pneumonia/bronchitis ($r = .019$), and to rates from certain diseases of infancy ($r = .111$) in these 165 populations. For males, on the other hand, death rates from cardiovascular disease are more strongly but *negatively* related to these diseases ($r = .170$, $-.198$, and $-.083$) (Table 2.4). In general, variations in causes of death tend to offset one another to a greater extent among males. Using the formula for the variance of a sum, the equation for the all-cause slope squared can be written as

$$\left(\frac{\sigma_M}{\sigma_F}\right)^2 = \frac{\sigma_{M_1}^2 + \sigma_{M_2}^2 + \cdots + \sigma_{M_{12}}^2 + \sum_i \sum_{k \neq i} \sigma_{M_{ik}}^2}{\sigma_{F_1}^2 + \sigma_{F_2}^2 + \cdots + \sigma_{F_{12}}^2 + \sum_i \sum_{k \neq i} \sigma_{F_{ik}}^2},$$

where $\sigma^2_{M_{ik}}$, $\sigma^2_{F_{ik}}$ = covariance between death rates from cause i and cause k for males and females, respectively. Because the covariance between causes of death — specifically, between a degenerative and an infectious disease — tends to be less strongly positive among males, the all-cause slope is much less than a weighted average of cause-specific slopes. This same phenomenon accounts for the fact that the intercept in the all-cause regression is much larger than the sum of intercepts in the cause-specific regression; the former takes explicit account of the greater tendency of causes to offset one another among males. It is readily shown that the difference between the all-cause intercept I and the sum of cause-specific intercepts, $\sum_i I_i$, is

$$I - \sum_i I_i = \sum_i \left(\frac{\sigma_{M_i}}{\sigma_{F_i}} - \frac{\sigma_M}{\sigma_F} \right) \bar{F}_i.$$

Since the term in parentheses is typically strongly positive, the all-cause intercept must be larger than the sum of cause-specfic intercept.

Aggregate Contribution of Individual Causes of Death to Sex Mortality Differentials

It is possible to make a preliminary assessment of the responsibility of particular causes of death for overall sex differentials by grouping populations according to the size of their differential and computing the average within-group contribution of the individual causes. Results of this procedure are shown in Table 6.3. It is clear from column 4 of the table that, when the differential is exceptionally large, the causes making the largest average contributions are, in order: cardiovascular disease (33.4%); "other and unknown causes" (17.0%); neoplasms (16.0%); influenza/pneumonia/bronchitis (14.9%); and respiratory tuberculosis (12.6%). When male mortality in a population is excessive, these are the causes most likely to be responsible. Likewise, when male mortality is deficient relative to female mortality (column 1), these same causes are typically responsible, and in the indentical order of average contribution. Diarrheal diseases and "other infectious and parasitic diseases," while major causes of death in the sample, are not, in general, influential contributors to sex mortality differentials. The reason is that deviations from the male/female relations for these diseases are minimal; the correlation coefficients of .996 and .994 between male and female death rates from the diseases are the highest of those for any cause of death. The composition of causes D_{cj} is likewise an insignificant factor (contributing less than 10% to the average value of D_j) in three of the four quartiles.

Table 6.3

Contribution of particular causes of death (D_{ij}) to sex mortality differentials (D_j) in populations grouped into quartiles according to the size of differential (D_j)

	Quartile			
	I	II	III	IV
Range of D_j	−4.93 to −.91	−.89 to +.05	.07 to 1.01	1.02 to 6.27
Mean of D_j	−1.771	−.460	.505	1.768
Mean of D_{ij}				
Resp. T.B.	−.197	−.071	.052	.222
Other infec. & para.	−.036	−.016	.023	.028
Neoplasms	−.279	−.057	.061	.281
Cardiovascular	−.625	−.046	.095	.591
Influ./pneu./bronch.	−.249	−.085	.077	.264
Diarrheal	−.046	.007	.019	.025
Certain chronic	−.074	−.035	.047	.064
Maternal	−.041	−.011	.022	.029
Certain dis. of inf.	.003	−.010	.004	.002
Auto accidents	−.008	−.001	.010	−.004
Other violence	.050	.076	−.056	−.072
Other and unknown	−.340	−.063	.111	.301
Composition of causes (D_{cj})	.073	−.148	.040	.035

Relations among the Differentials for Particular Causes of Death

If unusual sex mortality differentials are the product of an unusually debilitated condition for one sex, or of differential risk factors such as nutritional adequacy, restricted access to health care, or cigarette smoking that operate through several causes of death, then one would expect the differentials for particular causes of death to covary positively from population to population. On the other hand, if they are the product of factors that impinge uniquely on a particular disease, then no such covariation is to be expected. Table 6.4 indicates that positive covariation is the norm. Of the 66 coefficients of correlation between disease-specific sex mortality differentials in the table, 45 are positive. Nine of the 21 negative correlations involve "other violence," and 3 additional ones involve automobile accidents. Coefficients involving these causes of death are quite small. Clearly, the violent causes tend to operate on sex mortality differentials in large measure independently of the disease processes. We demonstrate below that the prevailing negative association between differentials from violence and diseases probably results from their opposite responsiveness to economic

Table 6.4

Coefficients of correlation among disease-specific sex mortality differentials (D_{ij}) in 165 populations

	Respir-atory T.B.	Other infec. & para.	Influ./ pneu./ bronch.	Diarrheal	Cert. dis. of inf.	Neo-plasms	Cardio-vascular	Maternal	Cert. chronic dis.	Auto acci-dents	Other violence	Other & unknown
Respiratory T.B.	—											
Other infec. & para.	.470	—										
Influ./pneu./ bronch.	.591	.389	—									
Diarrheal	.464	.665	.439	—								
Cert. dis. of inf.	.146	.232	.032	.282	—							
Neoplasms	.374	-.085	.495	.009	-.314	—						
Cardiovascular	.309	.046	.472	.115	-.131	.564	—					
Maternal	.083	-.195	.192	-.102	-.099	.472	.574	—				
Certain chronic dis.	.335	.011	.214	.054	-.124	.315	.317	.093	—			
Auto accidents	.076	.024	-.054	-.020	.149	.046	-.147	.054	.082	—		
Other violence	-.186	-.147	-.279	-.053	-.094	-.072	-.111	-.194	.088	.119	—	
Other & unknown	.636	.556	.512	.573	.159	.288	.358	-.593	.325	.052	-.089	

modernization, with violent causes showing reduced differentials in developed populations and other causes increased differentials.

Among correlations involving two disease groups, the highest occur within groups of diseases having similar etiology and age incidence. Areas in the table containing correlation coefficients of .380 or higher are demarcated. This level is attained by all correlations between two diseases in the infectious and parasitic group, comprising respiratory tuberculosis, other infectious and parasitic diseases, diarrheal diseases, and influenza/pneumonia/bronchitis. Excluding correlations involving "other and unknown" causes, the two highest correlations in the table occur within this group, one of which is between two infectious causes of death that affect the same organ system: respiratory tuberculosis and influenza/pneumonia/bronchitis. In populations where males have unusually high death rates relative to females for a particular infectious cause, they also tend to have abnormally high death rates from other infectious causes.

The second group that contains uniformly high correlations is cardiovascular disease, neoplasms, and maternal mortality. The inclusion of maternal mortality in this group is perhaps surprising, in view of the fact that a majority of deaths from this cause in high mortality populations are a result of infections following childbirth; that is, it might be expected that the differentials from the cause were more highly related to those from infectious diseases. One interpretation of the relationship between maternal mortality and cardiovascular disease or neoplasms is that both are jointly influenced by the extent of childbearing and by the status of women in a population. A heavy burden of childbearing and childrearing has been repeatedly suggested as a risk factor in the development of cardiovascular disease (cf. Moriyama, Woolsey, and Stamler, 1958) and cervical cancer (cf. Lundin, Erikson, and Sprunt, 1964). Kitagawa and Hauser (1973, pp. 112–13) show that the number of children a woman has borne past the third child, controlling her educational attainment, is positively associated with her subsequent mortality from all causes combined. Presumably, much of this effect works through the most important cause of death, cardiovascular disease. In addition, the level of maternal mortality is an indicator of the status of women, especially in health-related matters, since it reflects both the extent to which women are constrained to nonmarket activities and the adequacy of medical attention a women receives during childbirth. Their relative status should influence death rates from cardiovascular diseases and cancer for both material and pyschological reasons. The inclusion of maternal mortality in a sector of high correlation with degenerative diseases is clearly consistent with the implication of the preceding chapter that high rates of maternal mortality are significantly associated with high death rates in the postmaternal age interval of 40 to 59.

A plausible contributor to the positive correlation among deviations from neoplasms, cardiovascular disease, and influenza/pneumonia/bronchitis is variation in cigarette smoking behavior. Cigarette smoking affects male mortality more than female (absolutely and proportionately) both because males more commonly indulge and because they are more susceptible if they do. Neoplasms, cardiovascular disease, and bronchitis are the principal causes of death through which smoking affects mortality (United States Surgeon General, 1964). Bronchitis and cardiovascular diseases are synergistically and often inextricably related causes of death (Preston *et al.*, 1972, pp. 5–7), probably contributing further to the association between these causes of death. It is fitting that influenza/pneumonia/bronchtis deviations be linked with those of both the infectious and degenerative groups, since the category is itself a composite of infectious and degenerative causes.

The correlations in Table 6.4 suggest that there are certain factors, operating primarily within special age intervals, that influence simultaneously sex differentials in mortality from several major causes of death. Surprisingly, there is little systematic association between deviations for diseases whose principal impact occurs at different ages, suggesting that sex-specific influences (e.g., discrimination against females) do not typically span all ages in their mortality effects. Violent death shows essentially no association with any of the diseases in its contribution to overall deviations. The generally low correlations between deviations from different causes of death suggests the utility of studying determinants of the differentials separately for the various causes.

Sex Mortality Differentials in Each Population

The amount by which male mortality exceeds expected male mortality from all causes combined is shown for each population in Table 6.5. The deviations range from -4.79 in Costa Rica, 1960, to 6.27 in Taiwan, 1920. Two distinct tendencies are apparent from a careful examination of these values: values tend to be clustered geographically and culturally; and values for a particular country tend to increase over time.

In the second column of the table, deviations are presented with a linear time effect netted out. That is, a linear regression was computed of D_j on T, where T is the number of years between 1861 (the date of the earliest observation) and the year of observation. Values in the second column are deviations from that regression line. Nonlinearities in the relationship are not evident; the partial correlation between T^2 and D_j, controlling T, was

Table 6.5

Values of sex mortality differential (D_j = excess of actual over expected male death rate, all causes combined) for 165 populations

Country	Year	D_j	D_j*^a	Country	Year	D_j	D_j*^a
Australia	1911	.32	.88		1921	.25	.64
	1921	.07	.46		1931	.53	.75
	1933	.05	.24		1940	1.25	1.32
	1940	.59	.66		1951	1.36	1.24
	1951	1.06	.94		1960	1.34	1.07
	1960	1.37	1.10		1964	1.53	1.19
	1964	1.71	1.37	Finland	1921	1.83	1.71
Austria	1961	1.28	.99		1960	1.76	1.49
	1964	1.40	1.06		1964	2.02	1.68
Belgium	1960	1.25	.98	France	1951	1.49	1.37
	1964	1.04	.70		1960	1.57	1.30
Bulgaria	1964	− .89	− 1.23		1964	1.51	1.17
Canada	1921	− 1.80	− 1.41	West Germany	1960	.64	.37
	1931	− 1.55	− 1.33		1964	1.08	.74
	1941	− .58	− .53	Greece	1960	− 1.30	− 1.57
	1951	− .24	− .36		1964	− .73	− 1.07
	1960	.58	.31	Guatemala	1961	− 3.17	− 3.46
	1964	.75	.41		1964	− 2.13	− 2.47
Chile	1909	.30	.90	Hong Kong	1961	3.03	2.74
	1920	− .67	− .26		1964	3.24	2.90
	1930	− .44	.20	Hungary	1960	− .18	− .45
	1940	− .01	.06		1964	.13	− .21
	1950	1.35	1.25	Iceland	1964	− .02	− .36
	1959	1.26	1.01	Ireland	1951	− .77	− .89
	1964	1.27	.93		1961	− .07	− .36
Colombia	1960	− 1.04	− 1.31	Israel	1951	− 1.16	− 1.28
	1964	− .84	− 1.18		1960	− 1.31	− 1.58
Costa Rica	1960	− 4.79	− 5.06		1964	− 1.38	− 1.72
	1964	− 1.19	− 1.53	Italy	1881	− 3.04	− 1.97
Czechoslovakia	1934	− .56	− .39		1891	− 4.83	− 3.93
	1960	.35	.08		1901	− 2.40	− 1.67
	1964	1.01	.67		1910	− 2.22	− 1.64
Denmark	1921	− 2.17	− 1.78		1921	− 1.96	− 1.57
	1930	− 2.02	− 1.78		1931	− .91	− .69
	1940	− 1.70	− 1.63		1960	.30	.03
	1960	− .87	− 1.14		1964	.46	.12
	1964	− .13	− .47	Japan	1908	− 2.12	− 1.50
England & Wales	1861	− .33	1.08		1940	1.34	1.40
	1871	.26	1.50		1951	.24	.12
	1881	.26	1.33		1960	1.01	.74
	1891	1.02	1.92		1964	.79	.45
	1901	.73	1.46	Malta	1964	− .47	− .81
	1911	.58	1.42	Mexico	1960	− 1.25	− 1.52

Table 6.5 (*Continued*)

Country	Year	D_j	$D_j{}^a$	Country	Year	D_j	$D_j{}^a$
	1964	−1.42	−1.76	(White)	1941	.61	.66
Netherlands	1931	−2.18	−1.96	(Colored)	1951	1.26	1.14
	1940	−.99	−.92	(White)	1951	.96	.84
	1950	−1.57	−1.67	(Colored)	1960	1.85	1.58
	1960	−.76	−1.03	(White)	1960	1.13	.86
	1964	−.11	−.45	Spain	1930	.75	.99
New Zealand	1881	−.77	.30		1940	4.08	4.15
	1891	−.19	.71		1960	.08	−.19
	1901	−1.19	−.46	Sweden	1911	−1.00	−.44
	1911	−.61	−.05		1920	−1.28	−.87
	1921	−.90	−.51		1930	−1.79	−1.55
	1926	−.74	−.43		1940	−1.44	−1.37
	1936	−1.11	−.97		1951	−1.41	−1.53
	1945	−.32	−.34		1960	−.74	−1.01
	1951	−.11	−.23		1964	−.39	−.73
	1964	1.13	.79	Switzerland	1930	.29	.53
Northern Ireland	1960	.43	.16		1941	.07	.12
	1964	.64	.30		1951	.14	.02
Norway	1910	−1.08	−.50		1960	.31	.04
	1920	−1.15	−.74		1964	.63	.29
	1930	−1.14	−.90	Taiwan	1920	6.27	6.68
	1946	−1.16	−1.19		1930	3.92	4.16
	1951	−1.24	−1.36		1936	4.16	4.30
	1960	−.54	−.81		1960	1.11	.84
	1964	−.35	−.69		1964	.82	.48
Panama	1960	−.62	−.89	Trinidad	1963	1.22	.90
	1964	−.88	−1.22	United States	1900	−.94	−.19
Poland	1960	.66	.39		1910	−.30	.28
	1964	1.04	.70	(Nonwhite)	1920	−2.96	−2.55
Portugal	1930	1.24	1.48	(White)	1920	−1.59	−1.18
	1940	.56	.63		1930	−.44	−.20
	1960	.88	.61		1940	.28	.35
	1964	.89	.55	(White)	1950	.81	.71
Puerto Rico	1960	−.48	−.75	(Nonwhite)	1950	.11	.01
	1964	−.09	−.43		1960	1.31	1.04
Scotland	1951	.66	.54		1964	1.45	1.11
	1960	1.20	.93	Venezuela	1960	−.29	−.56
	1964	1.75	1.41		1964	−.61	−.95
South Africa (Colored)	1941	−2.31	−2.26	Yugoslavia	1961	−.68	−.97
					1964	−.24	−.58

a Controlled for date of observation.

only $+.039$, and the increase in R^2 from introduction of the second-degree term was insignificant.

The regional and temporal effects must be a consequence of variation either in the cause-specific differentials (D_{ij}) or in the composition of causes (D'_{cj}). Although values of these measures have been computed for each population, their presentation is excessively tedious. Instead, we shall in the next section demonstrate the contribution of causes of death to sex mortality differentials in regional blocs of countries and over time.

Regional and Temporal Variation in Sex Mortality Differentials

On the basis of values presented in Table 6.5, six groups of nations have been identified that are geographically contiguous (except where intervening territory is ocean or is a country for which data are missing) and whose pattern of deviations are highly similar and persistent over time after "date of observation" is controlled. These groups are:

NORTHWESTERN EUROPE
Denmark, Iceland, The Netherlands, Norway, and Sweden
25 observations, 1910–64
Sex mortality differentials are always negative, indicating lower than expected male mortality.

SOUTHEASTERN EUROPE
Bulgaria, Greece, Hungary, Italy, Malta, Yugoslavia
16 observations, 1881–1964
Sex mortality differentials are always negative except for 2 observations (Italy, 1960 and 1964, .03 and .12).

WESTERN AND CENTRAL EUROPE
Austria, Belgium, Czechoslovakia, England and Wales, France, West Germany, Northern Ireland, Poland, Portugal, Scotland, Spain, and Switzerland
43 observations, 1861–1964
Sex mortality differentials are always positive, except Czechoslovakia, 1934 $(-.39)$ and Spain, 1960 $(-.19)$.

TROPICAL LATIN AMERICA
Colombia, Costa Rica, Guatemala, Mexico, Panama, Puerto Rico, Trinidad and Tobago, Venezuela
15 observations, 1960–64
Sex mortality differentials are always negative (except Trinidad and Tobago, 1963, $+.90$).

FAR EAST
Hong Kong, Japan, Taiwan
12 observations, 1908–64
Sex mortality differential always positive (except Japan, 1908, -1.50).

REMAINDER
Australia, Canada, Chile, Finland, Ireland, Israel (Jewish), New Zealand,
United States, Republic of South Africa
54 observations, 1881–1964
No distinctive characteristic.

The geographic differentials are remarkable for their strength and persistence, particularly within Europe, where a band of nations with high relative male mortality separates two blocs with relatively high female mortality. The accompanying map, Figure 6.2, displays the geographic pattern of sex mortality differentials in Europe, 1964. Two peripheral nations alone, Finland and Ireland, are exceptions to the spatial pattern, and even Finland could be incorporated into the high male mortality band by expanding the region's boundaries in the northeast direction. Keys, Karnoren, and Fidanza (1958) demonstrate striking regional differentials within Finland in death rates from arteriosclerotic heart disease. The western areas show low rates, similar to those in Sweden and Norway, whereas the southeastern part, that closest to the western-central bloc, displays exceptionally high rates. Thus, there is a suggestion that two different mortality patterns, each congruent with that of neighboring areas, coexist in Finland. If finer division were practical, Finland may appear to be less of an outlier.

Ireland's excessively high female mortality has frequently been noted. Kennedy (1973, Chap. 3) attributes it to the highly subordinate family status of Irish girls and women, particularly as it affects the adequacy of their diets. We might also note that Ireland is distinguished from most of the remainder of Europe in the 1960's when our data are recorded, by its high proportion rural (slightly over one-half (Davis, 1969)). Kennedy shows that the comparative mortality rates of Irish women were particularly high in rural areas.

That social and cultural, as opposed to genetic, factors are at least partially responsible for the observed geographic pattern of differentials is indicated by their incomplete maintenance among derivative populations. The "remainder" group, primarily composed of nations populated by migrants from Europe, is particularly interesting in this respect. The population of New Zealand is drawn predominantly from England and Wales, but the high and persistent excess in male mortality in the latter is reversed in the former. The relatively high proportion of males in agricultural occupations in New Zealand is a plausible explanation of its peculiarity, in view of studies noted below that find agricultural pursuits and rural living to be more advantageous to males than to females. Australia, the most highly urbanized country in

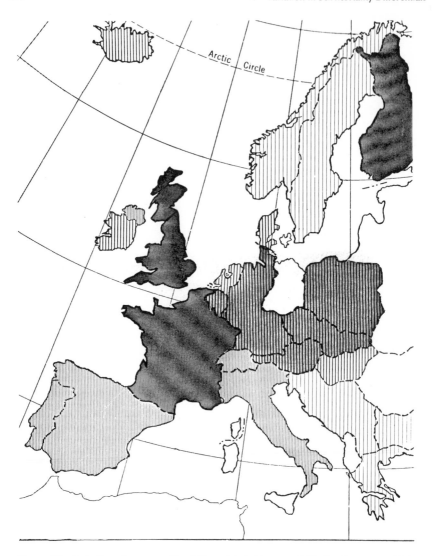

Figure 6.2   Quintiles of sex mortality differentials in Europe, 1964. (Darkest areas: highest masculinity of mortality; blank areas: no data.)

the world, maintains the British pattern. The United States and Canada, recipients of heavy volumes of migration from high and low male mortality areas of Europe, show no persistent tendency for positive or negative differentials, but rather a marked increase over time from what were negative differentials in the early years of the century. Chile differs markedly from the rest of Latin America by displaying a history of positive deviations;

this difference might be attributable to its higher level of urbanization than the other Latin countries represented (Davis, 1969, pp. 64–69), to its being the only Latin country represented that is in the temperate zone, or to its having a higher proportion of its population of European extraction than the other Latin countries.

Thus, we have identified three nations—Ireland, Chile, and New Zealand—whose pattern of sex differentials differs from that of culturally affiliated neighboring countries. In each case the deviant country is distinguished by an extreme level of urbanization, relatively low in New Zealand and Ireland, where the average deviation is relatively low, and relatively high in Chile, where the differential is relatively high. The importance of urbanization for sex mortality differentials is supported by the more comprehensive analysis presented below.

However, constitutional or genetic factors must also be suspected of playing a role in geographic differences, especially those uncovered within the European region. One interesting possibility is somatotype. Central Europeans tend to be more mesomorphic (stocky, muscular) than other Europeans (United States National Center for Health Statistics, 1965, p. 19). Such a body type has been implicated as an important risk factor in the development of coronary heart disease in males (Cady, Gertler, Gottsch, and Woodbury, 1961). Scandinavians tend to be taller than other Europeans and unusually large height seems to protect against the development of coronary heart disease (ibid.). Interestingly, Keys et al. (1968) found Finns in the lower mortality western area to be taller than those in the higher mortality, southeastern section. Scandinavians tend to retain some of their relative advantage in death rates from cardiovascular disease after migration to the United States (Sauer, 1962, p. 102). Differences in blood group types are also a possible explanation of regional disparities in sex mortality differential. The regional distribution of blood type A and D genes in Europe appears rather similar to that of sex mortality differentials, and persons with blood type A appear to be more susceptible to death from bronchopneumonia and stomach cancer (Mourant, 1954, pp. 182, 184, Maps 1 and 6).

The mortality zones identified here are rather distinct from those uncovered by Coale and Demeny (1966), who classified nations on the basis of their age patterns of mortality. The classifications are similar for the Northwestern European group, except that Denmark and the Netherlands are excluded from their "North" pattern. Our Southeastern European group includes nations that are members of each of the South and the East Tables of Coale and Demeny, and it also excludes nations (e.g., Spain, Portugal, Poland, Austria) that are members of each group. Most interesting, the level of the sex differential is similar in both our Northwestern and Southeastern groups, whereas the age patterns of mortality are radically different in the

Coale–Demeny "North" as opposed to their "South" or "East," with the former having exceptionally low and the latter two exceptionally high infant mortality. Our Western and Central European group includes representatives of the Coale–Demeny West, South, and East patterns. Our residual group, like theirs, is largely composed of overseas European nations, but we have found it feasible to extract Far Eastern populations and tropical Latin American populations from this group. It seems quite clear that the regional factors producing variation in mortality relations between the sexes are at least partially different from those producing variation in relations among the ages.

Table 6.6 presents the average sex mortality differential in these six regional groups as well as the average differential for each cause of death in each group, with "date of observation" controlled in all cases. This table identifies the causes of death responsible for a region's anomalous sex mortality differential. The cause-specific differentials sum to the differential for all causes combined (to within 1% or .0002). The values were obtained by classical least squares regression with date and region (the latter expressed as a set of dummy variables) employed as independent variables.

The table shows that the principal sources of regional differences are to be found among cardiovascular disease, neoplasms, and influenza/pneumonia/bronchitis. In three of the five distinct regions (excluding the Residual group), these diseases, always acting in the same direction, account for over 63% of the overall deviation D_j. The exceptions are Southeastern and Northwestern Europe, where they account, respectively, for 38.3% and 34.6% of D_j. In these regions, an important additional contribution is the composition of causes, accounting for 18.6% and 40.7%. The effect of this category can be further traced primarily to exceptionally low female death rates from neoplasms in Southeastern Europe and from cardiovascular diseases in Northwestern Europe.[2]

Other quantitatively important contributors to regional peculiarities ($D_{ij} > 0.35$) are respiratory tuberculosis in the Far East, with a high masculinity, and "other and unknown causes" in the Far East and in tropical Latin America. Maternal mortality never accounts for as much as 8% of the measured average regional differential and in 3 of 5 regions has a countervailing effect on D_j. "Other Infectious and Parasitic Diseases" and "Diarrheal Diseases" make essentially no contribution to regional differences in D_j. Perhaps surprisingly, the same is true of mortality from motor vehicle accidents. "Other violence" is highly feminine in the Far East and highly masculine in Latin America, acting in both cases to diminish the absolute

---

[2] This statement can be made because the formal expression for the "composition of cause" effect can itself be decomposed into specific causes of death in the identical manner used to estimate D_{mj} in Equation (6.6).

Table 6.6

Average sex mortality differential (controlling for time) from all causes combined, each of twelve causes of death, and the composition of causes in six mortality regions

Cause of death	Average deviation from grand mean in						Standard deviation controlled for date
	Western & Central Europe	Far East	South-eastern Europe	North-western Europe	Tropical Latin America	Remaining population	
All causes	.8696	1.9333	-1.1268	-1.0723	-1.5478	.1383	1.4465
Respiratory T.B.	.0641	.4326	-.0936	-.1779	-.0930	-.0112	.2438
Other infec. & para.	-.0016	.0709	-.0750	-.0093	-.0395	.0230	.0933
Neoplasms	.1606	.3710	.2540	-.1577	-.3648	-.1114	.3246
Cardiovascular	.2154	.5330	-.5936	-.0776	-.4027	.0336	.6141
Influ./pneu./bronch.	.1736	.3374	-.0924	-.1362	-.3081	-.0372	.2778
Diarrheal	.0264	.0504	-.0818	.0042	-.0423	.0018	.0881
Cert. chronic dis.	.0614	.1248	-.0030	-.0852	-.0480	-.0230	.1200
Maternal	.0423	-.0654	.0356	.0634	-.1013	-.0309	.0999
Cert. dis. of inf.	.0119	-.0245	-.0382	-.0050	.0271	.0020	.0430
Auto accidents	.0072	-.0166	.0156	-.0160	.0324	-.0083	.0445
Other violence	-.0724	-.3174	.0009	.0519	.3198	.0151	.3346
Other & unknown	.1734	.4002	-.2431	-.0899	-.3690	-.0108	.4248
Composition of causes	.0051	.0383	-.2100	-.4364	-.1572	.2953	.6307

143

value of regional D_j. The striking disparity in sex differentials from violent causes between these two regions undoubtedly reflects broader cultural differences and seems worthy of investigation.

The residual group of populations is marked by a very low average absolute value for the overall differential and for each cause-specific differential; typically, the $\bar{D}_{ij}$'s are smaller in absolute value in this group than in any other region. But the grouping conceals substantial diversity among the member nations. As is clear from Table 6.7, the overseas English-speaking populations (Australia, Canada, New Zealand, Republic of South Africa (white), and the United States) in general tend to retain the high cardiovascular masculinity of the western and central European group; but average values of D_j are lower than in the European group because deviations from neoplasms and influenza/pneumonia/bronchitis are usually small and frequently negative for these populations (until 1960). Australia and the Republic of South Africa (white) maintain a profile that would permit their classification with the Western–Central European nations, but the other three populations have neoplasm and respiratory differences that are too great for their inclusion. Thus, in general, the cardiovascular differential was exported but the neoplasm and respiratory differential was not. Climatic differences in the case of respiratory disease and dietary differences in the case of neoplasms must be suspected of contributing to the regional discrepancies.

Chile differs from tropical Latin America not because of any cause-specific sex differential. In fact, as shown in Table 6.7, differentials from neoplasms, cardiovascular disease, and influenza/pneumonia/bronchitis tend to be strongly negative and from "other violence" strongly positive in Chile, as in the tropical Latin American group. The difference is almost exclusively attributable to the "composition of causes" factor. In Chile, female death rates from cardiovascular disease, neoplasms, influenza/pneumonia/bronchitis, and "other violence" tend to be considerably higher than in the other Latin countries, with rates from diarrheal and "other infectious and parasitic diseases" much lower (Preston et al., 1972). Since these latter diseases typically display low sex ratios of standard deviations $(\sigma_{M_i}/\sigma_{F_i})$, the composition of causes in Chile is favorable to a high value of D_j and in tropical Latin America to a low value of D_j. The comparison between Chile and the rest of Latin America is a striking example of the influence of the composition of causes on the recorded differential from all causes combined.

Trends in Sex Mortality Differentials

Sex mortality differentials have generally increased during the twentieth century. This tendency is most pronounced when the ratio of death rates

Table 6.7

Comparison of average sex mortality differentials (controlling date of observation) in certain countries in "remainder" group to those in certain distinct mortality zones

	Average deviation from grand mean (controlling date of observation) from					
	All causes	Cardiovascular	Neoplasms	Influ./pneu./bronch.	Violence	Composition of causes
Western and Central Europe	.87	.22	.16	.17		
Australia	.80	.50	.07	.13		
Canada	−.48	.24	−.21	−.09		
New Zealand	−.12	.31	−.06	.07		
Republic of South Africa (white)	1.02	.47	.04	.16		
United States (excluding nonwhites in 1920 and 1950)	.24	.17	−.27	−.16		
Finland	1.63	.54	.51	−.05		
Tropical Latin America	−1.55	−.40	−.36	−.31	.32	−.16
Chile	.53	−.33	−.24	−.22	.56	1.46
Southeastern Europe	−1.13	−.59	.25	−.09		
Ireland	−.63	−.37	.01	−.06		

is used to measure differentials, but in large part this simply reflects the level-intercept relation identified above. But male mortality has also tended to increase relative to a given level of female mortality. The zero-order correlation between D_j and T, date of observation, is .262; controlled for regional composition, the partial correlation is .405. Causes of death responsible for this increase in the differential can be identified by computing a series of linear regressions of D_j and D_{ij} on T, the date of observation. Table 6.8 displays the results of this procedure. The value of .02078 at the top of the second column implies that each additional year is associated with a rise in the value of the differential (D_j) by .02 deaths per 1000 males when the regional composition of observation is controlled by a series of dummy variables.

The table shows clearly that increasing sex differentials from cardiovascular disease are by themselves responsible for over 80% of the increase in D_j. Large positive contributions are also made by neoplasms and influenza/pneumonia/bronchitis. Thus, the degenerative diseases are clearly the principal source of the rising sex mortality differentials from all causes combined in this international sample. Declining death rates from maternal mortality make a small additional contribution. These tendencies are broadly congruent with those documented by Retherford (1975) in his analysis of trends

Table 6.8

Coefficients of T, date of observation, in linear regressions of sex mortality differentials $(D_j$ and $D_{ij})$ on T, $N = 165$

	Regression with regional composition	
Cause of death	Uncontrolled	Controlled
All causes	.01698[a]	.02078[a]
Respiratory T.B.	.00375[a]	.00379[a]
Other infec. & para.	−.00018	−.00005
Neoplasms	.00794[a]	.00878[a]
Cardiovascular	.01595[a]	.01681[a]
Influ./pneu./bronch.	.00244[a]	.00314[a]
Diarrheal	.00002	.00011
Cert. chronic dis.	.00044	.00048
Maternal	.00382[a]	.00411[a]
Cert. dis. infancy	−.00024	−.00034[a]
Auto accidents	.00022	.00011
Other violence	−.00128	−.00213
Other and unknown	.00152	.00239
Composition of causes	−.01745[a]	−.01643[a]

[a] Significant at $\alpha = .05$.

in sex mortality differentials since 1910 in England, the United States, and New Zealand. Acting together, these causes would have produced a time trend almost twice as strong as that observed (when measured by the coefficient of T in the D_j regression). Their combined effects were partially offset by a change in the cause composition of female mortality that would, by itself, have tended to create a negative time trend. Decomposing equation (6.5) by cause of death, it can be shown that three-fourths of the influence of composition of causes on the time trend in D_j can be attributed to declining death rates from respiratory diseases and "other violence," causes with a higher male/female slope than that for all causes combined.

Environmental Factors Associated with Sex Mortality Differentials

In this section we will describe the extent of association between sex mortality differentials from all causes combined or from each cause and various national indices of social, economic, nutritional, and medical levels. Because of the high degree of collinearity among such indices, and the serious problems of measurement error that arise in cross-national research, it is unrealistic to expect definitive results. Furthermore, since every determinant of mortality is potentially a determinant of sex differentials in mortality, and since a score of plausible determinants could be listed for each of the twelve causes of death, most of them not measurable for all countries under consideration, the analysis can hardly purport to be exhaustive. However, the pattern of associations is highly suggestive of the factors that underlie the observed pattern of differentials. Listed below are sets of factors that have been suggested or may be presumed to affect sex mortality differentials, together with very brief statements regarding expected effects and citations to pertinent literature.

A. *Socioeconomic Discrimination against Females*

The factor most commonly mentioned as an influence on sex mortality differentials is the relative socioeconomic status of women and girls. El Badry (1969) suggests that the abnormally high sex ratios (M/F) recorded in censuses in India, East and West Pakistan, and Ceylon are attributable to higher female than male mortality. He suggests, following Coale and Hoover (1959, p. 351) and the Census Board of India itself, that the explanation is to be found in the subordinate position of women and the relative aversion to female children in these societies. El Badry's suggestion receives independent support from a study of health practices in rural Punjab villages.

Prior to death, female decedents in the villages had less frequently received medical attention than male decedents, and such care as given to the female decedents was provided by practitioners who were on average less competent (Singh, Gordon, and Wyon, 1962). Cowgill and Hutchinson (1963) also attribute a high sex ratio of population among native American populations in the Peten, Guatemala, to differential treatment of female children. In particular, they suggest that nutritional practices discriminate against females, who tended to be breastfed for shorter periods of time and occasionally even weaned while an older male sibling was still breastfeeding. Their evidence is highly impressionistic. Kennedy (1973, Chap. 3) amasses literary citation to and contemporary comment on the inferior status of Irish females to account for their high relative mortality. Their mortality disadvantage was much more severe in rural areas. Extreme physical demands on Irish rural housewives and a system of household food allocation giving priority to males were the two principal means through which sex discrimination was postulated to operate.

Six measures have been constructed in an attempt to represent the extent of discrimination against females in a society. They measure sex differentiation in labor force activity, school enrollment, and literacy. These indices are constructed in a manner identical to that used to measure sex mortality differentials. For example, we have computed the orthogonal regression of "percent illiterate-male" on "percent illiterate-female" and measured the degree of sex differentiation in a particular nation by the difference between actual and predicted male illiteracy for that nation. The variables and sources of data are described in Appendix 6A.

B. Economic Modernization

The procedure described above for measuring sex differentiation in effect controls for the level of socioeconomic development by computing deviations from normal patterns that cover the entire range of development levels. But the process of development itself may affect the sexes differentially, and such effects would not be captured by the discrimination variables. For example, Moriyama et al. (1958) cite opinions of medical "experts" that the attainment of a high level of economic modernization may have placed women in their optimal exercise range but deposited men below theirs. It is sometimes argued that cerebral occupations are more "stressful" than physical ones, although the importance of the link for mortality in an entire population has been questioned (Preston, 1970, Chap. IV). Since a higher proportion of men than women participate in the labor force, such mechanisms would presumably affect male mortality more than female. Variables representing economic modernization also reflect highly correlated unmeasured variables such as cigarette smoking, a habit that is more frequently indulged in by males and which affects male mortality more strongly in absolute value at every level of indulgence (Preston, 1970). More generally, Belloc (1973) finds with longitudinal data on Californians that male mortality is more strongly affected than female by personal health practices. Particularly important were sex differences in responsiveness to levels of exercise, cigarette smoking, and alcohol consumption. Most of these practices typically change in a deleterious manner with economic modernization, a tendency that would in itself increase the masculinity of mortality. Retherford (1975, Chap. 2) provides a more complete discussion of these factors insofar as they impinge on sex differentials.

Discrimination against women and girls, insofar as it is systematically reduced by economic modernization, is also reflected by such variables. It is reasonable to expect that the comparative value of males to the household is greater in an agricultural than in an urban setting, because of the typically larger contribution of sons to household production and to the support of aged parents. Consequently, more sex discriminatory practices may be expected in rural areas, a tendency confirmed in an extensive exploration by Williamson (1973, p. 174). She concludes after a review of the strength of relative preferences for sons around the world that urbanization is the strongest determinant of son preference. Martin (1956) demonstrates that the mortality advantage of rural over urban areas in England and Wales is much greater for males than for females from 1920–1922 to 1950–1952. Kennedy (1973) demonstrates the same tendency in Ireland. Initial results of an international World Health Organization study (1974:688) confirm that male death rates tend to be higher in urban areas, whereas no such tendency is evident for females. Kitagawa and Hauser (1973, p. 119), however, find no sex difference in the small mortality advantage of nonmetropolitan over metropolitan areas in the United States, 1960. Confounded with discrimination in its mortality effects is the apparently protective effect of agricultural work on males, probably in large measure a result of the greater habitual levels of exercise required. Moriyama and Guralnick (1956, p. 69) show that agricultural workers in both England and Wales and the United States had the lowest death rates of any major occupational group in all age intervals over 45, despite their low average level of income.

Our measures of economic modernization are the percentage of the labor force employed in agriculture, forestry, hunting, or fishing; percentage of the population residing in rural areas; percentage of the population residing in cities of more than a million inhabitants; per capita national income at factor cost (1963 U.S.$); and population per motor vehicle.

C. Social Psychological Modernization

Typically accompanying economic modernization, but logically separable from it, is a transformation in value and belief systems. Particularly relevant in the present context are an awareness of the dignity of others and a disposition to show respect for them, revealed particularly in attitudes toward women and children; and in the emergence of a belief that social rewards should be based upon achievements rather than upon such ascribed statuses as race, class of birth, or sex (Inkeles, 1966: 141–144). Such beliefs should by themselves result in reduced discrimination against females. Apart from the process of economic modernization itself, the educational system is presumably the most effective agent of change in belief systems. Hence, we will measure the extent of social-psychological modernization by the percent illiterate of the adult population and the proportion of school aged children who are enrolled.

D. Control Variables

Many variables influence mortality but are expected to be relatively indiscriminant with respect to sex. In order to influence mortality, they would probably have to interact with the extent of discrimination against females or males. For example, nutritional standards should have a greater impact on sex mortality differentials in populations where females are discriminated against than in those where discrimination is minimal. For this reason, the statistical importance of interaction between control variables and measures of sex discrimination will be considered. The control variables are: population per hospital bed; population per physician; calorie consumption as a percentage of daily requirements; grams of animal protein consumed per day; grams of total protein consumed per day; grams of total fat consumed per day; annual government health expenditures per capita (U.S.$); average number of rooms per dwelling; and average number of persons per room.

Data

Because problems of missing data become more severe for earlier populations, the analysis of factors associated with sex differentials is confined to the period 1960–1964. Mortality observations were recorded for 40 nations during this period, and latest available figures during the period are used. Because the period is so short, it is not necessary to control "date of observation," so that all observations remain in their raw, unadjusted form. We have included observations for three countries not represented on the original list of 165 populations, namely the Philippines, 1964, Mauritius, 1964, and Ceylon, 1964, bringing the total number of observations to 43. These populations were added, despite high proportions of deaths in the category "other and unknown causes," in order to provide better representation of less developed countries and to incorporate a nation, Ceylon, that is part of the South Asian bloc of high female mortality identified by El Badry. Sex mortality differentials in these nations are computed in a manner identical to that used for members of the original 165. Sources of data for the variables presumed to influence sex mortality differentials are described in Appendix 6A.

Correlation Results

The zero-order correlation between sex mortality differentials and the independent variables are shown in Table 6.9. It is clear that variables representing the degree of economic modernization are in general those most closely associated with the differential, particularly for all causes combined. Especially strongly associated with D_j are percent in agricultural activities, percent rural, and percent living in cities of over one million inhabitants. In part the higher association for these variables is attributable to Hong Kong's anomalous position. Hong Kong has 100% of its population living in urban areas of more than one million population and it also has the largest positive sex differential in 1964. However, when Hong Kong is omitted and the associations recomputed for 42 populations, percent in agriculture remains the variable most predictive of the mortality differential from all causes ($r = -.547$). Moreover, there is no *a priori* reason for excluding Hong Kong and its anomalous sex mortality differential may in fact be attributable to its unusual urban proportion.

Variables representing sex differentiation in the labor force or educational systems are poorly correlated with sex mortality differentials. Zero order correlations with D_j are quite small and in four cases out of six take on the wrong sign.[3] The largest correlation, between D_j and level 1 enrollment differentiation, is properly signed but insignificant at $\alpha = .05$. Likewise, social modernization and control variables perform poorly relative to those representing economic modernization. The control variables cannot be expected

---

[3] Except for the two illiteracy variables, the sign of the correlation should be negative; when females are relatively disadvantaged in the work force or educational systems, the value of these variables increases and the value of D_j should in theory increase in a negative direction. The sign on illiteracy should be positive; when a high proportion of males are illiterate relative to expected levels, male mortality should be relatively high.

Table 6.9

Coefficients of correlation between sex mortality differentials and various background variables

	Sex mortality differential from:				
	All causes	Resp. T.B.	Other infec. & para.	Neoplas.	Cardio-vascular
Male/female differential in					
% of adults in nonagricultural labor force	−.004	.123	.086	.096	−.092
% of adults in white collar occupations	.118	.107	−.017	.081	.100
Proportion enrolled in school, level 1	−.225	.253	−.215	.158	.001
Proportion enrolled in school, level 2	.104	.125	−.063	.148	−.011
Proportion illiterate	−.105	−.573	−.151	−.317	.000
Log, proportion illiterate	−.088	−.509	−.088	−.402	.091
Economic modernization					
Per capita income (U.S.$$)	.383	−.376	−.010	.157	.548
Percent of labor force in agriculture	−.574	.104	−.174	−.118	−.634
Motor vehicles per capita	.377	−.409	−.027	.079	.675
Percent of population in rural area	−.566	−.154	−.035	−.067	−.568
Percent in cities >1 million	.546	.570	.171	.243	.488
Social modernization					
Percent literate of adult pop.	.408	−.187	.160	.290	.342
School enrollment, 1st and 2nd level	.294	−.226	.162	.221	.387
Control variables: Health resources					
Population per hospital bed	−.194	.234	.146	−.057	−.174
Population per physician	−.217	.208	−.234	−.144	.002
Govt. health expenditures/cap (U.S.$$)	.328	−.058	−.054	.044	.383
Control variables: Nutrition					
Daily calories as % of requirements	.435	.035	−.043	.428	.238
Daily grams animal protein/cap	.464	−.292	−.007	.148	.609
Daily grams total protein/cap	.376	−.141	−.081	.343	.247
Daily grams animal fat/cap	.446	−.304	−.066	.157	.582
Daily grams total fat/cap	.390	−.322	−.095	.179	.520
Control variables: Housing					
Average # of rooms/dwelling	.243	−.438	−.014	.146	.445
Average # of persons/room	−.292	.452	−.053	−.230	−.312

Table 6.9 (*Continued*)

			Sex mortality differential from:					
Influ./ pneu./ bronch.	Diarrh.	Cert. chronic dis.	Maternal	Cert. dis. inf.	Auto accidents	Other violence	Unknown	Composition of causes
.028	.068	.083	.030	−.088	.107	−.052	.069	−.099
.208	−.031	.001	.123	−.217	.107	−.157	.185	−.073
−.230	−.282	.061	−.455	.277	.045	.067	−.453	−.310
.168	.085	.141	.177	.015	.130	−.403	.093	.149
−.059	−.215	−.386	−.161	.222	.182	.276	−.065	.187
−.076	−.164	−.273	−.318	.246	.128	.293	−.119	.184
.313	.165	−.188	.637	−.153	−.434	−.453	.153	.381
−.562	−.271	.047	−.603	.229	.334	.562	−.378	−.419
.357	.085	−.134	.451	−.189	−.487	−.345	.063	.281
−.467	−.169	−.082	−.504	.305	.438	.476	−.445	−.391
.352	.137	.430	.205	−.041	−.264	−.208	.354	.013
.425	.477	−.108	.777	−.324	−.286	−.557	.289	.354
.386	.339	−.309	.572	−.277	−.364	−.472	.219	.183
−.168	.150	.284	−.422	−.057	.029	.190	.156	−.307
−.287	−.516	.051	−.735	.345	.186	.333	−.273	−.285
.390	.223	−.176	.514	−.035	−.227	−.417	.120	.368
.578	.172	−.187	.755	−.192	−.249	−.442	.395	.213
.414	.243	−.161	.697	−.246	−.506	−.491	.244	.395
.439	.240	−.132	.823	−.394	−.361	−.483	.304	.330
.472	.199	−.148	.642	−.185	−.454	−.472	.181	.391
.416	.179	−.175	.721	−.228	−.389	−.580	.217	.368
.396	.131	−.122	.423	−.191	−.243	−.262	−.011	.115
−.411	−.270	.150	−.671	.241	.140	.457	−.113	−.294

to be related to the differential, apart from their association with the variables believed to be causally related to it. In fact, all correlations between D_j and a control variable are insignificant at $\alpha = .05$ when "percent in agriculture" is controlled by partial correlation. In order to test the importance of inter-action between health-related resources and sex discrimination in their mortality effects, we have constructed two sets of multiplicative variables. In one set the control variables, occasionally reconstituted by inversion so that values always increase when health conditions become poorer, are multi-plied by the measure of sex differentiation in level 1 enrollment. In the other case, they are multiplied by sex differentiation in percent engaged in non-agricultural activities.[4] The value of the variables are thus largest when health conditions are poor and females discriminated against. We expect the variables to be negatively related to D_j. The interactive variables in the former set are in every case negatively correlated with D_j, but the size of the correlation is quite similar to that between D_j and the equivalent non-interactive health-related variable. None of the interactive variables makes a statistically significant contribution to the variance in D_j explained ($\alpha = .05$) when its two components are also additively included in a regres-sion equation.

Regression Results

Since sex mortality differentials are undoubtedly a product of multiple factors, we cannot hope to identify all influential factors on the basis of zero-order correlations. In order to evaluate systematically but concisely the independent contribution of the many variables, we have employed ordinary least-squares regression in a stepwise fashion and allowed all variables, in interactive as well as noninteractive form, to enter the regres-sion equation. After three steps, the regression equation is

$$\hat{D}_j = .7363 - .02114 \cdot \text{PCTAG} + .02678 \cdot \text{LGCITY} - .59647 \cdot \text{INTERACT}$$
$$\phantom{\hat{D}_j = .7363} (.00854) \phantom{\cdot \text{PCTAG} + } (.00375) \phantom{\cdot \text{LGCITY} - } (.23819)$$

$$R^2 = .541 \tag{6.8}$$

where standard errors are in parentheses and PCTAG is the percentage of labor force in agriculture, forestry, hunting, and fishing; LGCITY the per-centage of population residing in cities of more than 1 million inhabitants; and INTERACT the reciprocal of daily grams of animal protein per capita

---

[4] In both cases the value of the discrimination variables is measured by distance from the minimum value of the variable in the 43 populations, in order that the values remain positive.

times extent of masculinity of school enrollments, level 1. All three coefficients are significant at $\alpha = .05$. When these three variables are controlled, the only variable significantly associated with D_j at $\alpha = .05$ is an interactive variable combining population per physician and sex differentials in school enrollment, level 1. But the sign of this partial correlation is positive, contrary to our prediction, and the stepwise procedure is thus terminated after three steps.

The causes of death through which the three variables identified in Equation (6.8) are affecting D_j can be identified by regressing each of the D_{ij} variables on the three variables in Equation (6.1). Since $\sum_i D_{ij} = D_j$, it must be the case that the β coefficients for a particular variable in the cause-specific regressions sum to the β coefficient for that variable in Equation (6.8) (Espenshade, 1973: Appendix A). Results of this procedure are presented in Table 6.10. They demonstrate that the cause of death most responsible for effects of the agricultural and large city variables on D_j is cardiovascular diseases, accounting respectively for 89% and 34% of beta coefficients for these variables in the all-cause regression. Other causes of death through which these variables contribute influentially to the differential

Table 6.10

Coefficients of linear regressions of sex mortality differentials on three independent variables. $N = 43$

Cause of death	R^2	Constant	Coef. of percent in: Agriculture	Cities >1 mill	Coef. of interactive term, nutrition & discrimination
All causes	.541	.73633	−.02114[a]	.02678[a]	−.59647[a]
Respiratory T.B.	.429	−.11473	.00297[a]	.00550[a]	−.01035
Other infec. & para.	.094	−.01753	−.00006	.00031	−.01693
Neoplasms	.065	.21822	−.00130	.00397	.04072
Cardiovascular	.504	.83851	−.01883[a]	.00912[a]	.14269
Influ./pneu./bronch.	.369	.17546	−.00525[a]	.00223	−.06340
Diarrheal	.143	.00244	−.00031[a]	.00014	−.01925
Cert. chronic dis.	.229	−.06407	.00175	.00376[a]	−.00306
Maternal	.535	.13372	−.00164[a]	.00007	−.05327[a]
Cert. dis. of inf.	.071	−.02219	.00038	.00007	.00880
Auto accidents	.138	−.02093	.00106	−.00057	−.00474
Other violence	.322	−.22840	.00920[a]	−.00017	−.03815
Other & unknown	.561	.05822	−.00026	.00551[a]	−.38926[a]
Composition of causes	.252	−.22811	−.00874	−.00317	−.18740
		$\sum .73061$	$\sum -.02103$	$\sum .02677$	−.59360

[a] Significant at $\alpha = .05$.

from all causes combined are neoplasms, influenza/pneumonia/bronchitis, and, for the urban variable, respiratory tuberculosis and certain chronic diseases. The association of economic modernization with sex mortality differentials clearly operates primarily through the chronic and degenerative causes of death, particularly cardiovascular diseases. "Other violence" displays a strong and significant tendency toward reduced masculinity of mortality with economic modernization, probably attributable in large part to reductions in exposure to the occupational hazards of farming. Their opposite association with economic modernization probably account for the prevailing negative correlations between sex differentials from violent and degenerative causes documented earlier in Table 6.4.

Unlike the economic modernization variables, the discrimination-nutrition interaction does not operate through the degenerative causes. An infectious group bears greater responsibility here; respiratory tuberculosis, other infectious and parasitic diseases, diarrheal diseases, influenza/pneumonia/bronchitis, and maternal mortality account together for approximately 27% of the effect of this variable on D_j. But a majority of its influence works through "other and unknown" causes of death. This disappointing outcome can be traced primarily to Guatemala and Ceylon, where sex mortality differentials from "other and unknown causes" are the highest in the sample in absolute value ($-.82$ and -1.50, representing more than half of D_j in both cases), and where the discrimination/poor nutrition variable is strongly positive. This is an instance where distinguishing among causes of death has not proven particularly fruitful, because of the imprecision of coding in pivotal populations. We can only speculate about the causes of death that should have been recorded in these populations. Because of well documented nutrition-infection interactions and because the interactive variable operates through infectious causes where assignment can be made, it seems likely that infectious diseases are primarily responsible for the relationship between D_j and the interactive variable. Thus, poor levels of nutrition when combined with discrimination against females appear to increase the femininity of mortality, especially for infectious diseases.

A declining percentage in agriculture could raise sex mortality differentials by increasing male mortality while lowering female mortality, by raising male mortality more than female, or by lowering male mortality less than female. In order to see which of these effects are occurring, we have regressed male and female death rates separately on these three variables, with the following results:

$$\hat{M} = 9.9387 + .04675 \cdot \text{PCTAG} + .02337 \cdot \text{LGCITY} + .5393 \\ \cdot \text{INTERACT} \tag{6.9}$$
$$R^2 = .446$$

$$\hat{F} = 6.3152 + .06723 \cdot \text{PCTAG} - .00348 \cdot \text{LGCITY} + 1.1271$$
$$\cdot \text{INTERACT} \qquad\qquad (6.10)$$
$$R^2 = .692$$

These equations indicate that a declining percentage in agriculture reduces male mortality but reduces female mortality much more vigorously; that an increasing percentage in large cities raises male mortality but lowers female mortality; and that, as expected, increments in the poor nutrition/discrimination interactive variable increases mortality for both sexes but do so much more vigorously for females.[5]

Discussion

Economic modernization appears to raise systematically the level of male mortality relative to a certain level of female mortality, and this effect is particularly important for cardiovascular diseases. Of the many standard components of economic modernization, nonagricultural employment and population concentration are the two having largest association with mortality differentials. As noted above, the importance of rural/urban residence for sex mortality differentials has also been documented within countries, and certain populations regionally deviant in their mortality differentials were also deviant in their level of urbanization. In all cases, rurality was associated with low masculinity of mortality. It is clear that changes in levels of economic modernization are also congruent with rising sex differentials previously documented.

Nevertheless, it is not plausible to argue that mere presence in a large city or pursuit of nonagricultural work causes by itself excessive male mortality. Undoubtedly these variables are acting as proxies for unmeasured variables that represent particular features of the urban environment or characteristics of persons living therein. That in some general sense it may be urban way of life is suggested by Syme, Hyman, and Enterline (1965), who show that urban birth adversely affects male mortality from coronary heart disease quite apart from urban residence. Similarly, Sauer (1962) demonstrates that

[5] The reader will note that the difference between β coefficients for males and females in Equations (6.9) and (6.10) are almost identical to the equivalent coefficient for that variable in Equation (6.8); the equivalence results from the expectation produced by the fitting procedure used to measure sex differentials that male and female death rates decline or rise by virtually equal absolute amounts from population to population. Thus, male and female death rates are expected to be equally responsive in absolute amount to environmental variation; any differential responsiveness appearing in equations (6.9) and (6.10) must be automatically translated into an effect on sex differentials in equation (6.8).

those born in the urban northeast of the United States carry with them high death rates from cardiovascular disease wherever they live, and that natives of rural regions retain some advantage as they move about. Whatever the factors represented by urban and industrial variables, they are apparently more effective in Western populations. Stocks (1969, p. 412) shows that female death rates from heart disease are very similar in 10 Latin American cities to those in cities of England and Wales (7% difference), whereas male death rates from the cause are 70% higher in the English than in the Latin cities. The factors represented by urbanization that seem most plausibly implicated in the changing pattern of sex differentials are reduced exercise levels, increased cigarette smoking, and reduced discrimination against women.

Socioeconomic Factors and Regional Patterns

Table 6.11 demonstrates the extent to which the regional discrepancies in sex mortality differentials previously identified can be accounted for by the three factors found to be significantly associated with D_j in 1960–1964. In four of the six mortality regions, the average sex differential is substantially reduced by controlling for the three variables. The average reduction in $\bar{D}_j$ in these four regions is 62%. The differentials in Southeastern Europe is essentially unchanged by the control procedure and in Northwestern Europe it is substantially raised in absolute value. The range of regional differentials

Table 6.11

Average sex mortality differential in regional blocs, 1960–64, before and after controlling for percent in agriculture, percent in large cities, and nutrition/discrimination interaction

| | Average differential, 1960–1964 | |
Region	Before control	After control[a]
Western and Central Europe	1.1118	.6481
Southeastern Europe	−.2900	−.2963
Northwestern Europe	−.0440	−.7674
Tropical Latin America	−.7425	−.4251
Far East	1.6167	.4620
Residual	.6943	−.0643
Added Countries		
Ceylon	−2.590	−.0156
Mauritius	1.020	1.5982
Philippines	−.980	−.4749

[a] Average residual for member nations from all-country multiple regression of D_j on the three independent variables.

is reduced from 2.3592 to 1.4155 (40.0%) by controlling these variables. Thus, they have substantial value in explaining the pattern of regional differentials previously described, although important regional variation remains and the position of the Northwestern European countries becomes even more anomalous after account is taken of their relatively low proportions in agriculture. The importance for regional differences of unmeasured variables, perhaps genetic or constitutional, is clearly suggested.

Summary

Relative to a particular level of female mortality, male mortality is lower than expected, currently and historically, in Northwestern Europe, Southeastern Europe, and tropical Latin America; it is higher than expected in Western-Central Europe and in the Far East. The geographic pattern of differentials is attributable primarily to variation in the masculinity of mortality from cardiovascular diseases, neoplasms, and influenza/pneumonia/bronchitis. Over time, male mortality has increased relative to a particular level of female mortality, and these same causes of death are principally responsible. In the 1960's, high masculinity of mortality was associated independently with low proportions in primary activities, high proportions living in large cities, and with high discrimination against females in school enrollment combined with poor general nutritional standards. The former two variables once again operate primarily through cardiovascular disease, neoplasms, and the respiratory diseases, whereas the discrimination–nutrition interaction appears to operate through infectious diseases. Variations in levels of economic modernization are capable of accounting for a substantial portion of the regional differences (although certain constitutional factors such as physiotype are also plausibly implicated) and they are also congruent with trends in sex mortality differentials.

Appendix 6A   Sources of Data and Construction of Measures Used in the Cross-Sectional Analysis

Measures of Sex Differentiation

RWHCOL   Sex differentiation in white collar employment.

For each of the 43 populations, we define the value of RWHCOL to be the difference between the observed and predicted percentages of the economically active male population in white collar occupations. The predicted percentages were calculated from a linear model fit to male and female data for the 43 populations by orthogonal regression. Thus, if (W_{fi}, W_{mi}), $i = 1, \ldots, 43$, denote the 43 pairs of female and male percentages in white collar occupations, we have

$$\text{RWHCOL}_i = W_{mi} - \left[\overline{W}_m + \frac{\sigma_{W_m}}{\sigma_{W_f}} (W_{fi} - \overline{W}_f) \right], \qquad i = 1, \ldots, 43.$$

The white collar category includes the professional, administrative, and clerical occupations, while the economically active population of either sex includes all males (or females) aged 15 to 64. Wherever possible, totals by sex in white collar occupations are restricted to the status of "salaried employees and wage earners." Accordingly, we have

$$W_{fi} = \frac{\text{total of salaried or wage earner females in white collar occupations}}{\text{total of females aged 15–64 in population}}.$$

A similar definition would hold for males W_{mi}.

Sources. International Labor Office. *Yearbook of Labor Statistics,* Geneva, various issues. United Nations. *Demographic Yearbook,* New York, various issues.

RNONAG   Sex differentiation in percent employed in nonagricultural activities

The definition of RNONAG is identical to that for RWHCOL, with the exception that RNONAG is based on salary or wage earners in nonagricultural industries. Hence, RNONAG is the difference between the observed and predicted percentage of the economically active male population in nonagricultural industries.

Sources.   Same as *RWHCOL.*

RGERL1 and RGERL2   Sex differentiation in gross enrollment ratios, levels 1 and 2.

Two other variables, RGERL1 and RGERL2, are based on male and female gross enrollment ratios for first and second levels of education, respectively. For example, RGERL1 is the difference between the observed male gross enrollment ratio (level 1) and the male ratio predicted by orthogonal regression from the female ratio.

Sources.   United Nations, Educational, Scientific, and Cultural Organization. *Statistical Yearbook* (various issues). New York. United Nations, *Demographic Yearbook* (various issues). New York.

RILLIT and RLOGIL   Sex differentiation in percentage illiterate and in log of percentage illiterate.

RILLIT is based on percentages of males and females over 15 years who are illiterate, while RLOGIL is based on the logarithms of these percentages illiterate. A logarithmic transformation is employed in RLOGIL to adjust for the heteroscedasticity arising from the fact that 17 of the 43 populations had illiteracy for both males and females at or below 1%. Again, RILLIT and RLOGIL are both male residuals from male/female orthogonal regressions.

Sources.   United Nations. *Demographic Yearbook* (various issues). New York. United Nations, Educational, Scientific, and Cultural Organization. *Statistical Yearbook* (various issues). New York, United Nations Educational, Scientific and Cultural Organization, *World Illiteracy at Mid-Century*, New York, 1957. *Gallatin Annual of International Business, 1965–66.* New York: American Heritage, 1967. D. Nortman. *Population and Family Planning: A Factbook* (Reports on Population/Family Planning). Population Council, #2, September, 1970, and #5, September, 1972.

Per Capita National Income

United Nations, *Statistical Yearbook, 1967,* Table 185. New York, 1968. Estimates for Ceylon, Ireland, Spain, Sweden and Soviet-bloc countries made by author and John McDonald. Details available upon request.

Percent of Labor Force in Primary Industries

International Labor Office, *Yearbook of Labor Statistics, 1971,* Table 2A. Geneva, 1972.

Motor Vehicles per Capita

Automobile Manufacturers Association. *Automobile Facts and Figures.* Various years.

Percent Living in Rural Areas and Percent Living in Cities of More than One Million Inhabitants

K. Davis, *World Urbanization, 1950–70,* Vol. 1. Berkeley Calif. Institute of International Studies, Univ. California, Berkeley, 1969. Population Monograph #4.

Percent Literate of Adult Population

A. S. Banks. *Cross-Polity Time Series Data.* MIT Press, 1971. For Israel (Jewish population), from United Nations. *Compendium of Social Statistics.* New York, 1967. For Taiwan, from Taiwan Department of Civil Affairs, *Taiwan Demographic Fact Book, 1965,* Table 12.

Combined Primary and Secondary Enrollment Ratio

International Bank for Reconstruction and Development, Economic Program Department, Socioeconomic Data Division. *World Tables,* Table 2. January, 1971.

Calorie Level as a Percent of Requirements, Inhabitants per Hospital Bed, and Inhabitants per Physician

United Nations. *Compendium of Social Statistics: 1967,* Tables 17, 18. New York, 1968. For calorie levels in countries not presented, estimated by author and John McDonald. Sources and procedures available upon request.

Government Health Expenditures per Capita in United States Dollars

World Health Organization. *World Health Statistics Report.* Geneva, various issues. For Spain, data from International Labor Office. *The Cost of Social Security.* Geneva, 1972.

Daily per Capita Grams of Animal Protein, Total Protein, Animal Fat, and Total Fat

Food and Agriculture Organization. *Production Yearbook, 1970,* Tables 136, 137, 138. Rome, 1971.

Average Number of Rooms/Dwelling and Average Number of Persons/Room

United Nations, *Statistical Yearbook, 1970,* Table 201. New York, 1971.

CHAPTER 7

Demographic and Social Consequences of Various Causes of Death in the United States

The previous chapters have attempted to study causes of death as sources of variation in mortality level and structure. But through their influence on level and structure, the causes also affect a wide variety of demographic and social processes. Perhaps their most significant impact has been on population size and growth rates. It is not unreasonable to suggest that the population of England and Wales would be larger by some 25–30% today were it not for the growth-inhibiting influence of respiratory tuberculosis in the nineteenth and early twentieth centuries.[1] The sudden reduction of mortality from such causes of death as malaria and smallpox has, of course, created

---

[1] The influence of a cause of death on population growth rates is closely approximated by formula 7.1 in the text. When this formula is applied to data from England decenially from 1861 to 1921, the reduction in annual female growth rates due to deaths from tuberculosis is evaluated as 0.00267, 0.00229, 0.00173, 0.00143, 0.00105, 0.00084, and 0.00078 (Preston *et al.*, 1972). A mean age at childbearing of 30 years is used. Assuming that the first figure applies to the previous 60-year period and that each subsequent figure applies to the preceding 10-year period, the cumulative impact on population size in 1921 and subsequently is 25.7%. That is, the population of 1921 and beyond would have been approximately 26% larger than it actually was if death rates from respiratory tuberculosis had been zero for the period 1801–1921. An alternative, cruder calculation (formula 7.2) is simply the exponential of the cumulative crude death rates from tuberculosis during the period. Making the same assumption, that rates are constant during some preceding period, we find that the population of 1921 would have been 27.3% larger without respiratory tuberculosis. Both calculations assume that modifying mortality rates would have had no impact on fertility or migration rates.

the condition of rapid population growth that today prevails in most of the less developed world.

This chapter examines the social and demographic impact of selected causes of death in a contemporary low mortality country, the United States. It may be widely believed that death rates have fallen to such low levels in developed countries that the influence of mortality from individual causes is trivial, but this is not the case. For example, with crude birth rates around 18/1000 and death rates around 9/1000, the typical Western country could increase its short-term growth rate by a factor of up to 2 through further advances against mortality. Furthermore, effects on age composition and on such related factors as birth rates and per capita income are likely to be greater when mortality declines from a low as opposed to a high level, since such declines are necessarily heavily concentrated in the span of ages above 50.

The procedure used in this chapter is straightforward. To gauge the impact of a cause of death on populations, a comparison is made between what the future population is expected to look like if the cause maintains its current level and what that population might look like if mortality from the cause were immediately reduced to zero within all age-sex groups. A standard form of population projection is the vehicle used to carry out this comparison. The projections will serve the purpose of indicating the effect of a cause on future population and can in no way be interpreted as predictions. The fictional quality is assured by assuming that a cause of death is eliminated instantaneously, rather than at an arbitrary pace over some course of years. However, it is important to note for analytic purposes that, whatever the pace, complete elimination of a cause of death would eventually produce identical characteristics in the projected population, with the sole exception of population size. This result is a consequence of the weak ergodic property of population movements through time (Lopez, 1961; McFarland, 1969).

The causes of death we shall examine are: all infectious and parasitic diseases, including influenza and pneumonia (B1–17, 30–32, 36, 40 in the Seventh Revision of the International Lists of Diseases, Injuries, and Causes of Death (World Health Organization, 1957); malignant and benign neoplasms (B18–19); cardiovascular disease (B22, 24–29; A85, 86); and accidents and violence (BE47–50). Each cause is examined with respect to its subsequent impact on population size, growth rate, age-sex composition, kinship ties, retirement age, and per capita income. It is hoped that the results of this investigation may, among other things, fill in a part of the background against which health policy decisions are made.

Persons "saved" from death due to a particular cause at some age will be exposed at all subsequent ages to the recorded United States schedules of birth rates and of death rates from other causes. Thus, we assume independence between age-specific birth and death rates and among age-specific death rates from the several causes of death. These assumptions are undoubtedly not completely accurate, but it is difficult to say in what direction they err. For example, death rates from infectious diseases are higher in lower social classes. Eliminating deaths from this cause may be expected to increase disproportionately the numbers in these lower classes, thus elevating birth rates. However, the persons "saved" may perhaps be among the less robust of their cohort and less likely to marry or to experience unimpaired fecundity. The assumption of independence among causes of death is likewise subject to error, but the errors unquestionably operate in both directions and the net effect cannot be appraised without much more effort than has thus far been expended on estimating empirically the size of interdependencies.

The projection procedure employed here differs from the traditional approach to studying the consequences of mortality variation, which focuses on changes in a cohort followed through life (e.g., Enke and Brown, 1972; Fuchs, 1966). While such an approach is useful, it is incomplete, since it takes no account either of the initial population structure or of the impact of mortality change on numbers of births. Thus, it neglects changing relations *among* cohorts. Mortality decline can only "age" a cohort; but an actual population is frequently rejuvenated through the impact on births of such declines (Hermalin, 1966).

United States Life Tables with Various Causes of Death Eliminated

The latest year for which cause-of-death life tables have been computed for the United States is 1964 (Preston *et al.*, 1972, pp. 768–71). Official United States cause-of-death life tables for 1969–1971 are not available at the time of this writing. Fortunately for our purposes, the mortality profile of the population is subject to quite small annual variation. For example, the life expectancy at birth in the 1964 life tables was 66.9 for males and 73.6 for females, while in 1968 the figures were 66.6 and 74.0 (United States National Center for Health Statistics, n.d. 1, pp. 5–7). There would appear to be minimal loss in using the 1964 tables even if we choose the base year of the projections to be somewhat later.

The survivorship columns in the various life tables for the United States population of 1964 are displayed in Table 7.1. To repeat, the basic assumption underlying these calculations is that the elimination of a cause of death would leave unaltered the force of mortality function (set of death rates at exact ages) for all other causes of death combined. The iterative technique developed by Nathan Keyfitz is utilized (Preston *et al.*, 1972).

Table 7.1

Survivorship proportions under United States life tables with specified causes eliminated, 1964

	PROPORTION OF THOSE ALIVE AT BEGINNING OF INTERVAL WHO SURVIVE TO END WITH SPECIFIED CAUSE ELIMINATED				
AGE INTERVAL BY SEX	No Causes	Neoplasms	Cardio-vascular Disease	All Infectious and Parasitic Diseases	Violence
Males					
0 to 0–4	0.97143	0.97172	0.97162	0.97514	0.97307
0–4 to 5–9	0.99597	0.99641	0.99606	0.99666	0.99735
5–9 to 10–14	0.99757	0.99797	0.99764	0.99778	0.99877
10–14 to 15–19	0.99545	0.99587	0.99561	0.99563	0.99855
15–19 to 20–24	0.99189	0.99241	0.99220	0.99213	0.99796
20–24 to 25–29	0.99088	0.99155	0.99144	0.99116	0.99732
25–29 to 30–34	0.99033	0.99128	0.99152	0.99070	0.99588
30–34 to 35–39	0.98746	0.98891	0.99029	0.98803	0.99277
35–39 to 40–44	0.98143	0.98399	0.98788	0.98227	0.98667
40–44 to 45–49	0.97076	0.97538	0.98348	0.97120	0.97620
45–49 to 50–54	0.95315	0.96159	0.97579	0.95505	0.95894
50–54 to 55–59	0.92663	0.94098	0.96450	0.92947	0.93266
55–59 to 60–64	0.89089	0.91284	0.94937	0.89496	0.89700
60–64 to 65–69	0.83989	0.87078	0.92807	0.84601	0.84602
65–69 to 70–74	0.77692	0.81554	0.90418	0.78564	0.78337
70–74 to 75–79	0.70277	0.74590	0.87809	0.71447	0.71008
75–79 to 80–84	0.60004	0.64684	0.86469	0.61710	0.60974
80–84 to 85–89	0.43143	0.48661	0.75377	0.47057	0.46127
85–89 to 90–94	0.29468	0.32335	0.69296	0.31665	0.30403
90–94 to 95–99	0.17361	0.19108	0.60485	0.19605	0.18193
95–99 to 100+[a]	0.10445	0.11478	0.60285	0.12496	0.11062
Life expectancy at birth	66.862	69.080	77.166	67.696	69.080
Females					
0 to 0–4	0.97768	0.97791	0.97784	0.98063	0.97899
0–4 to 5–9	0.99687	0.99721	0.99695	0.99748	0.99779
5–9 to 10–14	0.99833	0.99864	0.99842	0.99853	0.99891
10–14 to 15–19	0.99791	0.99821	0.99805	0.99811	0.99882
15–19 to 20–24	0.99681	0.99719	0.99712	0.99714	0.99829
20–24 to 25–29	0.99606	0.99660	0.99661	0.99652	0.99756
25–29 to 30–34	0.99475	0.99576	0.99562	0.99534	0.99625
30–34 to 35–39	0.99232	0.99425	0.99388	0.99303	0.99396
35–39 to 40–44	0.98870	0.99214	0.99151	0.98945	0.99042
40–44 to 45–49.	0.98308	0.98891	0.98793	0.98387	0.98488
45–49 to 50–54	0.97420	0.98334	0.98293	0.97517	0.97613
50–54 to 55–59	0.96227	0.97493	0.97719	0.96353	0.96435
55–59 to 60–64	0.94440	0.96053	0.97043	0.94616	0.94663
60–64 to 65–69	0.91426	0.93498	0.96037	0.91680	0.91680
65–69 to 70–74	0.86972	0.89489	0.94716	0.87367	0.87289
70–74 to 75–79	0.80090	0.82938	0.92903	0.80743	0.80517
75–79 to 80–84	0.69012	0.72425	0.92543	0.70228	0.69751
80–84 to 85–89	0.51564	0.54087	0.81081	0.52944	0.52368
85–89 to 90–94	0.31687	0.33890	0.74916	0.33494	0.32709
90–94 to 95–99	0.17658	0.19055	0.65884	0.19377	0.18594
95–99 to 100+[a]	0.10464	0.11299	0.69375	0.12017	0.11223
Life expectancy at birth	73.643	76.116	84.005	74.409	74.612

SOURCES: Compiled from Preston et al., 1972, and U.S. National Center for Health Statistics, 1964 and 1966.
[a] Ratio, person-years lived at ages over 100 to person-years lived, 95–99.

Additional information is introduced for ages over 85, since more than half of the population would survive to that age were cardiovascular disease to be eliminated. In the life tables for all causes combined, survivorship proportions over age 85 appearing in the official United States life tables for 1959–1961 (United States National Center for Health Statistics, 1964) are used. These calculations were based in turn upon the survival experience of Civil War veterans. For the other tables, the official figures were combined with data on the cause-distribution of deaths in age intervals above 85 in 1964 (United States National Center for Health Statistics, 1966).

Following Chiang (1968), it is assumed for these ages that the ratio of the force of mortality function from the cause eliminated to that from all other causes combined is constant within each five-year interval. This assumption is adopted for convenience since it permits a modification of the "all cause" table that relies completely on the ratio of deaths from the cause eliminated to deaths from all causes. Direct use of the cause-specific rates above age 85 is rejected because of the likelihood of large errors due to age misreporting.

Female Dominant Projections with Constant Fertility

All projections use a base year of 1969. This is the latest year for which age-specific birth rates for males and females were published at the time of computation (United States National Center for Health Statistics, 1973). The age-sex distribution of the population in 1969 is derived from the United States Bureau of Census (1970).

The sex ratio of births in the year 1969 was 1.0530, and this ratio is assumed to be constant throughout the projection period. The life tables shown in Table 7.1 are used throughout each set of projections. Zero net migration into each age interval is assumed throughout the projection period. This assumption is made partly for convenience and partly from a desire to derive the implications of mortality decline for current members of the population and their descendants.

The basic set of projections assumes that the age-specific female fertility rates of 1969 remain constant throughout the projection period. The total fertility rate for 1969 was 2.46. Although fertility has declined since 1969, the factors in the decline may well be transitory; the total fertility rate for 1969 was already quite close in its historical minimum. The fertility assumption is later modified by assuming male dominance and by adopting the Census Bureau's replacement-level fertility schedule. Table 7.2 summarizes the basic results of the five female-dominant, constant fertility projections based upon the five different mortality regimes.

Table 7.2

Parameters of the projected United States population under various assumptions regarding mortality, with female fertility constant at 1969 levels

Year and Parameters	All Causes	No Cancer	No Cardio-vascular Disease	No Infectious and Parasitic Diseases	No Violence
1979					
Population size (millions)	222.71	225.44	232.86	223.50	224.13
Proportion under age 15	0.258	0.255	0.247	0.258	0.257
Proportion 65+	0.101	0.107	0.133	0.103	0.102
Sex ratio (M/F)	0.962	0.963	0.966	0.963	0.967
Sex ratio at 65+	0.699	0.721	0.755	0.706	0.705
Growth rate[a]	0.0098	0.0107	0.0133	0.0101	0.0104
Birth rate[a]	0.0200	0.0198	0.0191	0.0199	0.0199
Death rate[a]	0.0101	0.0090	0.0058	0.0098	0.0095
1999					
Population size (millions)	265.31	271.22	288.59	267.30	269.57
Proportion under age 15	0.255	0.250	0.235	0.255	0.253
Proportion 65+	0.100	0.112	0.162	0.102	0.101
Sex ratio (M/F)	0.969	0.968	0.973	0.970	0.981
Sex ratio at 65+	0.651	0.681	0.762	0.663	0.667
Growth rate[a]	0.0077	0.0079	0.0086	0.0079	0.0081
Birth rate[a]	0.0181	0.0177	0.0166	0.0180	0.0179
Death rate[a]	0.0103	0.0097	0.0080	0.0101	0.0098
2049					
Population size (millions)	368.20	379.79	411.50	374.47	379.89
Proportion under age 15	0.245	0.239	0.220	0.244	0.242
Proportion 65+	0.120	0.134	0.198	0.122	0.123
Sex ratio (M/F)	0.971	0.970	0.980	0.973	0.989
Sex ratio at 65+	0.694	0.724	0.813	0.707	0.729
Growth rate[a]	0.0056	0.0057	0.0057	0.0058	0.0058
Birth rate[a]	0.0175	0.0170	0.0157	0.0174	0.0173
Death rate[a]	0.0119	0.0114	0.0100	0.0116	0.0114
Steady state					
Population size (millions)	...	...	...	...	...
Proportion under age 15	0.244	0.238	0.220	0.244	0.242
Proportion 65+	0.120	0.135	0.198	0.122	0.123
Sex ratio (M/F)	0.970	0.970	0.981	0.973	0.988
Sex ratio at 65+	0.692	0.723	0.817	0.705	0.728
Growth rate[a]	0.00563	0.00572	0.00568	0.00581	0.00587
Birth rate[a]	0.01748	0.01707	0.01573	0.01742	0.01728
Death rate[a]	0.01185	0.01135	0.01005	0.01161	0.01140

[a] Ten-year average centered on date.

A. Population Size and Growth

It is well known that additional mortality reductions would have relatively little effect on a modern country's intrinsic growth rate—the steady state growth rate that would ultimately be produced by the indefinite continuance of a given regime of age-specific mortality and fertility rates (Coale, 1959).

It has been shown that the gain in the intrinsic growth rate from a reduction in mortality is closely approximated by the average decline in the force of mortality function between ages zero and A_B, the mean age of childbearing in the stable population (Preston, 1974). Since mortality from any of the causes considered is relatively low prior to A_B, or indeed prior to the end of the childbearing period itself, the gain in the intrinsic growth rate is necessarily quite small. The largest gain results from the elimination of violence ($+.00024$) and the smallest from the elimination of cardiovascular disease ($+.00005$), even though the gain in female life expectancy is roughly ten times greater for cardiovascular disease. In both cases the effects on intrinsic growth rates are minor, and if we were to examine only this index, the effects of mortality reduction would appear inconsequential.

Yet this indicator can be quite misleading for developments in the near term. The increase in the instantaneous growth rate from eliminating a cause of death is simply equal to the crude death rate from that cause, which of course comprises events at ages after as well as before the end of childbearing. The difference is obvious from the following formulas:

$$\text{Increase in intrinsic growth rate} \simeq \frac{\int_0^{A_B} \mu^i(a)\, da}{A_B} \tag{7.1}$$

$$\text{Increase in instantaneous growth rate} = \int_0^{\infty} c(a)\mu^i(a)\, da \tag{7.2}$$

where $\mu^i(a)$ is the death rate from cause i at age a, $c(a)$ the proportion of the observed population at age a, A_B the average age of mother at childbirth in the stable population corresponding to observed age schedules of mortality and fertility. Both changes are averages of age-specific rates of death from cause i. The change in intrinsic growth rates in an (unweighted) average of death rates between birth and A_B; the change in instantaneous growth rates is a (population weighted) average of death rates at *all* ages.

Although cardiovascular disease has the least impact on intrinsic growth rates, it has the largest impact on population size through the first several centuries of projection. After 80 years, the population without cardiovascular disease is 11.8% larger than the population with all causes present. In fact, the gain in size from eliminating cardiovascular disease is at least double that from eliminating any other cause throughout the first century of projections. Cardiovascular disease has a trivial effect on annual arrivals at age 50 but a major effect on the numbers surviving beyond that point, and population size at a point in time depends upon both quantities.

A large majority of the gain in size from eliminating cardiovascular disease or cancer is realized within the first 30 years of the projection period. By

1999, the population is 8.8% larger with no cardiovascular disease and 2.2% larger with no cancer, compared to relative growth of 11.8% and 3.1% after 80 years. In contrast to the time pattern of impact from eliminating these chronic diseases, most of the relative growth from eliminating the other causes occurs after 1999. This results from the somewhat younger age incidence of death from the other causes, reflected in a roundabout way in Table 7.1. The relative increase from eliminating infectious and parasitic diseases or violence is 0.8% and 1.6% by 1999, compared to 1.7% and 3.2% by 2049. Here the additions to population act cumulatively, through births, but in the case of the chronic diseases they are essentially once-and-for-all gains at the older ages. The situation is analogous to increasing the volume of liquid in a container either by adding in the contents of another container or by turning up the tap slightly. Eventually, of course, population size with violence eliminated exceeds that of any other projection, but the date when this occurs is so distant as to be well beyond any realistic planning horizon.

Figure 7.1 displays the time sequence of growth rates for the various projections. Growth is most rapid in the no-cardiovascular projection during the first thirty years but its position changes rapidly thereafter and no-violence takes the lead. The no-cardiovascular series then shows a second period of relatively rapid growth, peaking around 2034. This oscillatory pattern is not a necessary outcome but is rather a product of coincidence. In 2034, the 75–90-year-olds, who are the principal beneficiaries of cardiovascular elimination, have been born into the exceptionally large birth cohorts of 1944–1959. Compared to the other projections, where the advantage at 75–90 is not so great, growth is quite rapid during this period. Fifteen years later this group is dying in the no-cardiovascular projection and its growth is exceptionally slow.

While the steady state growth rates differ little among the projections, the growth rates are attained with quite different combinations of birth and death rates. Intrinsic birth and death rates are within 5% of the "all cause" figures in the case of cancer, infectious and parasitic, and violence. But when cardiovascular disease is eliminated the birth rate falls by 9% and the death rate by 17%, reflecting the shifts in age composition that have been induced.

B. Age Distribution

From the preceeding discussion it is obvious that the elimination of cardiovascular disease or cancer produces an older population. After 30 years, the proportion over age 65 has increased by 62% (cardiovascular) and 12% (cancer), and in the steady state it has grown by 65% and 13%. Thus, the largest portion of the aging that will ultimately occur is realized in a rather

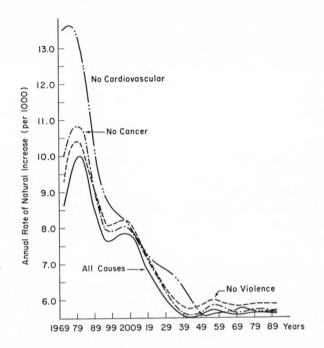

Figure 7.1   Time sequence of United States growth rates under various assumptions regarding mortality with female fertility constant at 1969 level, zero migration.

short length of time. This rapid adjustment is, once again, a consequence of the minor impact of these diseases on numbers of births. Most of the relative growth of the older population occurs at the expense of those 15–64 rather than of those 0–14. The proportion aged 0–14 falls by .006 (cancer) and .024 (cardiovascular) in the steady state, while the proportion 15–64 falls by .009 and .054.

Perhaps more surprising than the aging of the no-cardiovascular and no-cancer populations is the result that the elimination of infectious and parasitic diseases or violence also serves to age the population, although by relatively minor amounts. In the steady state, the proportion over age 65 grows by .002 (infectious) and .003 (violence). During the twentieth century, mortality declines in the United States have produced a slightly younger population (Hermalin, 1966). For the most part, these mortality reductions are attributable to declining death rates from infectious and parasitic diseases, which had a relatively young age incidence at the beginning of this period. But the age-incidence of those infectious deaths which remain (principally, influenza and pneumonia) is sufficiently old that further advances against even this group of causes are clearly unlikely to rejuvenate the population.

Abrupt changes in age composition such as produced by the elimination of cardiovascular disease or cancer could be expected to induce social, economic, and political adjustments. Some of these have been outlined in connection with discussions of the desirability of fertility declines (Coale, 1968; Sauvy, 1969, pp. 303–319). Among the most direct and concrete are implications for retirement systems. Many of these, including the United States federal retirement system administered by the Social Security Administration, operate in large part on a pay-as-you-go basis, so that the taxes on income of current labor force members finance the benefits of those currently retired. Any substantial aging of the population could be expected to place heavy strains on such systems, which in turn may act to decelerate the trend toward earlier retirement. To indicate the extent of adjustment required to reestablish a previous equilibrium, we calculate the age x that satisfies the following formula:

$$\frac{P_{x+}^{(-i)}}{P_{15+}^{(-i)}} = \frac{P_{65+}}{P_{15+}},$$

where $P_{a+}^{(-i)}$ is the number of persons above age a in the population with cause of death i eliminated. Thus x is the age in a population with cause i eliminated that divides the population above age 15 in the same proportion as age 65 divides the population in which all causes are still present, and is close to the new retirement age required to keep constant the ratio of the retired to the economically active. For the male stable population with cancer eliminated, this age is 66.7; for cardiovascular disease, it is 75.0. That is, to keep the same relationship between numbers of adults above and below retirement age, it would be necessary to increase the age at retirement by approximately two years if cancer were eliminated and by approximately ten years if cardiovascular disease were eliminated. To the extent that such changes fail to materialize, the incomes of the retired would be diminished or the contributions of workers to retirement systems would have to increase.

C. Sex Ratio

The sex ratio for all ages combined changes very little as a result of the projected mortality changes. In none of the projection years for any cause of death considered does the ratio of males to females change by as much as 2%. The elimination of violence, a heavily male-specific cause of death, produces the largest effect, raising the sex ratio by 1.9% in the steady state.

The relative invariance of the sex ratio is somewhat misleading because it reflects contrary tendencies. The sex ratio at every age past zero rises from the elimination of each cause of death (except cancer between ages 35 and

60), but in every case the population becomes older, resulting in greater weight for the ages with low sex ratios. But the overall sex ratio is surely less significant in social affairs than the sex ratio at particular ages, and the age-specific changes are quite large, particularly at the older ages. In the steady-state, the ratio of males to females in the age interval 65–69 has grown by 15.0% from the elimination of cardiovascular disease, 4.7% from violence, 2.1% from cancer and 1.1% from infectious and parasitic disease. These changes are a consequence of the greater rates of male than female mortality from the eliminated causes at prior ages. The sex ratio in a closed cohort at a particular age may be expressed as:

$$
\frac{M_a}{F_a} = \frac{M_0 \cdot \exp\left[-\int_0^a \mu^M(t)\,dt \right]}{F_0 \cdot \exp\left[-\int_0^a \mu^F(t)\,dt \right]}
$$

$$
= \text{SRB} \cdot \exp\left\{ -\int_0^a \left[[\mu_1{}^M(t) - \mu_1{}^F(t)] + [\mu_2{}^M(t) - \mu_2{}^F(t)] + \cdots \right.\right.
$$

$$
\left.\left. + [\mu_n{}^M(t) - \mu_n{}^F(t)] \right]\,dt \right\},
$$

where M_a, F_a is the number of males and females at age a, $\mu_i{}^M(t)$, $\mu_i{}^F(t)$ the annual death rates of cohort males and females at exact age t from cause i, and SRB the sex ratio at birth in the cohort. Thus the elimination of cause i increases the sex ratio at age x by the exponential of the *difference* between male and female death rates from that cause cumulated over all prior ages. If the cumulative difference is positive—male rates exceeding female—the sex ratio increases, even if that difference is absolutely or relatively less than the corresponding difference for all other causes combined. Since the male rate exceeds the female for all ages and causes considered (except neoplasms at ages 30–50), the elimination of a cause almost invariably raises the sex ratio at a particular age. For the older ages, in particular, a greater numerical equality of the sexes would be one of the most important benefits of progress against these causes of death, a benefit likely to be reinforced by the physical changes in the older population produced by the reduction of chronic afflictions.

D. Kinship Ties

We examine here the effect of eliminating a cause on two types of kinship relationships: lineal progenitors and spouses. We exclude siblings, offspring,

aunts, uncles, and cousins because the extent of these relationships depends
not only upon the *level* of fertility and mortality in a population but also
on the *distribution* of children ever born among families and the pattern of
childspacing. Calculation becomes exceedingly cumbersome and some of the
required information is not available for the United States population.

The probability that a person of a particular age has a living lineal progenitor of a particular type (father, mother, paternal grandfather, maternal
grandmother, etc.) is a function of the ages of parents at childbearing and of
mortality rates beyond those ages. A change in mortality rates affects both
of these elements, although the change in ages at childbearing tends to be
trivial for the cases discussed here since population age composition is altered
very little prior to the upper age of childbearing. Following Goodman,
Keyfitz, and Pullum (1974), we can estimate the proportion of persons at a
particular age with a living progenitor in the steady state by

$$\text{proportion with living mother for persons aged } a = M_1(a) = \int_\alpha^\beta p(a + x)m(x)e^{-ra}\,dx,$$

$$\text{proportion with living maternal grandmother for persons aged } a = M_2(a) = \int_\alpha^\beta M_1(a + x)p(x)m(x)e^{-ra}\,dx,$$

$$\text{proportion with living maternal/maternal great-grandmother for persons aged } a = M_3(a) = \int_\alpha^\beta M_2(a + x)p(x)m(x)e^{-ra}\,dx,$$

where $p(a + x)$ is the probability of surviving from birth to age $a + x$, $m(x)$
the birth rate of women aged x, r the intrinsic rate of natural increase, and α, β
are the minimum and maximum ages of mother at childbirth. Basic assump-
tions of these formulas are that survivorship is not conditioned by parent-
hood status and the survivorship is uncorrelated between the generations.

Table 7.3 shows the results of applying these formulas to the steady state
populations produced by 1964 fertility rates and the various assumptions
regarding mortality. Calculations referring to male progenitors employ
male fertility rates of the United States population in 1969 (United States
National Center for Health Statistics, 1973), scaled down by the factor,
constant with age, required in order that the male intrinsic growth rate equal
the female. Undoubtedly the most important categories in the table are the
proportions of persons with a living parent. For male progenitors, the
impact of eliminating cardiovascular disease exceeds that for cancer at all
ages and for all relationships. The proportion of persons aged 20 with a
living father increases from .906 to .942 and for persons aged 40 from .564
to .757 when cardiovascular disease is eliminated. For mothers, changes

Table 7.3

Proportion of persons with specified relatives still living in steady state population produced by 1969 United States fertility schedules (female and male) and various mortality schedules

	PROBABILITY THAT RELATIVE IS STILL ALIVE								
EXACT AGE OF PERSON	All Causes	No Cancer	No Cardio-vascular Disease	All Causes	No Cancer	No Cardio-vascular Disease	All Causes	No Cancer	No Cardio-vascular Disease
	Mother			Maternal Grandmother			Maternal Maternal Grandmother		
0	1.000	1.000	1.000	0.919	0.942	0.947	0.499	0.557	0.717
10	0.987	0.990	0.990	0.822	0.866	0.895	0.261	0.305	0.534
20	0.959	0.971	0.970	0.648	0.709	0.808	0.087	0.107	0.313
40	0.782	0.836	0.873	0.153	0.187	0.448	0.001	0.001	0.026
60	0.271	0.326	0.600	0.002	0.002	0.051	0.000	0.000	0.000
80	0.002	0.003	0.108	0.000	0.000	0.000	0.000	0.000	0.000
	Father			Paternal Grandfather			Paternal Paternal Grandfather		
0	1.000	1.000	1.000	0.771	0.803	0.869	0.180	0.219	0.416
10	0.969	0.973	0.978	0.576	0.628	0.756	0.058	0.077	0.231
20	0.906	0.920	0.942	0.343	0.399	0.595	0.011	0.016	0.092
40	0.564	0.623	0.757	0.034	0.047	0.200	0.000	0.000	0.000
60	0.100	0.134	0.376	0.000	0.000	0.008	0.000	0.000	0.000
80	0.000	0.001	0.032	0.000	0.000	0.000	0.000	0.000	0.000

produced by the elimination of cancer are as large as or larger than those produced by eliminating cardiovascular disease for persons up to age 20. Although cardiovascular disease has a much greater impact on female life expectancy, cancer death rates are higher in the age interval 25–50 for women (Preston *et al.*, 1972, p. 720). These latter are the crucial ages for orphanhood. Eliminating cancer would reduce the probability of having a *dead* mother by 23% for children aged 10 and by 29% for persons aged 20. Even though the duration and disagreeableness of cancer tends to inflate estimates of its importance relative to cardiovascular disease, it nonetheless exerts an important influence on maternal survivorship.

Although the survivorship of parents of young children would seem to have the greatest social significance, all forms of survivorship in the table are salient because of the responsibilities which one generation exercises on behalf of another. As the relationship moves through time and age, such responsibility typically shifts from the older onto the younger person. In this respect, it is awesome to contemplate that, if cardiovascular disease were eliminated, approximately 60% of persons aged 60 would still have a living mother, and 38% a living father. A living parent for a 60-year-old means a living grandparent for a 30-year-old and a living great-grandparent

for an infant, prospective developments which are equally apparent in Table
7.3. At age 80, 14% would still have at least one parent living, assuming
independence of fathers' and mothers' survival. The most obvious consequence is that the typical individual will be sandwiched between the two
adjacent generations for a much longer period of life.

Turning to the survivorship of marriages, we encounter immediately the
"problem of the sexes" to which no satisfactory solution has yet been mapped
out. The problem from our perspective is that alterations in mortality will
change age distributions and that age-specific marriage rates for males and
females in the United States, 1969, typically will, when applied to these new
age distributions, produce a different number of males than females marrying. We cannot predict satisfactorily steady state marriage patterns without
a complex and as yet unverified marriage function. We can, however, calculate the probabilities of marital survivorship for couples marrying at
particular ages under the old and new mortality regimes, and progress from
there to a very approximate calculation for the population as a whole.

Table 7.4 displays the survivorship experience of couples married at
specified ages, based upon the cause of death life tables. The factor of divorce
is ignored; the probabilities are most properly interpreted as the chance that
both male and female partners to a marriage will be alive after x years,
regardless of whether they are still married to one another. Because the
survivorship of both partners is by definition a function of joint survival,
the elimination of a cause tends to have a greater impact at a particular
"duration" than in the previous case. This impact increases both with age
at marriage and with duration of marriage, as the scope for mortality inter-
vention widens. Of 1000 marriages which both partners contract at the age of
30, 62 more will survive 30 years if cancer is eliminated, and 120 more will
survive this period if cardiovascular disease is eliminated. In this case, one
is not forced to examine only the very high ages for impressive effects. As in
the preceding table, the elimination of cardiovascular disease has a substantially greater impact than that of cancer except at the shortest durations.
With no deaths from cardiovascular disease, 62.8% of those marriages con-
tracted by people at age 20 would have both partners alive to celebrate their
50th anniversary, and 42.0% their 60th, the latter representing an increase of
more than threefold. It can be seen from Table 7.4 that eliminating cancer
or cardiovascular disease has an effect on marital survivorship roughly
equivalent to both partners marrying at an age five or ten years younger,
respectively.

One almost certain consequence of this improved marital survivorship is
an increase in the proportion of marriages ending in divorce. Such an increase follows on formal grounds alone. In a situation of competing risks,

Table 7.4

Proportion of marriages in which both husband and wife are alive after specified number of years under various mortality regimes and ages at marriage

AGE AT MARRIAGE AND ELIMINATED CAUSES OF DEATH	DURATION OF MARRIAGE (YEARS)					
	10	20	30	40	50	60
Both spouses age 20						
No causes	0.974	0.935	0.850	0.673	0.393	0.121
Cancer	0.977	0.944	0.877	0.754	0.484	0.180
Cardiovascular disease	0.976	0.945	0.892	0.791	0.628	0.420
Both spouses age 25						
No causes	0.970	0.912	0.785	0.552	0.249	0.039
Cancer	0.974	0.927	0.828	0.633	0.333	0.067
Cardiovascular disease	0.974	0.934	0.858	0.728	0.532	0.302
Both spouses age 30						
No causes	0.959	0.872	0.691	0.404	0.124	0.006
Cancer	0.966	0.898	0.753	0.496	0.184	0.012
Cardiovascular disease	0.968	0.913	0.811	0.643	0.426	0.184

when one risk function declines, the proportion of a cohort ultimately succumbing to the other risk must increase if that risk function itself is unchanged. There is also a possibility that reduced mortality would increase the divorce risk function itself (divorce rate as a function of marital duration), since a forward-looking spouse would anticipate unpleasant circumstances lasting longer if left to the natural course of events.

Despite reducing proportions widowed at each age, the elimination of these diseases scarcely changes the proportion for all ages combined. The age-specific reduction is largely offset by the older age structure of the population. Put another way, a smaller proportion becomes widowed at each age but such widows as are produced live longer, on average. The effect can be illustrated by assuming that all persons of both sexes marry at age 25, calculating the proportions widowed at each subsequent age, and weighting these proportions by the population's age distribution. Since widowhood is virtually absent between ages 20 and 25, the results also give an accurate indication of proportions widowed if all marry at 20, or at any combination of ages between 20 and 25. In formal terms, we are computing in the steady state

$$W^F = \frac{\int_{25}^{\infty} e^{-ra} P^F(a)[1 - P_{25}^M(a)]\, da}{\int_{0}^{\infty} e^{-ra} P^F(a)\, da} = C_{25+}^F - \frac{\int_{25}^{\infty} e^{-ra} P^F(a) P_{25}^M(a)\, da}{\int_{0}^{\infty} e^{-ra} P^F(a)\, da},$$

where W^F is the proportion of the female population ever-widowed, $P^F(a)$ the probability of a female surviving from birth to age a, $P^M_{25}(a)$ the probability of a male aged 25 surviving to age a, r the intrinsic growth rate, and C^F_{25+} the proportion of female population that is age 25 and over. Mortality change works through both terms in this equation. The first term represents the age-structural effect; without cardiovascular disease, the proportion of the population over age 25 rises, causing the proportion widowed to increase. The second term represents marital survival and tends to rise when mortality declines since the numerator includes a joint survival term and the denominator only female survival.

These two terms tend largely to offset one another and neither is consistently dominant. In the steady state population with all causes of death present, the ever-widowed as a proportion of the total population is .195 for females and .101 for males. The impact of eliminating various causes on these figures is relatively minor, as can be seen in Table 7.5. For females, the largest reduction in the prevalence of widowhood results from removing violence as a cause of death, since this cause is heavily male-specific and its removal has little effect on the female age distribution. Many more husbands are "saved" when cardiovascular disease is eliminated, but such widows as there are tend to live much longer, with relatively little net effect on the prevalence of widowhood. In fact, the elimination of cardiovascular disease for both sexes *raises* the proportion of males who are widowed; the age-structural term dominates. In general, we reach the somewhat surprising conclusion that eliminating these diseases would have minor effects on the prevalence of widowhood, and in one case would even serve to raise it.

E. Effect on Per Capita Income

Attempts to assess the economic value of eliminating deaths from a disease have a long history. Certainly the most important component of the calcula-

Table 7.5

Proportions ever widowed in steady state populations with fertility rates of United States 1969 and various mortality regimes

CAUSE OF DEATH ELIMINATED FOR BOTH SEXES SIMULTANEOUSLY	PROPORTION EVER-WIDOWED	
	Females	Males
No cause	0.195	0.101
Cancer	0.184	0.089
Cardiovascular disease	0.179	0.105
Infectious and parasitic		
diseases	0.192	0.100
Violence	0.176	0.097

tion is the value that people place on their own lives or on those of close relatives, but this element is usually neglected because of its attendant measurement problems. Instead, analysis has focused on estimating the future productive contribution of the persons hypothetically "saved" (see Cohen, 1972 for a review of various "production" approaches). But this approach generally ignores the fact that more persons are alive to share the fruits of production and that per capita production may actually fall. If it were applied to the analysis of births, the results would be vigorously pro-natalist, despite the nearly unanimous opinion of economists (using more sophisticated models) that higher fertility reduces economic well-being. The "production" approach to mortality reduction also neglects the fact that some of those "saved" will have offspring who will also become producers and consumers.

These omissions can be corrected by population projection in which persons of different ages at a particular time are weighted by an age schedule of production or earnings. A complete account would consider such matters as the impact of the new members on savings and the degree of diminishing returns to labor (Barlow, 1968), but the approach here will assume that added members produce at the average rate recorded for members of the population at the same age.

We are primarily interested in the ratio

$$K^{(-i)} = \frac{\sum_{x=1}^{2} \int_{0}^{\infty} c^{(-i)}(a, x) Y(a, x) \, da}{\sum_{x=1}^{2} \int_{0}^{\infty} c(a, x) Y(a, x) \, da},$$

where $c(a, x)$, $c^{(-i)}(a, x)$ is the proportion age a, sex x, in projected population with all causes present and with cause i eliminated, and $Y(a, x)$ is the earnings of persons aged a, sex x, in dollars. Thus $K^{(-i)}$ is the ratio of per capita income in the population with cause i eliminated to that with all causes present. The age schedule of earnings is the mean 1969 earnings for males and females, as recorded in the 1970 Census.[2] Values of $K^{(-i)}$ are shown in Table 7.6 at various points during the projection process.

The first-order effect of eliminating cancer, infectious and parasitic diseases, or violence is to change per capita income at future dates by no more than 1%. Eliminating violence has a small positive effect (in large part

---

[2] Earnings are clearly more appropriate to use than income, which includes a substantial amount of transfer payments, particularly among the elderly. Mean earnings figures by age for the population with earnings are derived from United States Bureau of Census, 1973, Tables 5, 6, 7, and 11. Nonearners are inferred from the difference between the total population of an age interval and the number of earners of that age.

Table 7.6

Index numbers of per capita earnings in future populations with particular causes of
death eliminated

YEAR	No CAUSES	CANCER	CARDIO-VASCULAR DISEASE	INFECTIOUS AND PARASITIC DISEASES	VIOLENCE
1979	1,000	998	984	998	1,003
1999	1,000	993	959	998	1,009
2049	1,000	991	946	998	1,010
Steady state	1,000	991	947	998	1,010

because of a relative increase in numbers of males), and a small negative
effect occurs in the other two instances. Only when cardiovascular disease
is eliminated does per capita income change by more than 1%; in this case
it declines by 5.3% in the steady state. Even this may seem a surprisingly
small change in view of the massive changes in age distribution produced.
But the higher proportion in the retirement ages is largely offset in its effects
by the higher ratio of males to females in the working ages and by an increase
in the proportion of the population in the later, highly productive working
ages. Moreover, the effects are smaller in the near term, which receives
greatest weight in policy considerations. After 10 years per capita income is
only 1.6% lower in the no-cardiovascular projection. Differences of 2% or
even 5% can be compensated for by one year of exceptional economic growth.
In general, the conclusion must be that disease elimination has quite minor
first-order effects on per capita income, effects that are surely trivial in comparison to the value that people place on their own lives.

Male-Dominant Projections. Tests were performed on the sensitivity of
the results with respect to two underlying assumptions: female dominance
in fertility, and the constancy of fertility. A second set of projections were
prepared in which *male* fertility was constant at its 1969 level. Both male and
female births are derived by applying these male fertility rates to the male
age distribution and assuming a constant sex ratio of births. Whether the
male- or female-dominant projections yield more reliable predictions depends on the resolution of the problem of the sexes which was alluded to
earlier. If births are more sensitive to the number of males in the population
than to the number of females, the male-dominant projections provide the
more appropriate predictions.

Dominance does make a large difference for future population size, as
indicated in Table 7.7, but a rather small difference for the consequences of
eliminating a particular cause of death. The elimination of a cause produces

Table 7.7

Parameters of the projected United States population under various assumptions regarding mortality, with male fertility constant at 1969 levels

	All causes	No cancer	No cardio-vascular	No infectious and parasitic	No violence
1979					
Population size (millions)	223.20	225.94	233.38	224.00	224.82
Proportion under age 15	.260	.257	.249	.260	.260
Proportion 65 +	.101	.107	.132	.103	.102
Sex ratio (M/F)	.962	.963	.966	.962	.967
Sex ratio at 65 +	.699	.721	.755	.706	.705
Growth rate[a]	.0094	.0114	.0140	.0107	.0112
Birth rate[a]	.0193	.0204	.0197	.0205	.0207
Death rate[a]	.0100	.0090	.0057	.0098	.0095
1999					
Population size (millions)	273.54	279.56	297.00	275.55	279.32
Proportion under age 15	.271	.266	.251	.271	.272
Proportion 65 +	.097	.109	.158	.099	.098
Sex ratio (M/F)	.971	.970	.975	.972	.983
Sex ratio at 65 +	.651	.681	.762	.662	.667
Growth rate[a]	.0091	.0093	.0099	.0093	.0098
Birth rate[a]	.0192	.0188	.0178	.0191	.0192
Death rate[a]	.0101	.0095	.0078	.0098	.0095
2049					
Population size (millions)	428.87	441.98	474.42	436.06	453.69
Proportion under age 15	.266	.260	.242	.265	.266
Proportion 65 +	.105	.118	.181	.107	.106
Sex ratio (M/F)	.978	.977	.982	.980	.996
Sex ratio at 65 +	.696	.725	.815	.709	.732
Growth rate[a]	.0086	.0087	.0086	.0088	.0094
Birth rate[a]	.0193	.0189	.0177	.0193	.0195
Death rate[a]	.0107	.0102	.0091	.0105	.0101
Steady state					
Population size (millions)	—	—	—	—	—
Proportion under age 15	.264	.259	.242	.265	.265
Proportion 65 +	.106	.120	.175	.108	.107
Sex ratio (M/F)	.977	.977	.988	.979	.995
Sex ratio at 65 +	.695	.725	.820	.707	.731
Growth rate[a]	.00864	.00876	.00873	.00883	.00938
Birth rate[a]	.01936	.01897	.01769	.01930	.01947
Death rate[a]	.01072	.01021	.00896	.01047	.01009

[a] Ten year average centered on date.

a somewhat larger increment in intrinsic growth rates in the male-dominant projections. This larger increment is a consequence of two factors. In terms of the previous formula for the change in intrinsic growth rates, μ_x^i is somewhat higher for males than for females, and A_B is also somewhat higher (childbearing is older). Since μ_x^i tends to rise with age, an older A_B produces a larger increment to intrinsic growth rates. If men were aged 60 at the birth of their children and women aged 30, for example, the growth consequences of eliminating cardiovascular disease would be radically different in the two set of projections. In reality the differences are rather minor. The order of causes with respect to their influence on the intrinsic growth rate is identical in the two sets of projections. Male dominance has the principal effect of reinforcing the incremental growth caused by eliminating violence, a cause that is heavily male-specific and that is quite active prior to the end of the fertile period. After 80 years the population without violence is 5.8% larger than the population with all causes present, compared to 3.2% larger in the female-dominant projections. In the other cases the effect on proportionate growth after 80 years is nearly identical in the two sets of projections. Even though the increment to the intrinsic growth rate is larger in every instance for the male dominant projections, the consequence is effectively obscured through the first 80 years (except for violence) by the higher fertility and younger age structure pertaining to the male dominant projections; in a younger population, the older ages receive less weight in the overall outcome. The population without violence is larger than that without cardiovascular disease after 158 years and beyond.

Because the elimination of a cause has a slightly larger impact on the intrinsic growth rate in the male-dominant projection, the tendency for the population to grow older is slightly attenuated. Again, this result is really noteworthy only for violence, whose elimination actually increases the proportion of the population under age 15 by a tiny amount and produces a slightly higher birth rate. Other changes in age composition induced by mortality reductions are very much the same as in the female-dominant case, and changes in sex ratios and widowhood proportions are nearly identical in the two sets of projections. We conclude that the original results are not sensitive to the assumption of female dominance, with the exception of certain calculations relating to violence. Most notably, the intrinsic growth rate increases by .74/1000 when violence is eliminated in the male dominant projection, compared to an increase of .24/1000 when females are dominant. This substantial difference is further indication of the need for a practicable solution to the problem of the sexes.

Declining Fertility Projections. A third set of projections were prepared to demonstrate how declining mortality interacts with declining fertility in its demographic effects. These projections utilize the United States Census

Table 7.8

Parameters of projected United States population under various assumptions regarding mortality, with female fertility following the Census Bureau's E-schedule after 1969

	All causes	No cancer	No cardio-vascular	No infectious and parasitic	No violence
1979					
Population size (millions)	214.83	217.55	224.97	215.60	216.23
Proportion under age 15	.231	.228	.221	.231	.230
Proportion 65+	.105	.111	.137	.107	.106
Sex ratio (M/F)	.959	.960	.963	.960	.964
Sex ratio at 65+	.699	.721	.755	.706	.705
Growth rate[a]	.0063	.0073	.0100	.0066	.0069
Birth rate[a]	.0167	.0165	.0159	.0167	.0167
Death rate[a]	.0104	.0092	.0059	.0101	.0097
1999					
Population size (millions)	239.78	245.62	263.01	241.61	243.79
Proportion under age 15	.224	.219	.205	.224	.222
Proportion 65+	.111	.124	.178	.113	.112
Sex ratio (M/F)	.961	.960	.967	.962	.974
Sex ratio at 65+	.651	.681	.762	.663	.667
Growth rate[a]	.0042	.0045	.0054	.0043	.0046
Birth rate[a]	.0154	.0150	.0140	.0153	.0152
Death rate[a]	.0112	.0106	.0086	.0110	.0106
2049					
Population size (millions)	256.36	265.91	296.11	260.93	264.91
Proportion under age 15	.205	.199	.179	.205	.203
Proportion 65+	.146	.164	.246	.149	.149
Sex ratio (M/F)	.956	.956	.965	.958	.976
Sex ratio at 65+	.686	.716	.803	.698	.721
Growth rate[a]	−.0004	−.0004	−.0003	−.0002	−.0001
Birth rate[a]	.0141	.0136	.0122	.0140	.0139
Death rate[a]	.0144	.0140	.0125	.0142	.0140
Steady state					
Population size (millions)	—	—	—	—	—
Proportion under age 15	.205	.199	.178	.204	.202
Proportion 65+	.151	.170	.249	.154	.155
Sex ratio (M/F)	.955	.955	.966	.957	.974
Sex ratio at 65+	.688	.718	.810	.700	.723
Growth rate[a]	−.00050	−.00042	−.00045	−.00032	−.00026
Birth rate[a]	.01399	.01357	.01218	.01392	.01380
Death rate[a]	.01449	.01399	.01263	.01424	.01406

[a]Ten-year average centered on date.

Bureau's E-schedule of fertility starting in 1974 (United States Bureau of Census, 1972).[3] In brief, this schedule assumes that cohorts of women who had not entered the childbearing period in 1969 would experience replacement level fertility, an average of 2.11 births per woman, and that women then in the childbearing years will progress smoothly toward the period fertility rates implied by the replacement-level schedule. Table 7.8 presents the results.

The most important consequence of incorporating fertility declines is to increase the factor by which the population grows when various causes are eliminated. Whereas the removal of cardiovascular disease produced an 11.8% larger population after 80 years of constant fertility, it is 15.5% larger with declining fertility. The corresponding figures for cancer are 3.1% in the constant fertility population and 3.7% with declining fertility, for infectious and parasitic 1.7% and 1.8%, and for violence, 3.2% and 3.3%. The reason for these increases in the amount of growth is that declining fertility gives greater weight to developments at the older ages, where all of these causes of death are most active. Calculations for cardiovascular disease, with the oldest age incidence of all, are most affected by declining fertility. However, changes in the intrinsic growth rates are, for all practical purposes, identical to those in the constant fertility population. The formal reason for this is obvious from the earlier expression for the change in the intrinsic growth rate, which depends only on the average value of μ_x^i in an interval whose length is subject to little variation.

Declining fertility produces an older population and reinforces the age-structural effects of eliminating a cause of death. After 30 years in the no-cardiovascular projection, there are almost as many people over age 65 as under age 15. When the steady state is achieved, the number above 65 exceeds that under 15 by some 40%. Simultaneous achievement of replacement level fertility and major progress against the diseases associated with aging would obviously have revolutionary consequences for the nature of the "dependency burden." It has been demonstrated repeatedly that the principal cause of population aging has been declining fertility, but this is not a necessary result and may not apply to future developments. With all causes present, for example, declining fertility increases the proportion over 65 from .120 to .151; but with *no* declines in fertility, the elimination of cardiovascular disease increases that proportion from .120 to .198.

Summary

This chapter has considered separately the consequences for the future United States population of eliminating deaths from neoplasms, cardio-

[3] For the period 1969–1974, preliminary fertility rates for 1972 were used.

vascular disease, all infectious and parasitic diseases, and violence. In a constant-fertility, female-dominant projection, none of these causes has a substantial effect on the intrinsic population growth rate. But major additions to population size would result from elimination of cardiovascular disease and cancer, as a consequence of improved survivorship among persons in the postreproductive ages. Most of the relative growth in these cases occurs within 30 years after disease eradication. After several centuries, well beyond the planning horizon, the population without violent death exceeds in size each of those without the other causes.

The population "ages" in each of the four cases. After 30 years, the proportion of the total population which is over age 65 has grown by 62% as a result of the elimination of cardiovascular disease and by 12% in the case of neoplasms. In order to retain the previous numerical relationship between the number of retired and of economically active males, age at retirement would eventually have to increase by approximately ten years and two years when these diseases are eliminated. The sex ratio (M/F) for all ages combined undergoes little change when a cause is eliminated, but it almost invariably increases at a particular age, and these changes can be quite large at the higher ages.

The probability of having a living mother or father for a person under 20 changes by less than 2% when cancer or cardiovascular disease is eliminated. Cancer has a bigger impact on orphanhood by death of mothers, cardiovascular disease on orphanhood by death of fathers. As age progresses, the elimination of a cause has a progressively larger impact on the probability of having a living parent. Without cardiovascular disease, 10.8% of survivors to age 80 would still have a living mother (versus 0.2% when all causes are present). Of 1000 marriages which both partners contract at age 30, 62 more will survive the risk of mortality for 30 years if cancer is eliminated and 120 more will survive this period if none die from cardiovascular disease. However, the tendency for the prevalence of widowhood to decline in the population as a whole is largely or completely offset by the longer survivorship of such widows as are produced.

The elimination of these diseases affects future per capita income by no more than 1% except in the case of cardiovascular disease, where income declines by some 5.3% in the steady state. The changes are undoubtedly inconsequential in comparison to the value that people place on their own lives or on those of close relatives and can be safely neglected for planning purposes.

The procedures used in the basic projections have probably produced underestimates of the effects of cause-of-death elimination on population size. Fertility has already declined substantially from its 1969 levels, and declining fertility weights more heavily developments at older ages. Using the Census Bureau's replacement-level fertility schedule, the population without cardiovascular disease is 15.5% larger after 80 years than the population with all causes present, instead of 11.8% larger, as in the projections with constant fertility. The effect of eliminating other causes also increases, but in smaller proportion. If reproduction is assumed to be male dominant rather than female dominant, the effect of elimination on size and growth is again enhanced, because of higher male mortality and older male fertility. The changes are particularly important for violence, whose elimination increases the population after 80 years by 5.8% rather than by 3.2%. The scope for additions to population size from further reductions in mortality is clearly much larger than indicated by comparison of female intrinsic growth rates.

References

Adlakha, A., 1972. Model life tables: An empirical test of their applicability to less developed countries. *Demography, 9*(4), 589–602.

Adelman, I., 1963. An econometric analysis of population growth. *American Economic Review, 53*, 314–39.

Arriaga, E. E. and K. Davis, 1969. The pattern of mortality change in Latin America. *Demography, 6*, 223–42.

Balfour, M. C., R. F. Evans, F. W. Notestein, and I. B. Taeuber, 1950. *Public Health and Demography in the Far East.* New York: Rockefeller Foundation.

Barlow, R., 1968. *The Economic Effects of Malaria Eradication.* Economic Research Series, 15. University of Michigan School of Public Health, Ann Arbor.

Belloc, N. B., 1973. Relationship of health practices and mortality. *Preventive Medicine, 2,* 67–81.

Blalock, H. M., 1960. *Social Statistics.* New York: McGraw-Hill.

Bongaarts, J. P., 1973. A review of the population sector in *The Limits to Growth. Studies in Family Planning, 4,* 327–34.

Bonte, J., and A. Kühner, 1971. Recent levels, characteristics and trends of mortality in Africa. United Nations Economic and Social Council; Economic Commission for Africa. African Population Conference, Accra, Ghana, December 9–18, 1971.

Brass, W. and A. J. Coale, 1968. Methods of analysis and estimation. In W. Brass, *et al.,* The *Demography of Tropical Africa.* Princeton University Press.

Buck, A., T. T. Sasaki, and R. I. Anderson, 1958. *Health and Disease in Four Peruvian Villages.* Baltimore: Johns Hopkins Press.

Cady, L. D., M. M. Gertler, L. Gottsch, and M. Woodbury, 1961. The factor structure of variables concerned with coronary artery disease. *Behavioral Science, 6*(1), 37–41.

Campbell, M., 1963. Death rates from diseases of the heart: 1876 to 1959. *British Medical Journal,* 528–35 (August 31).

Carrier, N., and J. Hobcraft, 1971. *Demographic Estimation for Developing Societies.* Population Investigation Committee, London School of Economics.

Case, R. A. M., 1956. Cohort analysis of cancer mortality in England and Wales, 1911–1954, by site and sex., *British Journal of Preventive and Social Medicine, 10,* 172–199.

Chiang, C. L., 1968. *Introduction to Stochastic Processes in Biostatistics.* New York: Wiley.

Cipolla, C. M., 1965. Four centuries of Italian demographic development. C. V. Glass and D. E. C. Eversley (Eds.), *Population in History*, 570–587. London: Edward Arnold.

Coale, A. J., 1959. Increases in expectation of life and population growth. *Proceedings, Intertional Population Conference, Vienna, 1959*.

Coale, A. J., 1968. Should the United States start a campaign for fewer births? *Population Index, 34*, 467–74.

Coale, A. J., and P. Demeny, 1966. *Regional Model Life Tables and Stable Populations*. Princeton University Press.

Coale, A. J., and Hoover, E. (1958). *Population Growth and Economic Development in Low Income Countries*. Princeton: Princeton University Press.

Cohen, J. E., 1972. *Livelihood Benefits of Small Improvements in the Life Table*. Unpublished manuscript, Harvard University Department of Biology.

Corsa, L. and D. Oakley, 1971. Consequences of population growth for health services in less developed countries—An initial appraisal. *Rapid Population Growth: Consequences and Policy Implications*. National Academy of Sciences. Baltimore: Johns Hopkins Press.

Cowgill, U. M., and G. E. Hutchinson, 1963. Sex-ratio in childhood and the depopulation of the Peten, Guatemala. *Human Biology, 35*(1), 90–103.

Daw, R. H., 1954. Some statistical aspects of mortality from degenerative heart disease. *Journal of the Institute of Actuaries, 8* (Part I), No. 354, 69–100.

Davis, K., 1956. The amazing decline of mortality in underdeveloped areas. *American Economic Review, 46*, 305–18.

Davis, K., 1969. *World Urbanization, 1950–70. Vol. I: Basic Data for Cities, Countries, and Regions*, Population Monograph No. 4. Institute of International Studies, University of California, Berkeley.

Demeny, P., 1965. Investment allocation and population growth. *Demography, 2*, 203–32.

Drake, M., 1969. *Population and Society in Norway, 1735–1865*. Cambridge: Cambridge University Press.

Dublin, L. I., 1919. *Mortality Statistics of Insured Wage-Earners and Their Families*. New York: Metropolitan Life Insurance Company.

Dublin, L. I., A. J. Lotka, and M. Spiegelman, 1949. *Length of Life* (Revised ed.). New York: Ronald Press.

El Badry, M. A., 1969. Higher female than male mortality in some countries of South Asia: A digest. *Journal of the American Statistical Association, 64*, 1234–44.

Enke, S., and R. A. Brown, 1972. Economic worth of preventing death at different ages in developing countries. *Journal of Biosocial Science, 4*, 299–306.

Enterline, P. E., 1961. Causes of death responsible for recent increases in sex mortality differentials in the United States. *Milbank Memorial Fund Quarterly, 34*(2), 312–25.

Epstein, F. H., 1965. The epidemiology of coronary heart disease. *Journal of Chronic Diseases, 18*, 735–74.

Espenshade, T., 1973. *The Cost of Children in the Urban United States*, Population Monograph No. 14. Institute of International Studies, University of California, Berkeley.

Frederiksen, H., 1961. Determinants and consequences of mortality trends in Ceylon. *Public Health Reports, 76*, 659–63.

Frederiksen, H., 1966a. Determinants and consequences of mortality and fertility trends. *Public Health Reports, 81*, 715–27.

Frederiksen, H., 1966b. Dynamic equilibrium of economic and demographic transition. *Economic Development and Cultural Change, 14*, 316–22.

Fuchs, V. J., 1966. The contribution of health services to the American economy. *Milbank Memorial Fund Quarterly, Health Services Research 44*(4), (Part 2), 65–103.

Gabriel, K. R., and I. Ronen, 1958. Estimates of mortality from infant mortality rates. *Population Studies, 12,* 164–69.

Goodman, Leo A., N. Keyfitz, and T. W. Pullum, 1974. Family formation and the frequency of various kinship relations. *Theoretical Population Biology,* 5(1), 1–27.

Gordon, J. E., M. Béhar, and N. S. Scrimshaw. 1964. Acute diarrheal disease in less developed countries: 1. An Epidemiological Basis for Control. *Bulletin of the World Health Organization, 31,* 1–8.

Gordon, J. E., M. A. Guzmán, W. Ascoli, and N. S. Scrimshaw, 1964. Acute diarrheal disease in less developed countries: 2. Patterns of epidemiological behavior in rural Guatamalan villages. *Bulletin of the World Health Organization, 31,* 9–20.

Gordon, J. E., M. Béhar, and N. S. Scrimshaw, 1964. Acute diarrheal disease in less developed countries: 3. Methods for prevention and control. *Bulletin of the World Health Organization, 31,* 21–28.

Gordon, J. E., J. B. Wyon, and W. Ascoli, 1967. The second year death rate in less developed countries. *American Journal of Medical Science, 254*(3), 357–80.

Hagen, E. E., 1962. *On the Theory of Social Change.* Homewood, Illinois: Dorsey Press.

Heer, D. M., 1968. *Readings on Population.* Englewood Cliffs, New Jersey: Prentice-Hall.

Hermalin, A., 1966. The effect of changes in mortality rates on population growth and age distribution in the United States. *Milbank Memorial Fund Quarterly, 44,* 451–69.

Inkeles, A., 1966. The modernization of Man. In M. Weiner (Ed.), *Modernization: The Dynamics of Growth,* pp. 138–150. New York: Basic Books.

International Labour Office, 1973. *Economic-Demographic Modelling Activities of the World Employment Programme.* Geneva. (Mimeographed).

Kennedy, R. E., 1973. *The Irish: Emigration, Marriage, and Fertility.* University of California Press, Berkeley.

Keyfitz, N., and W. Flieger, 1968. *World Population: An Analysis of Vital Data.* University of Chicago, Chicago.

Keyfitz, N., and W. Flieger, 1971. *Population: Facts and Methods of Demography.* W. H. Freeman, San Francisco.

Keys, A., 1950. *The Biology of Human Starvation,* Vol. I. University of Minnesota, Minneapolis.

Keys, A., M. J. Karnoven, and F. Fidanza, 1958. Serum cholesterol studies in Finland. *Lancet, 2,* 175–78.

Kitagawa, E. M., and P. M. Hauser, 1973. *Differential Mortality in the United States: A Study in Socioeconomic Epidemiology.* Harvard University Press, Cambridge, Mass.

Kuznets, S., 1956. Quantitative aspects of the economic growth of Nations. I. Levels and variability of rates of growth. *Economic Development and Cultural Change, V,* 5–94.

Kuznets, S., 1963. Quantitative aspects of the economic growth of nations. *Economic Development and Cultural Change, XI.*

Ledermann, S., 1969. *Nouvelles Tables—Types de mortalité.* Travaux et Documents, Book No. 53. Paris: Institut National d'Etudes Démographiques.

Leibenstein. H., 1954. *A Theory of Economic-Demographic Development.* Princeton University Press. Princeton.

Lopez, A., 1961. *Problems in Stable Population Theory.* Office of Population Research, Princeton University, Princeton.

Lundin, F. E., C. C. Erickson, and D. H. Sprunt, 1964. *Socioeconomic Distribution of Cervical Cancer: In Relation to Early Marriage and Pregnancy,* Public Health Monograph 73, Public Health Service. Washington, D.C.: Government Printing Office.

Mandle, J. R., 1970. The decline of mortality in British Guiana, 1911–1960. *Demography, 7,* 301–16.

Martin, W. J., 1951. A comparison of the trends of male and female mortality. *Journal of the Royal Statistical Society, 114*(3), 287–298.

Martin, W. J., 1956. A study of sex, age, and regional differences in the advantage of rural over urban mortality. *British Journal of Preventive and Social Medicine, 10,* 88–91.

McDermott, W., 1966. Modern medicine and the demographic-disease pattern of overly traditional societies: A technological misfit. *Journal of Medical Education, 41*(9), 138–62.

McFarland, D. D., 1969. On the theory of stable populations: A new and elementary proof of the theorems under weaker assumptions. *Demography, 6,* 301–322.

McKeown, T., 1965. Medicine and world population. In M. C. Sheps and J. C. Ridley (Eds.). *Public Health and Population Change.* University of Pittsburgh, Pittsburgh.

McKeown, T., and R. G. Record, 1962. Reasons for the decline of mortality in England and Wales during the 19th century. *Population Studies, 16,* 94–122.

Moore, H. A., E. du la Cruz, and O. Vergas-Mendez, 1965a. Diarrheal disease studies in Costa Rica: Morbidity and mortality from diarrhea. *American Journal of Epidemiology, 82*(2), 143–61.

Moore, H. A., E. du la Cruz, and O. Vergas-Mendez, 1965b. Diarrheal disease studies in Costa Rica: The influence of sanitation upon the prevalence of intestinal infection and diarrheal disease. *American Journal of Epidemiology, 82*(2), 162–84.

Moore, H. A., E. du la Cruz, and O. Vergas-Mendez, 1966a. Diarrheal disease studies in Costa Rica: Plan and methods of investigation. *American Journal of Public Health, 56*(2), 276–86.

Moore, H. A., E. du la Cruz, O. Vergas-Mendez, and F. I. Pérez, 1966b. Diarrheal disease studies in Costa Rica: The prevalence of certain enteric organisms and their relationship to diarrhea. *American Journal of Public Health, 56*(3), 442–51.

Moriyama, I. M., and L. Guralnick, 1956. Occupational and social class differences in mortality. *Trends and Differentials in Mortality,* 61–73. New York: Milbank Memorial Fund.

Moriyama, I. M., T. D. Woolsey, and J. Stamler, 1958. Observations on possible factors responsible for the sex and race trends in cardiovascular-renal mortality in the United States. *Journal of Chronic Diseases, 7*(5), 401–12.

Moriyama, I. M., D. E. Krueger and J. Stamler, 1971. *Cardiovascular Diseases in the United States.* Cambridge, Massachusetts: Harvard University Press.

Mourant, A. E., 1954. *The Distribution of the Human Blood Groups.* Oxford: Blackwell Scientific Publications.

Naeye, R. L., L. S. Burt, D. L. Wright, W. M. Blanc, and D. Tatter, 1971. Neonatal mortality, the male disadvantage. *Pediatrics, 48*(6), 902–06.

Nelson, R. R., 1956. A theory of the low level equilibrium trap in underdeveloped economies. *American Economic Review, XLVI,* 894–908.

Newman, P., 1965. *Malaria Eradication and Population Growth: With Special Reference to Ceylon and British Guiana,* Research Series No. 10. Ann Arbor, Michigan: Bureau of Public Health Economics, School of Public Health, University of Michigan.

Newman, P., 1970. Malaria control and population growth. *Journal of Development Studies,* 133–58.

Nicholson, J. L., 1949. Variations in working class family expenditure. *Journal of the Royal Statistical Society,* Series A, *112* (Part IV), 359–411.

Omran, A. R., 1971. The epidemiologic transition. *Milbank Memorial Fund Quarterly, XLIX* (Part I), 509–38.

Pascua, M., 1952. Evolution of mortality in Europe during the twentieth century. *Epidemiological and Vital Statistics Report* (World Health Organization), Vol. 5.

Petersen, W., 1967. Taiwan's population problem. In S. Chandrasekhar (Ed.), *Asia's Population Problem.* London: Allen and Unwin.

Preston, S. H., 1970. *Older Male Mortality and Cigarette Smoking: A Demographic Analysis*, (Population Monograph #7). Institute of International Studies, University of California, Berkeley.

Preston, S. H., N. Keyfitz and R. Schoen, 1972. *Causes of Death: Life Tables for National Populations*. New York: Seminar Press.

Preston, S. H., 1974. Effect of mortality change on stable population parameters. *Demography*, *11*(1), 119–30.

Preston, S. H., and V. E. Nelson, 1974. Structure and change in causes of death: An international summary. *Population Studies, 28*(1), 19–51.

Preston, S. H., 1972. Influence of cause of death structure on age patterns of mortality. In T. N. E. Greville (Ed.), *Population Dynamics*, pp. 201–50. New York: Academic Press.

Puffer, R. R., and G. W. Griffith, 1967. *Patterns of Urban Mortality*, Scientific Publication No. 151. Washington, D.C.: Pan American Health Organization.

Puffer, R. R., and C. V. Serrano, 1973. *Patterns of Mortality in Childhood*, Scientific Publication No. 262. Washington, D.C.: Pan American Health Organization.

Razzell, P. E., 1965. Population change in eighteenth century England: A re-appraisal. *Economic History Review, 18*, 312–32. Reprinted in Michael Drake (Ed.), *Population in Industrialization*. London: Methuen, 1969.

Retherford, R. D., 1975. *The Changing Sex Differential in Mortality*. Studies in Population and Urban Demography No. 1. Westport, Connecticut: Greenwood Press.

Sacher, G. A., 1960. The dimensionality of the life span. In Bernard L. Strehler (Ed.), *The Biology of Ageing: A Symposium*. American Institute of Biological Sciences.

Sauer, H. I., 1962. Epidemiology of cardiovascular mortality—geographic and ethnic. *American Journal of Public Health, 52*(1), 94–105.

Sauvy, A., 1969. *General Theory of Population*. New York: Basic Books.

Shamberger, R. J., S. Tytko, and C. E. Willis, 1972. Antioxidants in cereals and in food preservatives and declining gastric cancer mortality. *Cleveland Clinic Quarterly, 39*(2), 119–24.

Shettles, L. B., 1958. Biological sex differences with special reference to disease, resistance, and longevity. *Journal of Obstetrics and Gynecology of the British Empire, 65*(2), 288–95.

Shils, M. E., 1968. Nutrition in neoplastic diseases. In M. Wohl and R. Goodhart (Eds.), *Modern Nutrition in Health and Disease* (4th ed). Philadelphia: Lea and Febiger.

Shrewsbury, J. F. D., 1970. *A History of Bubonic Plague in the British Isles*. Cambridge: Cambridge University Press.

Singh, S., J. E. Gordon, and J. B. Wyon, 1962. Medical care in fatal illness of a rural Punjab population: Some social biological, and cultural factors and their implications. *Indian Journal of Medical Research, 50*(6), 865–80.

Sloan, F., 1971. *Survival of Progeny in Developing Countries: An Analysis of Evidence from Costa Rica, Mexico, East Pakistan, and Puerto Rico*. Report prepared for the Agency for International Development. Santa Monica, California: Rand Corporation.

Springett, V. H., 1960. A comparative study of tuberculosis mortality rates. *Journal of Hygiene, 48*(3), 361–95.

Stocks, P., 1969. Heart disease mortality in cities of Latin America and in cities and regions of England and Wales. *Bulletin of the World Health Organization, 40*, 409–23.

Stolnitz, G., 1955. A century of international mortality trends: I. *Population Studies, 9*, 24–55.

Stolnitz, G., 1956. A century of international mortality trends: II. *Population Studies, 10*(1), 17–42.

Stolnitz, G., 1965. Recent mortality trends in Latin America, Asia, and Africa. *Population Studies*, 117–38.

length

Sullivan, J. M., 1973. The influence of cause-specific mortality conditions at the age pattern of mortality with special reference to Taiwan. *Population Studies, 27*(1), 135–58.

Syme, S. L., M. M. Hyman, and P. E. Enterline, 1965. Cultural mobility and the occurrence of coronary heart disease. *Journal of Health and Human Behavior, 6,* 178–89.

Taeuber, I. B., 1958. *The Population of Japan.* Princeton, New Jersey: Princeton University Press.

Taylor, C. E., and M.-F. Hall, 1967. Health, population, and economic development. *Science, 157*(3789), 651–57.

Todd, G. F., 1963. *Tobacco Consumption in Various Countries.* Research Paper No. 6. London: Tobacco Research Council.

Tromp, S. W., 1963. *Medical Biometerology.* New York: Elsevier.

United Nations, Department of Social Affairs, Population Branch, 1955. *Age and Sex Patterns of Mortality,* Population Studies No. 22. New York.

United Nations, Department of Social and Economic Affairs, Population Branch, 1961. *Report on the World Social Situation.* New York.

United Nations, Department of Social and Economic Affairs, Population Branch, 1963a. *Population Bulletin of the United Nations, No. 6.* (With special reference to the situation and recent trends of mortality in the world). New York.

United Nations, Department of Social and Economic Affairs, Population Branch, 1963b. *1963 Report on the World Social Situation.* New York.

United Nations, Department of Social and Economic Affairs, Population Branch, 1965. *1965 Report on the World Social Situation.* New York.

United Nations, Department of Social and Economic Affairs, Population Branch, 1966. *World Population Prospects As Assessed in 1963,* Population Studies No. 41. New York.

United Nations, Department of Social Affairs, Population Branch, 1967. *Methods of Estimating Basic Demographic Measures from Incomplete Data* (Manual IV), Population Study No. 42. New York.

United Nations, Department of Social Affairs, Population Branch, 1971. *The World Population Situation in 1970,* Population Study No. 49. New York.

United Nations, Economic Commission for Europe, 1970. *Economic Survey of Europe in 1969. Part I. Structural Trends and Prospects in the European Economy.* New York.

United Nations, Educational, Scientific, and Cultural Organization, 1966. *Statistical Yearbook 1964.* New York.

United States Bureau of the Census, 1970. Current Population Reports. *Estimates of the Population of the United States by Age, Race, and Sex: July 1, 1967 to July 1, 1969* (Series P-24, No. 441). Washington, D.C.: Government Printing Office.

United States Bureau of the Census 1972. Current Population Reports. *Projections of the Population of the United States by Age and Sex: 1972 to 2020* (Series P-25, No. 493). Washington, D.C.: Government Printing Office.

United States Bureau of the Census 1973. 1970 Census of Population. *Earnings by Occupation and Education.* Subject Reports (Series PC(2)-8B). Washington, D.C.: Government Printing Office.

United States Department of Commerce, Bureau of Census, 1938. Classification of joint causes of death. *Vital Statistics-Special Reports, 5*(47), 385–469.

United States, Department of Health, Education, and Welfare, 1963. Comparability of mortality statistics for the fifth and sixth revision. *Vital Statistics-Special Reports, Selected Studies, 51*(2).

United States National Center for Health Statistics, 1964. *United States Life Tables: 1959–1961,* Vol. 1, No. 1. Public Health Service Publication No. 1252. Washington, D.C.

United States National Center for Health Statistics, 1965. *Weight, Height, and Selected Body Dimensions of Adults. United States, 1960–1962.* Vital and Health Statistics, Series 11, No. 8. Washington, D.C.: U.S. Department of Health, Education, and Welfare.

United States National Center for Health Statistics, 1966. *Vital Statistics of the United States, 1964,* Vol. II, Mortality, Part A. Washington, D.C.

United States National Center for Health Statistics, 1973. *Monthly Vital Statistics Report, Summary Report, Final Natality Statistics, 1969,* Vol. 22, No. 7. Supplement.

United States National Center for Health Statistics, 1974. *Vital Statistics of the United States, 1970.* (Vol. II.) *Mortality. Part A.* Rockville, Maryland.

United States National Center for Health Statistics, n.d. (1). *Vital Statistics of the United States, 1968.* Vol. II, Section 5, Life Tables. Washington, D.C.

United States National Center for Health Statistics, n.d. (2). *Vital Statistics of the United States, 1970,* Vol. II, Section 5, Life Tables. Washington, D.C.

United States Public Health Service, National Office of Vital Statistics, 1950. *Vital Statistics of the United States, 1950,* Vol. I. Washington, D.C.

United States Surgeon General, Department of Health, Education, and Welfare, 1964. *Smoking and Health,* Public Health Service Publication No. 1103. Washington, D.C.: Government Printing Office.

Vallin, J., 1968. La mortalite dans les pays du Tiers Monde: evolution et perspectives. *Population,* 845–68.

Verhoestraete, L. J., and R. R. Puffer, 1958. Diarrheal disease with special reference to the Americas. *Bulletin of the World Health Organization, 19,* 27.

Williamson, N. E., 1973. *Preference for Sons Around the World.* Unpublished Ph.D. dissertation, Department of Sociology, Harvard University.

World Health Organization, 1948. *Bulletin,* Supplement 1. *Manual of the International Statistical Classification of Diseases, Injuries, and Causes of Death. Sixth Revision of the International Lists of Diseases, Injuries, and Causes of Death.* (Adopted 1948). Geneva.

World Health Organization, 1952. Comparability of statistics of causes of death according to the fifth and sixth revisions of the International Lists. *World Health Organization Bulletin,* Supplement 4. Geneva.

World Health Organization, 1957. *Manual of the International Statistical Classification of Disease, Injuries, and Causes of Death,* Vol. I. Geneva.

World Health Organization, 1964. *World Health Statistics Annual.* Geneva.

World Health Organization, 1967a. The accuracy and comparability of death statistics. *World Health Organization Chronicle, 21,* 12–13.

World Health Organization, 1967b. *Third Report on the World Health Situation, 1961–1964.* Official Records of the World Health Organization, No. 155. Geneva.

World Health Organization, 1974. Health trends and prospects, 1950–2000. *World Health Statistics Report, 27*(10), 672–706.

Wynder, E. L., and D. Hoffman, 1966. Current concepts of environmental cancer research. *Medical Clinics of North America, 50*(3), 631–50.

Index